THE HARMONY GUIDE TO
KNITTING STITCHES
VOLUME TWO

Lyric Books Limited

© 1987 Lyric Books Limited
P.O. Box 152, Mill Hill, London NW7,
England
ISBN 07111 00330
Printed in Belgium

The following titles are available in this series

The Harmony Guide to Decorative Needlecraft
ISBN 07111 00128

The Harmony Guide to Knitting Stitches
ISBN 07111 00136

The Harmony Guide to Knitting Stitches Volume Two
ISBN 07111 00330

The Harmony Guide to Crochet Stitches
ISBN 07111 00284

SOLE IMPORTERS

AUSTRALIA

Panda Yarns (International) Pty Ltd.,
17-27 Brunswick Road, East Brunswick,
Victoria 3057, Australia.

Distributors of:

Panda Twilleys Hayfield HOLIDAY

Hand Knitting Yarns

CANADA

A. Bruneau Canada Inc.,
338 est. St-Antoine East,
Montreal, Canada H2Y 1A3

Distributors of:
Art Needlework Accessories

INDIA

The Variety Book Depot,
31 Mohan Singh Place,
P.O. Box 505, New Delhi-110001,
India.

NEW ZEALAND

ALLTEX International NEW ZEALAND

Distributors of:

Fontana Kaiapoi *Shepherd* SIRDAR
Hand Knitting Yarns

UNITED STATES OF AMERICA

SusanBates® Inc. Manufacturers Since 1873

Your Complete Art Needlework Source

212 Middlesex Avenue, Chester, Ct. 06412

CONTENTS

Yarns and Needles

Knitting needles

Knitting needles are used in pairs to produce a flat knitted fabric. They are pointed at one end to form the stitches and have a knob at the other end to retain the stitches. They may be made in plastic, wood, steel or alloy and range in size from 2mm to 17mm in diameter. In the UK needles used to be sized by numbers — the higher the number, the smaller the needle. Metric sizing has now been adopted almost everywhere. Needles are also made in different lengths. Choose a length that will comfortably hold the stitches required for each project.

It is useful to have a range of sizes so that tension swatches can be knitted up and compared. Discard any needles that become bent. Points should be fairly sharp, blunt needles reduce the speed and ease of working.

Circular and double-pointed needles are used to produce a tubular fabric or flat rounds. Many traditional fisherman's sweaters are knitted in the round. Double-pointed needles are sold in sets of four or six. Circular needles consist of two needles joined by a flexible length of plastic. The plastic varies in length. Use the shorter lengths for knitting sleeves, neckband etc, and the longer lengths for larger pieces such as sweaters and skirts.

Cable needles are short needles used to hold the stitches of a cable to the back or front of the main body of the knitting.

Needle gauges are punched with holes corresponding to needle sizes and are marked with both the old numerical sizing and the metric sizing so you can easily check the size of any needle.

Stitch holders resemble large safety pins and are used to hold stitches while they are not being worked, for example, around a neckline when the neckband stitches will be picked up and worked after back and front have been joined. As an alternative, thread a blunt-pointed sewing needle with a generous length of contrast-coloured yarn, thread it through the stitches to be held while they are still on the needle, then slip the stitches off the needle and knot both ends of the contrast yarn together.

Wool sewing needles are used to sew completed pieces of knitting together. They are large with a broad eye for easy threading and a blunt-pointed that will slip between the knitted stitches without splitting and fraying the yarn. Do not use sharp pointed sewing needles to sew up knitting. A tapestry needle is also suitable.

A row counter is used to count the number of rows that have been knitted. It is a cylinder with a numbered dial that is pushed onto the needle and the dial is turned at the completion of each row.

A tape measure is essential for checking tension swatches and for measuring the length and width of completed knitting. For an accurate result, always smooth knitting out (without stretching) on a firm flat surface before measuring it.

A crochet hook is useful for picking up dropped stitches.

Knitting yarn

Yarn is the term used for strands of spun fibre which are twisted together into a continuous thread of the required thickness.

Yarn can be of animal origin (wool, angora, mohair, silk, alpaca), vegetable origin (cotton, linen) or man-made (nylon, acrylic, rayon). Knitting yarn may be made up from a combination of different fibres.

Each single strand of yarn is known as a ply. A number of plys are twisted together to form the yarn. The texture and characteristics of the yarn may be varied by the combination of fibres and by the way in which the yarn is spun. Wool and other natural fibres are often combined with man-made fibres to make a yarn that is more economical and hard-wearing. Wool can also be treated to make it machine washable. The twist of the yarn can be varied too. A tightly twisted yarn is firm and smooth and knits up into a hard-wearing fabric. Loosely twisted yarn has a softer finish when knitted.

Buying yarn

Yarn is most commonly sold ready wound into balls of specific weight measured in grams or ounces. Some yarn, particularly very thick yarn, is also sold in a coiled hank or skein and must be wound up into a ball before you begin knitting.

Yarn manufacturers (called spinners) wrap each ball with a paper band on which is printed a lot of necessary information. The ball band states the weight of the yarn and its composition. It will give instructions for washing and ironing and may state the ideal range of needle sizes to be used with the yarn. The ball band also carries the shade number and dye lot number. It is important that you use yarn of the same dye lot for a single project. Different dye lots vary subtly in shading which may not be apparent when you are holding two balls, but which will show as a variation in shade on the finished piece of knitting.

Always keep the ball band as a reference. The best way is to pin it to the tension swatch (see page 7) and keep them together with any left over yarn and spare buttons or other trimmings. That way you can always check the washing instructions and also have materials for repairs.

Holding the needles 1

The right needle is held in the same position as holding a pencil. For casting on and working the first few rows the knitted piece passes over the hand, between the thumb and the index finger. As work progresses let the thumb slide under the knitted piece, grasping the needle from below.

Holding the needles 2

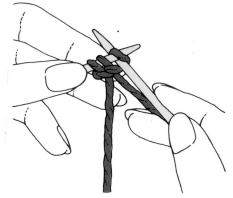

The left needle is held lightly over the top, using the thumb and index finger to control the tip of the needle.

Holding the yarn method 1

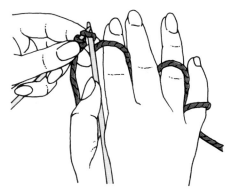

Holding yarn in right hand, pass yarn under the little finger, then around same finger, over third finger, under centre finger and over index finger. The index finger is used to pass the yarn around needle tip. The yarn circled around the little finger creates the necessary tension for knitting evenly.

Holding the yarn method 2

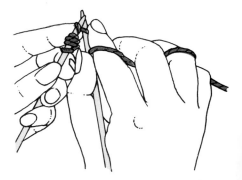

Holding yarn in right hand, pass under the little finger, over third finger, under centre finger and over index finger. The index finger is used to pass the yarn around the needle tip. The tension on the yarn is controlled by gripping the yarn in the crook of the little finger.

Casting On

There are two 'best ways' of casting on each serving a rather different purpose. The Thumb Method is used whenever a very elastic edge is required or when the rows immediately after the cast-on edge are to be worked in garter stitch or stocking stitch. The second method is the Cable or 'between stitches' method. This gives a very firm neat finish and is best for use before ribbing or any other firm type of stitch.

Both these methods commence with a slip knot and this is the starting-off point for almost everything you do in knitting.

Slip knot

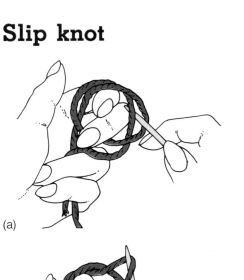

(a)

(b)

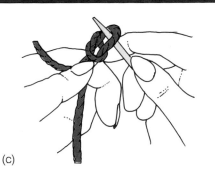

(c)

(a) Wind the yarn around two fingers and over the two fingers again to the back of the first thread.
(b) Using a knitting needle pull the back thread through the front one to form a loop.
(c) Pull end to tighten the loop.

Thumb method

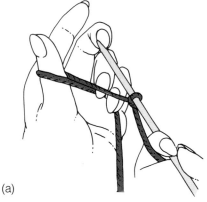

(a)

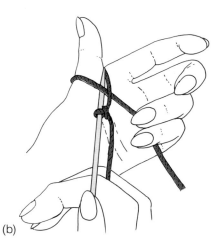

(b)

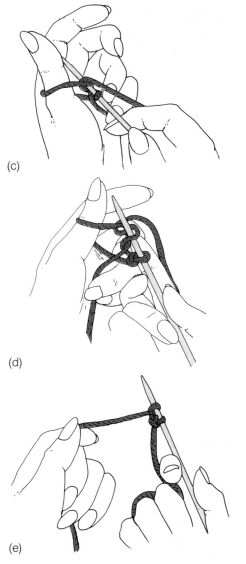

(c)

(d)

(e)

(a) Make a slip knot about 1 metre (depending on the number of stitches required) from the end of the yarn. Place the slip knot on a needle and hold the needle in the right hand with the ball end of the yarn over your first finger. *Wind the loose end of the yarn around the left thumb from front to back.
(b) Insert the needle through the yarn on the thumb.
(c) Take the yarn with your right forefinger over the point of the needle, (diagram c).
(d) Pull a loop through to form the first stitch.
(e) Remove your left thumb from the yarn and pull the loose end to secure the stitch. Repeat from * until the required number of stitches has been cast on.

For North American Readers

English terms are used throughout this book.
Please note equivalent American terms:
Tension — Gauge
Cast Off — Bind Off
Stocking Stitch — Stockinette Stitch
Yf, yfon, yfrn, yon and yrn — Yarn over

The Basic Stitches

Cable method

(a)

(b)

(c)

(d)

(e)

(f)

The Basic Stitches
Knit stitch

(a)

(b)

(c)

(d)

Purl stitch

(a)

(b)

(c)

(d)

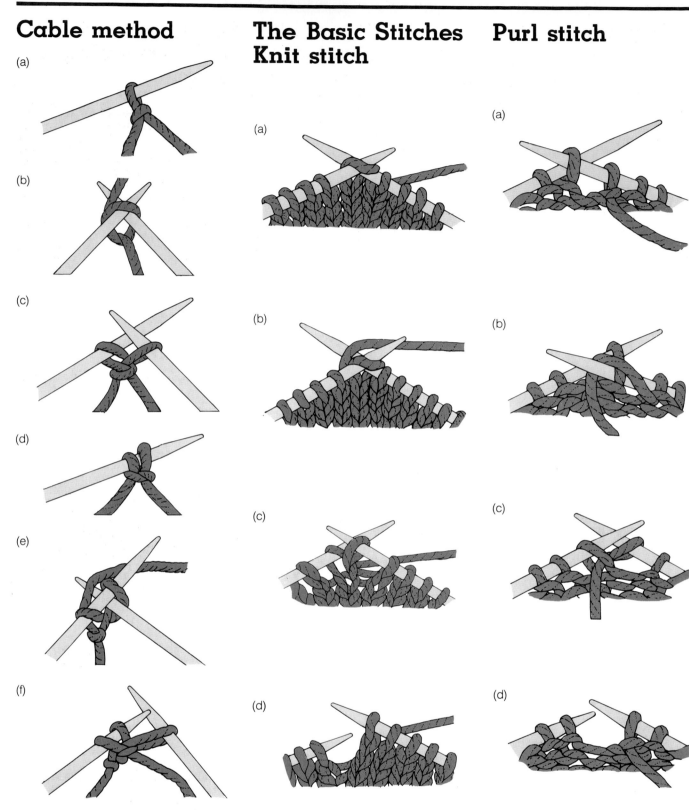

This method requires the use of two needles.

(a) Make a slip knot about 10 cms from the end and place on left hand needle.

(b) Insert right hand needle through the slip knot and pass the yarn over the right needle.

(c) Pull a loop through.

(d) Place this loop on the left hand needle.

(e) Insert right hand needle between the two stitches on the left hand needle. Wind yarn round point of right hand needle.

(f) Draw a loop through, place this loop on left hand needle.

Repeat steps (e) and (f) until the required number of stitches are on the needle.

(a) With the yarn at the back of the work insert the right hand needle from left to right through the front of the first stitch on the left hand needle.

(b) Wind the yarn over the right hand needle.

(c) Pull through a loop.

(d) Slip the original stitch off the left hand needle.

Repeat this until all stitches have been transferred from left needle to right needle.

(a) With the yarn at the front of the work insert the right hand needle from right to left through the front of the first stitch on the left hand needle.

(b) Wind the yarn round the right hand needle.

(c) Draw a loop through to the back.

(d) Slip the original stitch off the left hand needle.

Repeat this until all stitches are transferred to right hand needle.

Casting off

Always cast off in pattern. This means that in stocking stitch you cast off knitwise (see below) on a knit row and purlwise on a purl row. Casting off ribbing should always be done as if you were continuing to rib and most pattern stitches can also be followed during the course of the casting off.

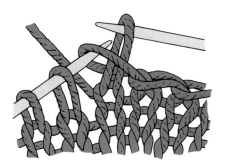

1) Knitwise

Knit the first two stitches. *Using the left hand needle lift the first stitch over the second and drop it off the needle. Knit the next stitch and repeat from the *.

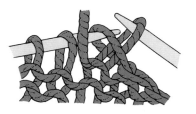

2) Purlwise

Purl the first two stitches, then *using the left hand needle lift the first stitch over the second and drop if off the needle. Purl the next stitch and repeat from the *.

Using a crochet hook to cast off can be extremely time saving. Treat the crochet hook as if it were the right hand needle and knit or purl the first two stitches in the usual way. *Pull the second stitch through the first, knit or purl the next stitch and repeat from the *. This method is extremely useful when a loose elastic cast off edge is required as you can gently loosen the stitch still on the crochet hook to ensure that the elasticity is retained.

Tension or gauge

The correct tension (or gauge) is the most important contribution to the successful knitting of a garment. The information under this heading given at the beginning of all patterns refers to the number of stitches required to

fill a particular area; for example a frequent tension indication would be '22 sts and 30 rows = 10 cms square measured over stocking stitch on 4mm needles'. This means that it is necessary to produce fabric made up of the proportion of stitches and rows as given in the tension paragraph in order to obtain the correct measurements for the garment you intend to knit, regardless of the needles **you** use. The needle size indicated in the pattern is the one which **most** knitters will use to achieve this tension but it is the tension that is important, not needle size.

The way to ensure that you do achieve a correct tension is to work a tension sample or swatch before starting the main part of the knitting. Although this may seem to be time wasting and a nuisance it can save the enormous amount of time and aggravation that would result from having knitted a garment to the wrong size.

Tension swatch

The instructions given in the tension paragraph of a knitting pattern are either for working in stocking stitch or in pattern stitch. If they are given in pattern stitch is is necessary to work a multiple of stitches the same as the multiple required in the pattern. If in stocking stitch any number can be cast on but whichever method is used this should always be enough to give at least 12 cms in width. Work in pattern or stocking stitch according to the wording of the tension paragraph until the piece measures at least 10 cms in depth. Break the yarn about 15 cms from the work and thread this end through the stitches, then remove the knitting needle. Place a pin vertically into the fabric a few stitches from the side edge. Measure 10 cms carefully and insert a second pin. Count the stitches. If the number of stitches between the pins is less than that specified in the pattern (even by half a stitch) your garment will be too large. Use smaller needles and knit another tension sample. If your sample has more stitches over 10 cms, the garment will be too small. Change to larger needles. Check the number of rows against the given tension also.

It is most important to get the width measurement correct before starting to knit. Length measurements can usually be adjusted during the course of knitting by adjusting the length to underarm or sleeve length, which is frequently given as a measurement and not in rows.

Increasing and Decreasing

There are various methods of increasing and decreasing and they serve two purposes. The first is to make the knitting wider or narrower, to shape it. The second purpose is to create the decorative effects in lacy or in textured patterns.

Using increasing and decreasing to shape

When knitting the various parts of a garment, increases or decreases are worked in pairs at each end of the row on the symmetrical peices — (back, sleeves etc) to given a balanced shape. The fronts of a cardigan however are shaped differently on each side to give the correct shape for the armhole on one side and the neck shaping at the other.

It is very important to follow the instructions given in the knitting pattern very carefully. The designer will have worked out the various shapings to give the best possible results for each piece of material, and to ensure that the pieces fit together correctly when made up.

Slip stitch decrease

(a)

(a) Slip next stitch onto the right hand needle without knitting it then knit the next stitch.

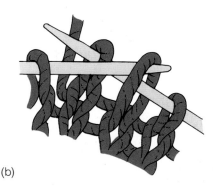

(b)

(b) Lift the slipped stitch over the knitted stitch and drop it off the needle. The abbreviation is **sl 1, k1, psso** (slip 1, knit 1, pass slipped stitch over). On a purl row the abbreviation is **sl 1, p1, psso.**

Increasing and Decreasing

Working two stitches together

This decrease is worked simply by inserting the right hand needle through two stitches instead of one and then knitting them together as one stitch. On a purl row, insert the needle purlwise through the two stitches and purl in the usual way. The abbreviation is **k2tog** or **p2tog.**

Yarn forward increase

knit row

To make the yarn forward increase in a knit row, bring the yarn to the front, take it over the right hand needle and knit the stitch. The completed increase creates a visible hole and is often used in lace patterns. The increase is abbreviated in knitting patterns as **yf** (yarn forward) or as **yfwd.**

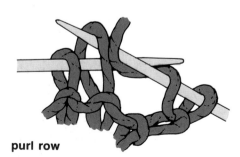

purl row

In a purl row, take the yarn over the right hand needle to the back of the work, then under the needle to the front. The abbreviation is **yrn** (yarn round needle).

Sometimes the abbreviation **yo** (yarn over) is used as a general term on knit or purl rows to indicate that a stitch has to be increased

at that position by the method of winding the yarn round the needle, as opposed to the 'front and back' method described below. In this case it is necessary to ensure that you wind the yarn correctly; after you have worked the next stitch check to see that you have actually made an extra stitch and not just carried the yarn from front to back or vice versa!

Working into the front and back of a stitch

knit row

Knit into the stitch and before slipping it off the needle, knit again into the back of the loop. This is abbreviated in patterns as **Inc 1,** or inc in next st.

purl row

The method on a purl row is similar. Purl into the front of the stitch then purl into the back of it before slipping it off the needle.

Make 1

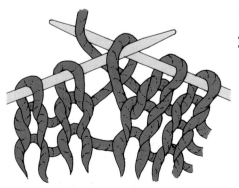

Lift the yarn lying between the stitch just worked and the next stitch and place it on left hand needle, then knit (or purl) into back of this loop. This increase is abbreviated as **M1** (make 1).

Joining and Finishing

Picking up dropped stitches

If a stitch drops off the needle it is usually easy to pick it up immediately, even if it has slipped through to the row below. Simply pick up the stitch and the strand above it on the right hand needle. Then insert the left hand needle through the stitch and pull the strand through the stitch using the right hand needle to form the stitch once more in its correct place.

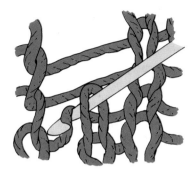

However, if a stitch drops unnoticed it can easily form a ladder running down a number of rows. In this case the stitch must be re-formed all the way up the ladder using a crochet hook. Always work from the front or knit side of the work. Insert hook through centre of loose st, pick up next horizontal strand above and draw through the stitch below to form a new stitch. Continue all the way up the ladder.

If more than one stitch has dropped, secure the others with a safety pin until you are ready to pick them up.

Grafting

Grafting invisibly joins two pieces of knitting. The edges are not cast off, and the knitting can be joined either while is it still on the needles or after it has been taken off.

Knitting on the needles

Thread a wool or tapestry needle with a length of knitting yarn. Place the two pieces to be joined with right side facing and hold the knitting needles in the left hand. *Pass the wool needle knitwise through the first stitch on the front needle and slip the stitch off the knitting needle. Pass the wool needle purlwise through the second stitch on the same needle, leaving the stitch on the needle. Pass purlwise through the first stitch on the back knitting needle and slip the stitch off, then pass knitwise through the second stitch on the same needle, leaving the stitch on the needle. Repeat from *. Pull the yarn through so as to form stitches of the same size as the knitted ones. To finish, darn in loose ends at the back of the work.

Thread a wool or tapestry needle with the knitting yarn. Place the pieces to be joined right sides together. Ensure that they match pattern for pattern and row for row. Work backstitch along the seam close to the edge.

This method of sewing is the most commonly used but to give a really professional finish to your garments you should use a Mattress Stitch for sewing all the seams.

(c)

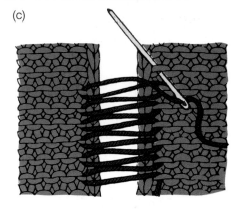

Knitting taken off the needles

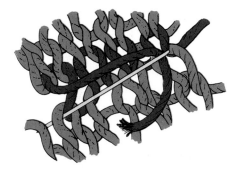

Mattress stitch seam

You will see in the diagrams below visual descriptions of the mattress stitch that we use for almost every seam in the garments we make as this gives the neatest, most professional finish.

Mattress stitch can be worked either one stitch in from the edge (diagram a) or half a stitch in from the edge (diagram b) according to how neat the edge of the fabric is, and how thick the yarn is. Where the knit side of the work is the right side work under two rows at a time (as shown in diagrams a and b); where purl is used as the right side it is better to work under only one row at a time (diagram c) although experience will tell you what is actually required.

The secret of good mattress stitching is to keep the seam elastic without allowing it to stretch too much. The best way to do this is to work the mattress stitch loosely for 1 or 2 centimetres and then pull the thread very firmly so that the stitches are held together quite tightly. Now stretch this seam slightly to give the required amount of elasticity, then continue with the next section of the seam.

If you are used to sewing your knitting together by other means it may take a little while to get used to using mattress stitch. However — practise makes perfect and the professional finish you will achieve will make it worth while. One advantage of mattress stitch is that it can be used to sew shaped edges together quite easily; because you are working on the right side of the work all the time it is much easier to see where you are and to keep the seam neat.

Carefully lay the pieces to be joined close together, with the stitches on each side corresponding to those opposite. Thread a wool or tapestry needle with the knitting yarn. Beginning on the right hand side, bring the needle up through the first stitch of the upper piece, bring it down through the first stitch of the lower piece and bring it up again through the next stitch to the left. *On the upper piece, pass the needle down through the same stitch it came up through before and bring it up through the next stitch to the left. On the lower piece, take the needle down through the stitch it came up through before and bring it up through the next stitch on the left. Repeat from *.

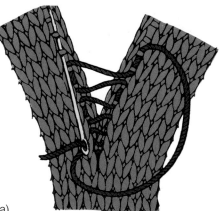

(a)

Picking up stitches along an edge

Once the main body of the knitting is complete, it is often necessary to add some extra rows to finish the work, to make a border or an edging. Sometimes these sections are knitted separately and sewn on, but it is quicker and neater to pick up stitches along the edge and knit directly onto these.

To pick up stitches along a cast on or cast off edge, for example to add a border or to work a collar, insert the point of the knitting needle under the first stitch, pass the yarn around the needle and draw a loop through to form a stitch. Continue for as many stitches as are required.

To pick up stitches along side edges, for example to work the button band on a cardigan, insert the point of the needle between the first and second rows 1 stitch or ½ stitch in from the edge, pass the yarn over the needle and draw a loop through. Often, the number of stitches that must be picked up are not the same as the number along the edge or the number of rows. It is easier to pick up the stitches evenly if you divide the length of the edge in half, then in half again and again, so the edge is divided into eighths. Mark each division with a pin. Divide the number of stitches to be picked up by eight and pick up approximately that number of stitches in each section.

Backstitch seam

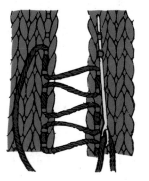

(b)

Hints and Tips

Making a Twisted Cord

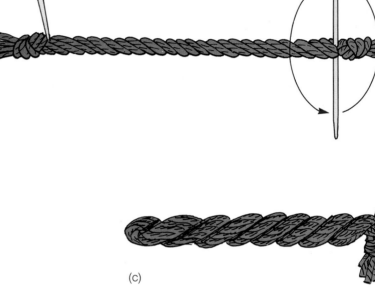

(a)

A Twisted Cord requires several strands of yarn each about 2½-3 times the required finished length. 4 strands will give you a finished cord 8 strands thick.

(a) Cut the strands of yarn as indicated and knot together at each end making sure that the lengths are even.

(b) Attach one end to a pin, hook or door handle.

(b)

(c) Insert a knitting needle through the other end. Twist the knitting needle anticlockwise until the strands are well twisted together. Holding the centre of the cord, place the needle end and the hook end together, keeping the cord taut to avoid tangling.

(d) Release the centre of the cord and allow the two halves to twist together smoothing out the bumps.

Knot and trim both ends.

(c)

Pompoms

(a) Cut 2 rings of card. The finished diameter of the ring will indicate the approximate finished size of the Pompom. Mark and cut a smaller circle at the centre of each piece to thread the wool through.

(b) Hold the 2 pieces of card together and wind the yarn round the ring until the card is covered. It is quicker to wind several strands at the same time.

(c) Using a pair of sharp scissors cut between the 2 pieces of card, through all the yarn around the outside edge, until the full circle has been separated.

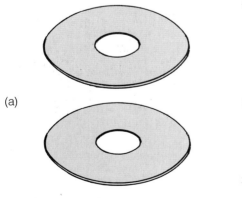

(a)

(b)

(c)

The larger the centre hole, the fuller and more compact the Pompom will be.

(d) Before taking the pieces of card away, thread a piece of yarn between the 2 rings and tie into a tight knot, securing the centre of the Pompom and leaving enough yarn to attach the Pompom where required.

Now pull the 2 pieces of card away and fluff out the ball. Trim the ends until the required shape and size is achieved.

(d)

Fringing

Fringes can be worked along the edge of knitted material as follows: Cut 1 or more lengths of yarn (just over twice the required finished length of the fringe). Fold in half and draw a loop through the edge stitch using a crochet hook. Now draw the loose ends of strands through the loop and pull down tightly to form a knot.

Working with Colour

Joining in a new yarn

It is better to join new yarn in at the beginning of a row. If it is not possible to do this and the yarn has to be joined in the middle of a row simply pick up the new yarn and continue knitting. After you have knitted a few more rows darn in the ends of the old and new yarns neatly at the back of the work.

Stranding colours

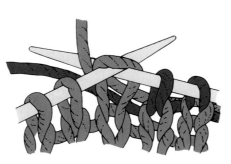

Use this method for colour patterns with small repeats. Hold the second colour in the left hand and carry it loosely across the wrong side of the work. To change colours exchange the position of the two yarns and insert the needle into the next stitch. Lift the old yarn over the right hand needle with your left hand and bring the new yarn ready to work the stitch. Before pulling the loop through take the old yarn back again then complete the stitch in the usual way. The old and new colours will thus be twisted together; this is necessary at the joining point to avoid making a hole. The secret of working good 2-colour knitting is to carry the colour not in use **loosely** across the wrong side of the work and take care not to pull it tight when changing the colours over.

Weaving

It is possible to work every alternate stitch of a fairisle pattern as given above for Stranding. This gives a neat appearance at the back of the work but distorts the shape of the stitches and alters the tension. Unless the pattern specifically calls for this method it is not recommended.

Colour patterns

Where colours are used in large blocks or over large areas at a time, it is best to use a separate ball of yarn for each section.

When using separate balls of yarn, the yarns must be twisted over each other otherwise a hole will be formed between the colours. When the colour change is in a vertical line, cross the yarns on both knit and purl rows.

When the colour change is on a slanting line, the yarns need be crossed only on alternate rows.

(a)

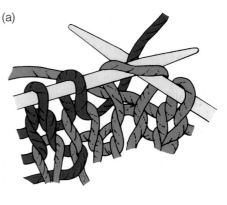

(a) When the colour change slants to the right, cross the yarns on the knit row. Take the first colour in front of the second colour, drop it, then pick up and knit with the second colour. On the purl row the diagonal slants in such a way that the yarns automatically cross.

(b)

(b) When the colour change slants to the left, the yarns must be crossed on the purl row. On the knit row the diagonal slant causes the yarns to cross automatically.

Following a Pattern and Abbreviations

Swiss darning

Swiss darning is a form of embroidery on knitting that exactly covers the knitted stitches so that the finished embroidery looks as if it had been knitted in. It is a useful and versatile technique. When a pattern calls for very small or widely spaced colour motifs, or for a very thin vertical stripe as in many plaids, it is often much easier to darn in afterwards than to knit it in.

To exactly duplicate the knitted stitches, use yarn of the same type as the knitting. For more obviously decorative effects, any suitable knitting or embroidery yarn can be used.

(a)

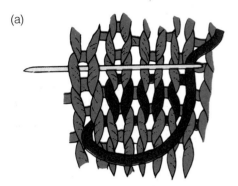

(a) To work Swiss darning horizontally, work from right to left. Darn in the yarn invisibly at the back. Bring the needle out in the centre of a stitch, take it up and around the head of the stitch (under the stitch above), then take the needle back through the centre of the **same** stitch.

(b)

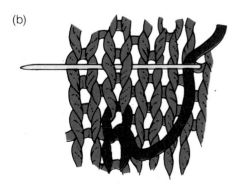

(b) To work the embroidery vertically, work from bottom to top. Bring the needle out in the centre of the stitch, then take it up and around the head of the stitch (under the stitch above). Take the needle back through the centre of the **same** stitch then up through the centre of the stitch above.

Following a Pattern and Abbreviations

Knitting patterns are written in a language all of their own. Abbreviations are used for many of the repetitive words which occur in the instructions and although all manufacturers do not use exactly the same abbreviations, an experienced knitter can follow the terminology.

Before starting to knit any pattern, always read it right through. Even if you are not experienced, this will give you an idea of how the pattern is structured and you will know what to expect. After knitting one or two patterns you will understand how the pattern works.

Multiples

A certain number of stitches are required to form one complete pattern, say a cable, a zigzag or a leaf shape. The number of stitches on the needle must be divisible by this number. The information is given at the beginning of a pattern. For example: multiple of 4 sts; multiple of 8 plus 1 sts. Some patterns also specify the number of rows required to complete the pattern.

Asterisks and Brackets

These are used to indicate repetition of a sequence of stitches. For example: *k3, p1; rep from * to end. This means knit 3 stitches and purl 1 stitch to the end of the row. The instructions within brackets are worked for the number of times required. For example: [k3, p1] 4 times. This means that the stitches within the brackets are worked 4 times in all.

Work Straight

This instruction means that you knit with the number of stitches on the needle for the required length or number of rows without increasing or decreasing.

Abbreviations

Below, the common pattern abbreviations are explained in detail. Opposite are some Special Abbreviations which usually occur in cable and other highly textured patterns.

Alt = Alternate This usually occurs during an instruction for shaping, for example: increase 1 stitch at end of next and every **alt** row until there are X sts. This means that, counting the next row as row 1, the increase is worked on rows 1, 3, 5, 7 etc., until the required number of stitches is reached. If the instruction reads 'increase 1 stitch at end of every **alt** row...' then the increases are worked on rows 2, 4, 6, 8 etc.

Beg = beginning

Cms = centimetres

Dec = decrease This is a shaping instruction. 1, 2 or even 3 stitches can be decreased in one go during knitting, but if more than this is required it is usually necessary to 'cast off' some stitches. See page 7 for this. For a description of the usual ways to work a decrease see pages 7 and 8.

Inc = increase This is a shaping instruction. 1 or 2 stitches can be increased in one place (see page 8). However, if more than 1 or 2 are required it is usually necessary to 'cast on' some stitches, (see page 6).

K = knit   P = purl These abbreviations describe all the detailed working of a pattern. Example: K1, p3, k1. This means that you knit 1 stitch, then you purl 3 stitches then you knit 1 stitch.

Psso = pass slipped stitch over This abbreviation occurs after a slip abbreviation. Example: K9, sl 1, k1, psso, k2. This means that you knit 9 stitches, slip the next stitch, knit 1 more stitch; then you lift the slipped stitch (using the point of the left hand needle) over the 1 knit stitch and drop if off the needle, then you knit the last 2 stitches. This is a frequently used method of decreasing.

Rep = repeat

Sl = slip Example: Sl 1, k1. This means that you slip the next stitch on to the right hand needle without knitting it, then you knit the next stitch.

St = stitch

Sts = stitches

St st = stocking stitch This consists of 1 row knit, 1 row purl, and gives a fabric which is smooth on one side and rough on the other. To facilitate sewing always keep the stitch at the beginning and end of each row in stocking stitch. Some knitters slip the first stitch of a knit row, or knit the first stitch of a purl row. If you use a mattress stitch seam (see page 9) keep the edge stitches in true stocking stitch.

Tbl = through back of loop

Tog = together Usually used as a method of decreasing. For example: k2tog.

Yb = yarn back

Yf = yarn forward

Yfon = yarn forward and over needle Yarn forward, as if to purl. Used to make a stitch at the beginning of a row.

Yfrn = yarn forward and round needle Used to make a stitch between a knit and purl stitch. Take the yarn right round the needle, finishing at the front.

Yon = yarn over needle Used to make a stitch between a purl and a knit stitch.

Yrn = yarn round needle Used to make a stitch between 2 purl stitches.

Alt = alternate; beg = begininning; cms = centimetres; dec = decrease; inc = increase; ins = inches; k = knit; m = metres; p = purl; psso = pass slipped stitch over; p2sso = pass 2 slipped sts over; rep = repeat; sl = slip; st = stitch; st(s) = stitch(es); st st = stocking stitch (1 row k, 1 row p); tbl = through back of loop; tog = together; yb = yarn back; yf = yarn forward; yfon = yarn forward and over needle; yfrn = yarn forward and round needle; yo = yarn over; yon = yarn over needle; yrn = yarn round needle.

M1 (Make 1 Stitch) = pick up horizontal strand of yarn lying between stitch just worked and next st and knit into back of it.

MB (Make Bobble) = knit into front, back and front of next st, turn and k3, turn and p3, turn and k3, turn and sl 1, k2tog, psso (bobble completed).

K1B (Knit 1 below) = insert needle through centre of st below next st on needle and knit this in the usual way, slipping the st above off needle at the same time.

Sl 2tog knitwise = insert needle into the next 2 sts on left-hand needle as if to k2tog then slip both sts onto right-hand needle without knitting them.

KB1 = knit into back of next stitch.

PB1 = purl into back of next stitch.

C2B or C2F (Cross 2 Back or Cross 2 Front) = knit into back (or front) of 2nd st on needle, then knit first st, slipping both sts off needle at the same time.

C2L (Cross 2 Left) = slip next st onto cable needle and hold at front of work, knit next st from left-hand needle, then knit st from cable needle.

C2R (Cross 2 Right) = slip next st onto cable needle and hold at back of work, knit next st from left-hand needle, then knit st from cable needle.

C2P (Cross 2 Purl) = purl into front of 2nd st on needle, then purl first st, slipping both sts off needle together.

T2 (Twist 2) = slip next st onto cable needle and hold at back of work, PB1 from left-hand needle then PB1 from cable needle.

T2L (Twist 2 Left) = slip next st onto cable needle and hold at front of work, purl next st from left-hand needle, then KB1 from cable needle.

T2R (Twist 2 Right) = slip next st onto cable needle and hold at back of work, KB1 from left-hand needle, then purl st from cable needle.

T2F (Twist 2 Front) = slip next st onto cable needle and hold at front of work, purl next st from left-hand needle, then knit st from cable needle.

T2B (Twist 2 Back) = slip next st onto cable needle and hold at back of work, knit next st from left-hand needle, then purl st from cable needle.

C3 (Cross 3) = knit into front of 3rd st on needle, then knit first st in usual way slipping this st off needle, now knit 2nd st in usual way, slipping 2nd and 3rd sts off needle together.

C3B (Cross 3 Back) = slip next st onto cable needle and hold at back of work, knit next 2 sts from left-hand needle, then knit st from cable needle.

C3F (Cross 3 Front) = slip next 2 sts onto cable needle and hold at front of work, knit next st from left-hand needle, then knit sts from cable needle.

C3L (Cable 3 Left) = slip next st onto cable needle and hold at front of work, knit next 2 sts from left-hand needle, then knit st from cable needle.

C3R (Cable 3 Right) = slip next 2 sts onto cable needle and hold at back of work, knit next st from left-hand needle, then knit sts from cable needle.

T3B (Twist 3 Back) = slip next st onto cable needle and hold at back of work, knit next 2 sts from left-hand needle, then purl st from cable needle.

T3F (Twist 3 Front) = slip next 2 sts onto cable needle and hold at front of work, purl next st from left-hand needle, then knit sts from cable needle.

T3L (Twist 3 Left) = slip next st onto cable needle and hold at front of work, work [KB1, p1] from left-hand needle, then KB1 from cable needle.

T3R (Twist 3 Right) = slip next 2 sts onto cable needle and hold at back of work, KB1 from left-hand needle, then [p1, KB1] from cable needle.

C4B or C4F (Cable 4 Back or Cable 4 Front) = slip next 2 sts onto cable needle and hold at back (or front) of work, knit next 2 sts from left-hand needle, then knit sts from cable needle.

C4L (Cross 4 Left) = slip next st onto cable needle and leave at front of work, knit next 3 sts from left-hand needle, then knit st from cable needle.

C4R (Cross 4 Right) = slip next 3 sts onto cable needle and leave at back of work, knit next st from left-hand needle then knit sts from cable needle.

T4B (Twist 4 Back) = slip next 2 sts onto cable needle and hold at back of work, knit next 2 sts from left-hand needle, then purl the 2 sts from cable needle.

T4F (Twist 4 Front) = slip next 2 sts onto cable needle and hold at front of work, purl next 2 sts from left-hand needle, then knit sts from cable needle.

T4L (Twist 4 Left) = slip next 2 sts onto cable needle and hold at front of work, k1, p1 from left-hand needle, then knit sts from cable needle.

T4R (Twist 4 Right) = slip next 2 sts onto cable needle and hold at back of work, knit next 2 sts from left-hand needle, then p1, k1 from cable needle.

C5 (Cable 5) = slip next 3 sts onto cable needle and hold at back of work, knit next 2 sts from left-hand needle, then knit sts from cable needle.

C5B or C5F (Cross 5 Back or Cross 5 Front) slip next 3 sts onto cable needle and hold at back (or front) of work, knit next 2 sts from left-hand needle, slip the purl st from point of cable needle back onto left-hand needle, purl this st, then k2 from cable needle.

C5L (Cross 5 Left) = slip next 4 sts onto cable needle and hold at front of work, purl next st on left-hand needle, then knit sts on cable needle.

C5R (Cross 5 Right) = slip the next st onto cable needle and hold at back of work, knit next 4 sts on left-hand needle, then purl the st on cable needle.

T5B (Twist 5 Back) = slip next 2 sts onto cable needle and hold at back of work, knit next 3 sts from left-hand needle, then purl sts from cable needle.

T5F (Twist 5 Front) = slip next 3 sts onto cable needle and hold at front of work, purl next 2 sts from left-hand needle, then knit sts from cable needle.

T5L (Twist 5 Left) = slip next 2 sts onto cable needle and hold at front of work, k2, p1 from left-hand needle, then k2 from cable needle.

T5R (Twist 5 Right) = slip next 3 sts onto cable needle and hold at back of work, knit next 2 sts from left-hand needle, then work [p1, k2] from cable needle.

T5FL (Twist 5 Front Left) = slip next 2 sts onto cable needle and hold at front of work, purl next 3 sts from left-hand needle, then knit the 2 sts from cable needle.

T5BR (Twist 5 Back Right) = slip next 3 sts onto cable needle and leave at back of work, knit next 2 sts from left-hand needle, then purl the 3 sts from cable needle.

C6 (Cross 6) = slip next 4 sts onto cable needle and hold at front of work, knit next 2 sts from left-hand needle, then slip the 2 purl sts from cable needle back to left-hand needle. Pass the cable needle with 2 remaining knit sts to back of work, purl 2 sts from left-hand needle, then knit the 2 sts from cable needle.

C6B or C6F (Cable 6 Back or Cable 6 Front) = slip next 3 sts onto cable needle and hold at back (or front) of work, knit next 3 sts from left-hand needle, then knit sts from cable needle.

T6B (Twist 6 Back) = slip next 3 sts onto cable needle and hold at back of work, knit next 3 sts from left-hand needle, then purl sts from cable needle.

T6F (Twist 6 Front) = slip next 3 sts onto cable needle and hold at front of work, purl next 3 sts from left-hand needle, then knit sts from cable needle.

T6L (Twist 6 Left) = slip next 2 sts onto cable needle and hold at front of work, work k2, p2 from left-hand needle, then knit the 2 sts from cable needle.

T6R (Twist 6 Right) = slip next 4 sts onto cable needle and hold at back of work, knit next 2 sts from left-hand needle, then work p2, k2 from cable needle.

C7F or C7B (Cable 7 Front or Cable 7 Back) = slip next 4 sts onto cable needle and hold at front (or back) of work, knit next 3 sts on left-hand needle, slip purl st from cable needle onto left-hand needle and purl it, then k3 from cable needle.

C8B or C8F (Cable 8 Back or Cable 8 Front) = slip next 4 sts onto cable needle and hold at back (or front) of work, knit next 4 sts from left-hand needle, then knit sts from cable needle.

C9B (Cable 9 Back) = slip next 4 sts onto cable needle and hold at back of work, knit next 5 sts from left-hand needle, then knit sts from cable needle.

C9F (Cable 9 Front) = slip next 5 sts onto cable needle and hold at front of work, knit next 4 sts from left-hand needle, then knit sts from cable needle.

C10B or C10F (Cable 10 Back or Cable 10 Front) = slip next 5 sts onto cable needle and hold at back (or front) of work, knit next 5 sts from left-hand needle, then knit sts from cable needle.

C12B or C12F (Cable 12 Back or Cable 12 Front) = slip next 6 sts onto cable needle and hold at back (or front) of work, knit next 6 sts from left-hand needle, then knit sts from cable needle.

Knit and Purl Patterns

Seed Stitch I

Multiple of 4 sts + 3.
1st row (right side): P1, k1, *p3, k1; rep from * to last st, p1.
2nd row: K3, *p1, k3; rep from * to end.
Rep these 2 rows.

Seed Stitch II

Worked as Seed Stitch I, using reverse side as right side.

Banded Rib

Multiple of 2 sts + 1.
1st row (right side): K1, *p1, k1; rep from * to end.
2nd row: P1, *k1, p1; rep from * to end.
Rep the last 2 rows twice more.
7th row: P1, *k1, p1; rep from * to end.
8th row: K1, *p1, k1; rep from * to end.
Rep the last 2 rows twice more.
Rep these 12 rows.

Waffle Stitch

Multiple of 3 sts + 1.
1st row (right side): P1, *k2, p1; rep from * to end.
2nd row: K1, *p2, k1; rep from * to end.
3rd row: As 1st row.
4th row: Knit.
Rep these 4 rows.

Seeded Texture

Multiple of 5 sts + 2.
1st row (right side): K2, *p3, k2; rep from * to end.
2nd row: Purl.
3rd row: *P3, k2; rep from * to last 2 sts, p2.
4th row: Purl.
Rep these 4 rows.

Space Invaders

Multiple of 6 sts + 3.

1st row (right side): K1, p1, k1, *p3, k1, p1, k1; rep from * to end.
2nd row: P3, *k3, p3; rep from * to end.
3rd row: P1, k1, *p5, k1; rep from * to last st, p1.
4th row: K1, p1, *k5, p1; rep from * to last st, k1.
5th row: P3, *k1, p1, k1, p3; rep from * to end.
6th row: K3, *p1, k1, p1, k3; rep from * to end.
7th row: P3, *k3, p3; rep from * to end.
8th row: K4, p1, *k5, p1; rep from * to last 4 sts, k4.
9th row: P4, k1, *p5, k1; rep from * to last 4 sts, p4.
10th row: P1, k1, p1, *k3, p1, k1, p1; rep from * to end.
Rep these 10 rows.

Box and Stripe Pattern

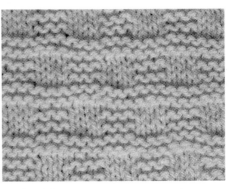

Multiple of 6 sts + 3.
Work 5 rows in garter stitch (1st row is right side).
6th row: K3, *p3, k3; rep from * to end.
7th row: Knit.
8th row: As 6th row.
Work 5 rows in garter stitch.
14th row: P3, *k3, p3; rep from * to end.
15th row: Knit.
16th row: As 14th row.
Rep these 16 rows.

Little Arrows

Mutliple of 8 sts + 1.

1st row (right side): K2, p2, k1, p2, *k3, p2, k1, p2; rep from * to last 2 sts, k2.

2nd row: P3, k1, p1, k1, *p5, k1, p1, k1; rep from * to last 3 sts, p3.

3rd row: K1, *p1, k5, p1, k1; rep from * to end.

4th row: P1, *k2, p3, k2, p1; rep from * to end.

Rep these 4 rows.

Oblong Texture

Multiple of 10 sts + 1.

1st row (right side): K3, p5, *k5, p5; rep from * to last 3 sts, k3.

2nd row: P3, k5, *p5, k5; rep from * to last 3 sts, p3.

3rd row: As 2nd row.

4th row: As 1st row.

Rep these 4 rows.

Basketweave Stitch I

Multiple of 8 sts + 3.

1st row (right side): Knit.

2nd row: K4, p3, *k5, p3; rep from * to last 4 sts, k4.

3rd row: P4, k3, *p5, k3; rep from * to last 4 sts, p4.

4th row: As 2nd row.

5th row: Knit.

6th row: P3, *k5, p3; rep from * to end.

7th row: K3, *p5, k3; rep from * to end.

8th row: As 6th row.

Rep these 8 rows.

Basketweave Stitch II

Worked as Basketweave Stitch I, using reverse side as right side.

Fancy Box Stitch

Multiple of 8 sts + 6.

1st row (right side): K2, *p2, k2; rep from * to end.

2nd row: P2, *k2, p2; rep from * to end.

3rd row: As 1st row.

4th row: K1, p4, *k4, p4; rep from * to last st, k1.

5th row: P1, k4, *p4, k4; rep from * to last st, p1.

6th row: As 4th row.

Rep these 6 rows.

Diagonal Texture

Multiple of 8 sts.

1st row (right side): *K1, p1, k1, p5; rep from * to end.

2nd row: *K5, p1, k1, p1; rep from * to end.

3rd row: *K1, p1, k5, p1; rep from * to end.

4th row: *K1, p5, k1, p1; rep from * to end.

5th row: As 4th row.

6th row: As 3rd row.

7th row: As 2nd row.

8th row: *K1, p1, k1, p5; rep from * to end.

9th row: P4, *k1, p1, k1, p5; rep from * to last 4 sts, [k1, p1] twice.

10th row: [K1, p1] twice, *k5, p1, k1, p1; rep from * to last 4 sts, k4.

11th row: K3, p1, k1, p1, *k5, p1, k1, p1; rep from * to last 2 sts, k2.

12th row: P2, k1, p1, k1, *p5, k1, p1, k1; rep from * to last 3 sts, p3.

13th row: As 12th row.

14th row: As 11th row.

15th row: As 10th row.

16th row: As 9th row.

Rep these 16 rows.

Diamond Web

Multiple of 6 sts + 1.

1st row (right side): P3, *k1, p5; rep from * to last 4 sts, k1, p3.

2nd row: K3, *p1, k5; rep from * to last 4 sts, p1, k3.

Rep these 2 rows once more.

5th row: P2, *k1, p1, k1, p3; rep from * to last 5 sts, k1, p1, k1, p2.

6th row: K2, *p1, k1, p1, k3; rep from * to last 5 sts, p1, k1, p1, k2.

Rep the last 2 rows once more.

9th row: P1, *k1, p3, k1, p1; rep from * to end.

10th row: K1, *p1, k3, p1, k1; rep from * to end.

Rep the last 2 rows once more.

13th row: K1, *p5, k1; rep from * to end.

14th row: P1, *k5, p1; rep from * to end.

Rep the last 2 rows once more.

17th row: As 9th row.

18th row: As 10th row.

Rep the last 2 rows once more.

21st row: As 5th row.

22nd row: As 6th row.

Rep the last 2 rows once more.

Rep these 24 rows.

Knit and Purl Patterns

Knife Pleats

Multiple of 13 sts.
1st row (right side): *K4, [p1, k1] 3 times, p3; rep from * to end.
2nd row: *K3, [p1, k1] 3 times, p4; rep from * to end.
Rep these 2 rows.

Multiple of 6 sts + 1.
1st row (right side): K1, *p2, k1; rep from * to end.
2nd row: P1, *k2, p1; rep from * to end.
Rep the last 2 rows once more.
5th row: K1, *p5, k1; rep from * to end.
6th row: P1, *k5, p1; rep from * to end.
Rep the last 2 rows once more.
9th and 11th rows: As 1st row.
10th and 12th rows: As 2nd row.
13th row: P3, *k1, p3; rep from * to end.
14th row: K3, *p1, k3; rep from * to end.
Rep the last 2 rows once more.
Rep these 16 rows.

2nd row: P1, k2, *p2, k2; rep from * to last st, p1.
3rd row: *P4, k2; rep from * to end.
4th row: *P2, k4; rep from * to end.
5th row: As 2nd row.
6th row: K1, p2, *k2, p2; rep from * to last st, k1.
7th row: *K2, p6, k2, p2; rep from * to end.
8th row: *K2, p2, k6, p2; rep from * to end.
Rep 1st to 6th rows once more.
15th row: [P2, k2] twice, *p6, k2, p2, k2; rep from * to last 4 sts, p4.
16th row: K4, p2, k2, p2, *k6, p2, k2, p2; rep from * to last 2 sts, k2.
Rep these 16 rows.

Vertical Dash Stitch

Multiple of 6 sts + 1.
1st row (right side): P3, k1, *p5, k1; rep from * to last 3 sts, p3.
2nd row: K3, p1, *k5, p1; rep from * to last 3 sts, k3.
Rep the last 2 rows once more.
5th row: K1, *p5, k1; rep from * to end.
6th row: P1, *k5, p1; rep from * to end.
Rep the last 2 rows once more.
Rep these 8 rows.

Fancy Track Pattern

Multiple of 12 sts + 1.
1st row (right side): K3, p3, k1, p3, *k5, p3, k1, p3; rep from * to last 3 sts, k3.
2nd row: K6, p1, *k11, p1; rep from * to last 6 sts, k6.
Rep the last 2 rows once more.
5th row: K3, p2, k1, p1, k1, p2, *k5, p2, k1, p1, k1, p2; rep from * to last 3 sts, k3.
6th row: K5, p1, k1, p1, *k9, p1, k1, p1; rep from * to last 5 sts, k5.
Rep the last 2 rows once more.
Rep these 8 rows.

Random Dash Pattern

Broken Chevron

Multiple of 12 sts.
1st row (right side): K1, p2, *k2, p2; rep from * to last st, k1.

Seed Pearl Grid

Multiple of 8 sts + 1.
1st and every alt row (wrong side): Purl.
2nd row: P1, *k1, p1; rep from * to end.
4th row: Knit.
6th row: P1, *k7, p1; rep from * to end.
8th row: Knit.
10th row: As 6th row.
12th row: Knit.
Rep these 12 rows.

Simple Seed Stitch

Multiple of 4 sts + 1.
1st row (right side): P1, *k3, p1; rep from * to end.
2nd and every alt row: Purl.
3rd row: Knit.
5th row: K2, p1, *k3, p1; rep from * to last 2 sts, k2.
7th row: Knit.

8th row: Purl.
Rep these 8 rows.

Ripple Pattern

Multiple of 8 sts + 6.
1st row (right side): K6, *p2, k6; rep from * to end.
2nd row: K1, *p4, k4; rep from * to last 5 sts, p4, k1.
3rd row: P2, *k2, p2; rep from * to end.
4th row: P1, *k4, p4; rep from * to last 5 sts, k4, p1.
5th row: K2, *p2, k6; rep from * to last 4 sts, p2, k2.
6th row: P6, *k2, p6; rep from * to end.
7th row: As 4th row.
8th row: K2, *p2, k2; rep from * to end.
9th row: As 2nd row.
10th row: P2, *k2, p6; rep from * to last 4 sts, k2, p2.
Rep these 10 rows.

Zigzag Moss Stitch

Multiple of 6 sts + 1.
1st row (right side): Knit.
2nd row: Purl.
3rd row: P1, *k5, p1; rep from * to end.
4th row: P1, *k1, p3, k1, p1; rep from * to end.
5th row: P1, *k1, p1; rep from * to end.
6th row: As 5th row.
7th row: K2, p1, k1, p1, *k3, p1, k1, p1; rep from * to last 2 sts, k2.
8th row: P3, k1, *p5, k1; rep from * to last 3 sts, p3.
9th row: Knit.
10th row: Purl.

11th row: K3, p1, *k5, p1; rep from * to last 3 sts, k3.
12th row: P2, k1, p1, k1, *p3, k1, p1, k1; rep from * to last 2 sts, p2.
13th row: K1, *p1, k1; rep from * to end.
14th row: As 13th row.
15th row: K1, *p1, k3, p1, k1; rep from * to end.
16th row: K1, *p5, k1; rep from * to end.
Rep these 16 rows.

Vertical Zigzag Moss Stitch

Multiple of 7 sts.
1st row (right side): *P1, k1, p1, k4; rep from * to end.
2nd row: *P4, k1, p1, k1; rep from * to end.
3rd row: *[k1, p1] twice, k3; rep from * to end.
4th row: *P3, [k1, p1] twice; rep from * to end.
5th row: K2, p1, k1, p1, *k4, p1, k1, p1; rep from * to last 2 sts, k2.
6th row: P2, k1, p1, k1, *p4, k1, p1, k1; rep from * to last 2 sts, p2.
7th row: K3, p1, k1, p1, *k4, p1, k1, p1; rep from * to last st, k1.
8th row: [P1, k1] twice, *p4, k1, p1, k1; rep from * to last 3 sts, p3.
9th row: *K4, p1, k1, p1; rep from * to end.
10th row: *K1, p1, k1, p4; rep from * to end.
11th and 12th rows: As 7th and 8th rows.
13th and 14th rows: As 5th and 6th rows.
15th and 16th rows: As 3rd and 4th rows.
Rep these 16 rows.

Caterpillar Stitch

Multiple of 8 sts + 6.
1st row (right side): K4, p2, *k6, p2; rep from * to end.
2nd row: P1, k2, *p6, k2; rep from * to last 3 sts, p3.
3rd row: K2, p2, *k6, p2; rep from * to last 2 sts, k2.
4th row: P3, k2, *p6, k2; rep from * to last st, p1.
5th row: P2, *k6, p2; rep from * to last 4 sts, k4.
6th row: Purl.
Rep these 6 rows.

Diagonals I

Multiple of 8 sts + 6.
1st row (right side): P3, *k5, p3; rep from * to last 3 sts, k3.
2nd row: P4, *k3, p5; rep from * to last 2 sts, k2.
3rd row: P1, k5, *p3, k5; rep from * to end.
4th row: K1, p5, *k3, p5; rep from * to end.
5th row: K4, *p3, k5; rep from * to last 2 sts, p2.
6th row: K3, *p5, k3; rep from * to last 3 sts, p3.
7th row: K2, p3, *k5, p3; rep from * to last st, k1.
8th row: P2, k3, *p5, k3; rep from * to last st, p1.
Rep these 8 rows.

Diagonals II

Worked as Diagonals I, using reverse side as right side.

Knit and Purl Patterns

Diamond Pattern

Multiple of 8 sts + 1.
1st row (right side): P1, *k7, p1; rep from * to end.
2nd row: K2, p5, *k3, p5; rep from * to last 2 sts, k2.
3rd row: K1, *p2, k3, p2, k1; rep from * to end.
4th row: P2, k2, p1, k2, *p3, k2, p1, k2; rep from * to last 2 sts, p2.
5th row: K3, p3, *k5, p3; rep from * to last 3 sts, k3.
6th row: P4, k1, *p7, k1; rep from * to last 4 sts, p4.
7th row: As 5th row.
8th row: As 4th row.
9th row: As 3rd row.
10th row: As 2nd row.
Rep these 10 rows.

Slanting Diamonds

Multiple of 10 sts.
1st row (right side): *K9, p1; rep from * to end.
2nd row: *K2, p8; rep from * to end.
3rd row: *K7, p3; rep from * to end.
4th row: *K4, p6; rep from * to end.
5th and 6th rows: *K5, p5; rep from * to end.
7th row: K5, p4, *k6, p4; rep from * to last st, k1.
8th row: P2, k3, *p7, k3; rep from * to last 5 sts, p5.
9th row: K5, p2, *k8, p2; rep from * to last 3 sts, k3.
10th row: P4, k1, *p9, k1; rep from * to last 5 sts, p5.
11th row: K4, p1, *k9, p1; rep from * to last 5 sts, k5.

12th row: P5, k2, *p8, k2; rep from * to last 3 sts, p3.
13th row: K2, p3, *k7, p3; rep from * to last 5 sts, k5.
14th row: P5, k4, *p6, k4; rep from * to last st, p1.
15th and 16th rows: *P5, k5; rep from * to end.
17th row: *P4, k6; rep from * to end.
18th row: *P7, k3; rep from * to end.
19th row: *P2, k8; rep from * to end.
20th row: *P9, k1; rep from * to end.
Rep these 20 rows.

Polperro Laughing Boy

Multiple of 6 sts.
1st row (right side): Knit.
2nd row: P2, k2, *p4, k2; rep from * to last 2 sts, p2.
Rep these 2 rows once more.
Work 4 rows in st st, starting knit.
Rep these 8 rows.

Cross Motif Pattern I

Multiple of 12 sts.
1st row (right side): P1, k10, *p2, k10; rep from * to last st, p1.
2nd row: K1, p10, *k2, p10; rep from * to last st, k1.
Rep the last 2 rows once more.

5th row: P3, k6, *p6, k6; rep from * to last 3 sts, p3.
6th row: K3, p6, *k6, p6; rep from * to last 3 sts, k3.
7th row: As 1st row.
8th row: As 2nd row.
Rep the last 2 rows once more.
11th row: Knit.
12th row: Purl.
13th row: K5, p2, *k10, p2; rep from * to last 5 sts, k5.
14th row: P5, k2, *p10, k2; rep from * to last 5 sts, p5.
Rep the last 2 rows once more.
17th row: K3, p6, *k6, p6; rep from * to last 3 sts, k3.
18th row: P3, k6, *p6, k6; rep from * to last 3 sts, p3.
19th row: K5, p2, *k10, p2; rep from * to last 5 sts, k5.
20th row: P5, k2, *p10, k2; rep from * to last 5 sts, p5.
Rep the last 2 rows once more.
23rd row: Knit.
24th row: Purl.
Rep these 24 rows.

Cross Motif Pattern II

Worked as Cross Motif Pattern I, using reverse side as right side.

Lizard Lattice

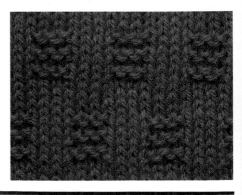

Multiple of 6 sts + 3.
Work 4 rows in st st, starting knit (1st row is right side).
5th row: P3, *k3, p3; rep from * to end.
6th row: Purl.
Rep the last 2 rows once more, then 5th row again.
Work 4 rows in st st, starting purl.
14th row: P3, *k3, p3; rep from * to end.
15th row: Knit.
Rep the last 2 rows once more, then 14th row again.
Rep these 18 rows.

Looe Eddystone

Multiple of 11 sts.
1st and every alt row (right side): Knit.
2nd row: P2, k7, *p4, k7; rep from * to last 2 sts, p2.
4th row: P3, k5, *p6, k5; rep from * to last 3 sts, p3.
6th row: P4, k3, *p8, k3; rep from * to last 4 sts, p4.
8th and 10th rows: P5, k1, *p10, k1; rep from * to last 5 sts, p5.
Work 4 rows in st st.
Rep these 14 rows.

Alans Pattern I

Multiple of 8 sts + 4.
1st row (right side) Knit.
2nd row: K4, *p4, k4; rep from * to end.
3rd row: P4, *k4, p4; rep from * to end.
4th row: Knit.
5th row: As 3rd row.

6th row: As 2nd row.
7th row: Knit.
Rep last 3 rows once more.
11th row: As 2nd row.
12th row: As 3rd row.
Rep these 12 rows.

Alans Pattern II

Worked as Alans Pattern I, using reverse side as right side.

Polperro Horizontal Diamonds

Multiple of 12 sts + 1.
Work 3 rows in garter st (1st row is right side).
Work 3 rows in st st, starting purl.
7th row: K6, p1, *k11, p1; rep from * to last 6 sts, k6.
8th row: P5, k1, p1, k1, *p9, k1, p1, k1; rep from * to last 5 sts, p5.
9th row: K4, p1, k3, p1, *k7, p1, k3, p1; rep from * to last 4 sts, k4.
10th row: P3, k1, *p5, k1; rep from * to last 3 sts, p3.
11th row: K2, p1, k7, p1, *k3, p1, k7, p1; rep from * to last 2 sts, k2.
12th row: P1, *k1, p9, k1, p1; rep from * to end.
13th row: P1, *k11, p1; rep from * to end.
14th row: As 12th row.
15th row: As 11th row.
16th row: As 10th row.
17th row: As 9th row.
18th row: As 8th row.

19th row: As 7th row.
Work 3 rows in st st, starting purl.
Rep these 22 rows.

Polperro Musician

Multiple of 23 sts.
1st row (wrong side): K1, p2, k1, [p7, k1] twice, p2, *k2, p2, k1, [p7, k1] twice, p2; rep from * to last st, k1.
2nd row: K10, p1, k1, p1, *k20, p1, k1, p1; rep from * to last 10 sts, k10.
3rd row: P1, k2, p6, k1, p3, k1, p6, k2, *p2, k2, p6, k1, p3, k1, p6, k2; rep from * to last st, p1.
4th row: K8, p1, k5, p1, *k16, p1, k5, p1; rep from * to last 8 sts, k8.
5th row: K1, p6, k1, p7, k1, p6, *k2, p6, k1, p7, k1, p6; rep from * to last st, k1.
6th row: K6, p1, k9, p1, *k12, p1, k9, p1; rep from * to last 6 sts, k6.
7th row: P1, k2, p2, k1, p11, k1, p2, k2, *p2, k2, p2, k1, p11, k1, p2, k2; rep from * to last st, p1.
8th row: K4, p1, k13, p1, *k8, p1, k13, p1; rep from * to last 4 sts, k4.
Rep these 8 rows.

Polperro Northcott

Multiple of 4 sts + 2.
Work 3 rows in garter st (1st row is right side).
4th row: K2, *p2, k2; rep from * to end.
5th row: Knit.
Rep the last 2 rows 10 times more.
Work 2 rows in garter st.
28th row: Purl.
Rep these 28 rows.

Knit and Purl Patterns

Maze Pattern

Multiple of 13 sts.
1st row (right side): Knit.
2nd row: Purl.
3rd row: Knit.
4th row: P1, k11, *p2, k11; rep from * to last st, p1.
5th row: K1, p11, *k2, p11; rep from * to last st, k1.
6th row: As 4th row.
7th row: K1, p2, k7, p2, *k2, p2, k7, p2; rep from * to last st, k1.
8th row: P1, k2, p7, k2, *p2, k2, p7, k2; rep from * to last st, p1.
9th row: As 7th row.
10th row: P1, k2, p2, k3, *[p2, k2] twice, p2, k3; rep from * to last 5 sts, p2, k2, p1.
11th row: K1, p2, k2, p3, *[k2, p2] twice, k2, p3; rep from * to last 5 sts, k2, p2, k1.
Rep the last 2 rows once more.
14th row: As 8th row.
15th row: As 7th row.
16th row: As 8th row.
17th row: As 5th row.
18th row: As 4th row.
19th row: As 5th row.
20th row: As 2nd row.
Rep these 20 rows.

Stripes in Relief

Multiple of 14 sts + 6.
1st row (wrong side): K6, *p3, k2, p3, k6; rep from * to end.
2nd row: P6, *k3, p2, k3, p6; rep from * to end.

3rd row: P9, k2, *p12, k2; rep from * to last 9 sts, p9.
4th row: K9, p2, *k12, p2; rep from * to last 9 sts, k9.
5th row: P2, k2, *p12, k2; rep from * to last 2 sts, p2.
6th row: K2, p2, *k12, p2; rep from * to last 2 sts, k2.
7th row: P2, k2, *p3, k6, p3, k2; rep from * to last 2 sts, p2.
8th row: K2, p2, *k3, p6, k3, p2; rep from * to last 2 sts, k2.
9th row: As 5th row.
10th row: As 6th row.
11th row: As 3rd row.
12th row: As 4th row.
Rep these 12 rows.

Diamond and Lozenge Pattern I

Multiple of 12 sts.
1st row (right side): *K6, p6; rep from * to end.
2nd row: *K6, p6; rep from * to end.
3rd and 4th rows: *P1, k5, p5, k1; rep from * to end.
5th and 6th rows: K1, p1, k4, p4, *[k1, p1] twice, k4, p4; rep from * to last 2 sts, k1, p1.
7th and 8th rows: P1, k1, p1, k3, p3, *[k1, p1] 3 times, k3, p3; rep from * to last 3 sts, k1, p1, k1.
9th and 10th rows: [K1, p1] twice, k2, p2, *[k1, p1] 4 times, k2, p2; rep from * to last 4 sts, [k1, p1] twice.
11th and 12th rows: *P1, k1; rep from * to end.
13th and 14th rows: *K1, p1; rep from * to end.
15th and 16th rows: [P1, k1] twice, p2, k2, *[p1, k1] 4 times, p2, k2; rep from * to last 4 sts, [p1, k1] twice.
17th and 18th rows: K1, p1, k1, p3, k3, *[p1, k1] 3 times, p3, k3; rep from * to last 3 sts, p1, k1, p1.
19th and 20th rows: P1, k1, p4, k4, *[p1, k1] twice, p4, k4; rep from * to last 2 sts, p1, k1.
21st and 22nd rows: *K1, p5, k5, p1; rep from * to end.
23rd and 24th rows: *P6, k6; rep from * to end.

25th and 26th rows: *P5, k1, p1, k5; rep from * to end.
27th and 28th rows: *P4, [k1, p1] twice, k4; rep from * to end.
29th and 30th rows: *P3, [k1, p1] 3 times, k3; rep from * to end.
31st and 32nd rows: *P2, [k1, p1] 4 times, k2; rep from * to end.
33rd and 34th rows: As 11th and 12th rows.
35th and 36th rows: As 13th and 14th rows.
37th and 38th rows: *K2, [p1, k1] 4 times, p2; rep from * to end.
39th and 40th rows: *K3, [p1, k1] 3 times, p3; rep from * to end.
41st and 42nd rows: *K4, [p1, k1] twice, p4; rep from * to end.
43rd and 44th rows: *K5, p1, k1, p5; rep from * to end.
Rep these 44 rows.

Diamond and Lozenge Pattern II

Multiple of 12 sts.
Rep rows 1 to 24 of Diamond and Lozenge Pattern I.

Diamond and Block

Multiple of 14 sts + 5.
1st row (right side): P5, *k4, p1, k4, p5; rep from * to end.

2nd row: K5, *p3, k3, p3, k5; rep from * to end,
3rd row: K7, p5, *k9, p5; rep from * to last 7 sts, k7.
4th row: P6, k7, *p7, k7; rep from * to last 6 sts, p6.
5th row: K5, *p9, k5; rep from * to end.
6th row: As 4th row.
7th row: As 3rd row.
8th row: As 2nd row.
Rep these 8 rows.

Divided Boxes

Multiple of 5 sts.
1st row (right side): Knit.
2nd row: *K1, p4; rep from * to end.
3rd row: *K3, p2; rep from * to end.
4th row: As 3rd row.
5th row: As 2nd row.
6th row: Knit.
Rep these 6 rows.

Staircase Pattern I

Multiple of 16 sts.
1st and 3rd rows (right side): *K5, p11; rep from * to end.
2nd row: *K11, p5; rep from * to end.
4th and 6th rows: Purl.
5th row: Knit.
7th and 9th rows: P4, *k5, p11; rep from

* to last 12 sts, k5, p7.
8th row: K7, *p5, k11; rep from * to last 9 sts, p5, k4.
10th and 12th rows: Purl.
11th row: Knit.
13th and 15th rows: P8, *k5, p11; rep from * to last 8 sts, k5, p3.
14th row: K3, *p5, k11; rep from * to last 13 sts, p5, k8.
16th and 18th rows: Purl.
17th row: Knit.
19th and 21st rows: K1, p11, *k5, p11; rep from * to last 4 sts, k4.
20th row: P4, *k11, p5; rep from * to last 12 sts, k11, p1.
22nd row: Purl.
23rd row: Knit.
24th row: Purl.
Rep these 24 rows.

Staircase Pattern II

Worked as Staircase Pattern I, using reverse side as right side.

Textured Triangle Stack

Multiple of 10 sts + 1.
1st row (right side): P5, *k1, p9; rep from * to last 6 sts, k1, p5.
2nd row: K5, *p1, k9; rep from * to last 6

sts, p1, k5.
3rd row: P4, *k3, p7; rep from * to last 7 sts, p3, k4.
4th row: K4, *p3, k7; rep from * to last 7 sts, k3, p4.
5th row: P3, *k5, p5; rep from * to last 8 sts, k5, p3.
6th row: K3, *p5, k5; rep from * to last 8 sts, p5, k3.
7th row: P2, *k7, p3; rep from * to last 9 sts, k7, p2.
8th row: K2, *p7, k3; rep from * to last 9 sts, p7, k2.
9th row: P1, *k9, p1; rep from * to end.
10th row: K1, *p9, k1; rep from * to end.
Rep these 10 rows.

Windmill Pattern

Multiple of 20 sts.
1st row (right side): *P1, k9, p9, k1; rep from * to end.
2nd row: *P2, k8, p8, k2; rep from * to end.
3rd row: *P3, k7, p7, k3: rep from * to end.
4th row: *P4, k6, p6, k4; rep from * to end.
5th row: *P5, k5; rep from * to end.
6th row: *P6, k4, p4, k6; rep from * to end.
7th row: *P7, k3, p3, k7; rep from * to end.
8th row: *P8, k2, p2, k8; rep from * to end.
9th row: *P9, k1, p1, k9; rep from * to end.
10th row: *P10, k10; rep from * to end.
11th row: *K10, p10; rep from * to end.
12th row: *K9, p1, k1, p9; rep from * to end.
13th row: *K8, p2, k2, p8; rep from * to end.
14th row: *K7, p3, k3, p7; rep from * to end.
15th row: *K6, p4, k4, p6; rep from * to end.
16th row: *K5, p5; rep from * to end.
17th row: *K4, p6, k6, p4; rep from * to end.
18th row: *K3, p7, k7, p3; rep from * to end.
19th row: *K2, p8, k8, p2; rep from * to end.
20th row: *K1, p9, k9, p1; rep from * to end.
21st row: As 10th row.
22nd row: As 11th row.
Rep these 22 rows.

Knit and Purl Patterns

Flag Pattern I

Multiple of 11 sts.
1st row (right side): *P1, k10; rep from * to end.
2nd row: *P9, k2; rep from * to end.
3rd row: *P3, k8; rep from * to end.
4th row: *P7, k4; rep from * to end.
5th row: *P5, k6; rep from * to end.
6th row: As 5th row.
7th row: As 5th row.
8th row: As 4th row.
9th row: As 3rd row.
10th row: As 2nd row.
11th row: As 1st row.
12th row: *K1, p10; rep from * to end.
13th row: *K9, p2; rep from * to end.
14th row: *K3, p8; rep from * to end.
15th row: *K7, p4; rep from * to end.
16th row: *K5, p6; rep from * to end.
17th row: As 16th row.
18th row: As 16th row.
19th row: As 15th row.
20th row: As 14th row.
21st row: As 13th row.
22nd row: As 12th row.
Rep these 22 rows.

Flag Pattern II

Worked as Flag Pattern I, using reverse side as right side.

Divided Triangles

Multiple of 14 sts + 1.
1st row (wrong side): Knit.
2nd row: Knit.
3rd row: K1, *p13, k1; rep from * to end.
4th row: K1, *p1, k11, p1, k1; rep from * to end.
5th row: P1, *k2, p9, k2, p1; rep from * to end.
6th row: K1, *p3, k7, p3, k1; rep from * to end.
7th row: P1, *k4, p5, k4, p1; rep from * to end.
8th row: K1, *p5, k3, p5, k1; rep from * to end.
9th row: P1, *[k6, p1] twice; rep from * to end.
10th and 11th rows: Purl.
12th row: K7, p1, *k13, p1; rep from * to last 7 sts, k7.
13th row: P6, k1, p1, k1, *p11, k1, p1, k1; rep from * to last 6 sts, p6.
14th row: K5, p2, k1, p2, *k9, p2, k1, p2; rep from * to last 5 sts, k5.
15th row: P4, k3, p1, k3, *p7, k3, p1, k3; rep from * to last 4 sts, p4.
16th row: K3, p4, k1, p4, *k5, p4, k1, p4; rep from * to last 3 sts, k3.
17th row: P2, k5, p1, k5, *p3, k5, p1, k5; rep from * to last 2 sts, p2.
18th row: K1, *p6, k1; rep from * to end.
Rep these 18 rows.

Compass Check Pattern

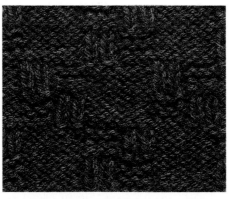

Multiple of 14 sts + 7.
1st row (right side): [P1, KB1] twice, *k10, [p1, KB1] twice; rep from * to last 3 sts, k3.
2nd row: K3, [PB1, k1] twice, *p7, k3, [PB1, k1] twice; rep from * to end.
Rep the last 2 rows once more.
5th row: Knit.
6th row: [K1, PB1] twice, *p10, [k1, PB1] twice; rep from * to last 3 sts, p3.
7th row: P3, [KB1, p1] twice, *k7, p3, [KB1, p1] twice; rep from * to end.
Rep the last 2 rows once more.
10th row: P7, *[k1, PB1] twice, p10; rep from * to end.
11th row: K7, *p3, [KB1, p1] twice, k7; rep from * to end.
Rep the last 2 rows once more.
14th row: Purl.
15th row: K7, *[p1, KB1] twice, k10; rep from * to end.
16th row: P7, *k3, [PB1, k1] twice, p7; rep from * to end.
Rep the last 2 rows once more.
Rep these 18 rows.

Rib and Arrow Pattern I

Multiple of 14 sts + 2.
1st row (right side): K2, *p4, k4, p4, k2; rep from * to end.
2nd row: P2, *k4, p4, k4, p2; rep from * to end.
3rd row: K2, *p3, k6, p3, k2; rep from * to end.
4th row: P2, *k3, p6, k3, p2; rep from * to end.
5th row: K2, p2, k2, [p1, k2] twice, *[p2, k2] twice, [p1, k2] twice; rep from * to last 4 sts, p2, k2.
6th row: P2, k2, p2, [k1, p2] twice, *[k2, p2] twice, [k1, p2] twice; rep from * to last 4 sts, k2, p2.
7th row: K2, *p1, k2, [p2, k2] twice, p1, k2; rep from * to end.
8th row: P2, *k1, p2, [k2, p2] twice, k1, p2; rep from * to end.
9th row: K4, p3, k2, p3, *k6, p3, k2, p3; rep from * to last 4 sts, k4.
10th row: P4, k3, p2, k3, *p6, k3, p2, k3; rep from * to last 4 sts, p4.
11th row: K3, p4, k2, p4, *k4, p4, k2, p4;

rep from * to last 3 sts, k3.
12th row: P3, k4, p2, k4, *p4, k4, p2, k4; rep from * to last 3 sts, p3.
13th row: K2, *p5, k2; rep from * to end.
14th row: P2, *k5, p2; rep from * to end.
Rep these 14 rows.

Rib and Arrow Pattern II

Worked as Rib and Arrow Pattern I, using reverse side as right side.

Ridge and Diamond Stripes

Multiple of 8 sts + 7.
1st row (right side): P7, *k1, p7; rep from * to end.
2nd row: K3, p1, *k2, p3, k2, p1; rep from * to last 3 sts, k3.
3rd row: P2, k3, *p2, k1, p2, k3; rep from * to last 2 sts, p2.
4th row: K1, p5, *k3, p5; rep from * to last st, k1.
5th row: K7, *p1, k7; rep from * to end.
6th row: As 4th row.
7th row: As 3rd row.
8th row: As 2nd row.
9th row: As 1st row.

10th, 11th and 12th rows: Purl.
Rep these 12 rows.

Spiral Pattern

Multiple of 7 sts.
1st row (right side): P2, k4, *p3, k4; rep from * to last st, p1.
2nd row: K1, p3, *k4, p3; rep from * to last 3 sts, k3.
3rd row: P1, k1, p2, *k2, p2, k1, p2; rep from * to last 3 sts, k2, p1.
4th row: K1, p1, k2, p2, *k2, p1, k2, p2; rep from * to last st, k1.
5th row: P1, k3, *p4, k3; rep from * to last 3 sts, p3.
6th row: K2, p4, *k3, p4; rep from * to last st, k1.
7th row: P1, k5, *p2, k5; rep from * to last st, p1.
8th row: K1, p5, *k2, p5; rep from * to last st, k1.
Rep these 8 rows.

Zigzag and Stripe Columns

Multiple of 10 sts.
1st row (right side): P1, k1, p2, k5, *p2, k1, p2, k5; rep from * to last st, p1.
2nd row: K1, p4, k2, p2, *k2, p4, k2, p2; rep from * to last st, k1.

3rd row: P1, k3, *p2, k3; rep from * to last st, p1.
4th row: K1, p2, k2, p4, *k2, p2, k2, p4; rep from * to last st, k1.
5th row: Purl.
6th row: Knit.
7th row: P1, k4, p2, k2, *p2, k4, p2, k2; rep from * to last st, p1.
8th row: K1, p3, *k2, p3; rep from * to last st, k1.
9th row: P1, k2, p2, k4, *p2, k2, p2, k4; rep from * to last st, p1.
10th row: K1, p5, k2, p1, *k2, p5, k2, p1; rep from * to last st, k1.
Rep these 10 rows.

Valentine Hearts

Multiple of 12 sts + 9.
1st row (right side): P4, k1, *p11, k1; rep from * to last 4 sts, p4.
2nd row: K3, p3, *k9, p3; rep from * to last 3 sts, k3.
3rd row: P3, k3, *p9, k3; rep from * to last 3 sts, p3.
4th row: K2, p5, *k7, p5; rep from * to last 2 sts, k2.
5th row: P1, k7, *p5, k7; rep from * to last st, p1.
6th row: P9, *k3, p9; rep from * to end.
7th row: K9, *p3, k9; rep from * to end.
8th row: As 6th row.
9th row: K4, p1, *k4, p3, k4, p1; rep from * to last 4 sts, k4.
10th row: K1, p2, k3, p2, *k2, p1, k2, p2, k3, p2; rep from * to last st, k1.
11th row: P10, *k1, p11; rep from * to last 11 sts, k1, p10.
12th row: As 7th row.
13th row: As 6th row.
14th row: As 5th row.
15th row: As 4th row.
16th row: As 3rd row.
17th row: As 2nd row.
18th row: As 3rd row.
19th row: K3, p3, *k4, p1, k4, p3; rep from * to last 3 sts, k3.
20th row: P2, k2, p1, k2, *p2, k3, p2, k2, p1, k2; rep from * to last 2 sts, p2.
Rep these 20 rows.

Knit and Purl Panels

Ridge and Furrow

Worked over 23 sts on a background of st st.
1st row (right side): P4, k7, p1, k7, p4.
2nd row: K1, p2, k1, p5, [k1, p1] twice, k1, p5, k1, p2, k1.
3rd row: P4, k4, [p1, k2] twice, p1, k4, p4.
4th row: K1, p2, [k1, p3] 4 times, k1, p2, k1.
5th row: P4, k2, [p1, k4] twice, p1, k2, p4.
6th row: K1, p2, k1, p1, [k1, p5] twice, k1, p1, k1, p2, k1.
Rep these 6 rows.

Tree of Life

Worked over 23 sts on a background of st st.
1st row (right side): P4, k7, p1, k7, p4.
2nd row: K1, p2, k1, p6, k1, p1, k1, p6, k1, p2, k1.
3rd row: P4, k5, p1, k3, p1, k5, p4.
4th row: K1, p2, k1, p4, [k1, p2] twice, k1, p4, k1, p2, k1.
5th row: P4, k3, p1, k2, p1, k1, p1, k2, p1, k3, p4.
6th row: [K1, p2] 3 times, k1, p3, [k1, p2] 3 times, k1.
7th row: P4, k1, [p1, k2] 4 times, p1, k1, p4.
8th row: K1, p2, k1, p3, k1, p2, k1, p1, k1, p2, k1, p3, k1, p2, k1.
9th row: P4, [k2, p1] twice, k3, [p1, k2] twice, p4.
10th row: As 4th row.
11th row: As 5th row.

12th row: K1, p2, k1, p5, k1, p3, k1, p5, k1, p2, k1.
13th row: P4, k4, [p1, k2] twice, p1, k4, p4.
14th row: As 2nd row.
15th row: As 3rd row.
16th row: K1, p2, k1, [p7, k1] twice, p2, k1.
17th row: P4, k6, p1, k1, p1, k6, p4.
18th row: K1, p2, k1, p15, k1, p2, k1.
19th row: As 1st row.
20th row: As 18th row.
Rep these 20 rows.

Triple Wave

Worked over 14 sts on a background of st st.
1st row (right side): P3, k8, p3.
2nd row: [K1, p1] twice, k2, p2, k2, [p1, k1] twice.
3rd row: P3, k3, p2, k3, p3.
4th row: K1, p1, k1, p8, k1, p1, k1.
5th row: P3, k1, p2, k2, p2, k1, p3.
6th row: K1, p1, k1, p3, k2, p3, k1, p1, k1.
Rep these 6 rows.

Anchor

Worked over 17 sts on a background of st st.
1st row (right side): P3, k11, p3.

2nd row: K1, p1, [k1, p5] twice, k1, p1, k1.
3rd row: P3, k4, p1, k1, p1, k4, p3.
4th row: K1, p1, k1, p3, [k1, p1] twice, k1, p3, k1, p1, k1.
5th row: P3, k2, p1, k5, p1, k2, p3.
6th row: [K1, p1] twice, [k1, p3] twice, [k1, p1] twice, k1.
7th row: P3, k1, p1, k7, p1, k1, p3.
8th row: K1, p1, [k1, p5] twice, k1, p1, k1.
9th row: As 1st row.
Rep the last 2 rows once more.
12th row: K1, p1, k1, p3, k5, p3, k1, p1, k1.
13th row: P3, k3, p5, k3, p3.
14th row: As 12th row.
15th row: As 1st row.
16th row: As 8th row.
Rep the last 2 rows once more.
19th row: As 3rd row.
20th row: K1, p1, [k1, p3] 3 times, k1, p1, k1.
21st row: As 3rd row.
22nd row: As 2nd row.
23rd row: As 1st row.
24th row: K1, p1, k1, p11, k1, p1, k1.
Rep these 24 rows.

Diamond Net Mask

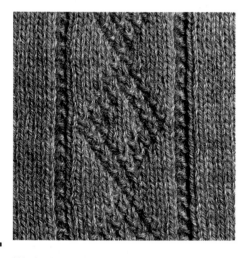

Worked over 19 sts on a background of st st.
1st row (right side): P3, k6, p1, k6, p3.
2nd row: K1, p1, k1, [p6, k1] twice, p1, k1.
3rd row: P3, k5, p1, k1, p1, k5, p3.
4th row: K1, p1, k1, [p5, k1, p1, k1] twice.
5th row: P3, k4, [p1, k1] twice, p1, k4, p3.
6th row: K1, p1, k1, p4, [k1, p1] twice, k1, p4, k1, p1, k1.
7th row: P3, k3, [p1, k1] 3 times, p1, k3, p3.
8th row: K1, p1, k1, p3, [k1, p1] 3 times, k1, p3, k1, p1, k1.
9th row: P3, k2, p1, k1, p1, k3, p1, k1, p1, k2, p3.
10th row: K1, p1, k1, p2, k1, p1, k1, p3, k1, p1, k1, p2, k1, p1, k1.
11th row: P3, [k1, p1] twice, k5, [p1, k1] twice, p3.
12th row: [K1, p1] 3 times, k1, p5, [k1, p1] 3 times, k1.
13th row: As 9th row.
14th row: As 10th row.
15th row: As 7th row.

16th row: As 8th row.
17th row: As 5th row.
18th row: As 6th row.
19th row: As 3rd row.
20th row: As 4th row.
Rep these 20 rows.

Ladder

Worked over 11 sts on a background of st st.
1st row (right side): P2, k7, p2.
2nd row: K2, p7, k2.
Rep the last 2 rows once more.
5th row: Purl.
6th row: As 2nd row.
7th row: As 1st row.
Rep the last 2 rows once more.
10th row: Knit.
Rep these 10 rows.

Marriage Lines

Worked over 17 sts on a background of st st.
1st row (right side): P3, k6, p1, k2, p1, k1, p3.
2nd row: K1, p1, [k1, p2] twice, k1, p5, k1, p1, k1.
3rd row: P3, k4, p1, k2, p1, k3, p3.
4th row: K1, p1, k1, p4, k1, p2, k1, p3, k1, p1, k1.

5th row: P3, [k2, p1] twice, k5, p3.
6th row: K1, p1, k1, p6, k1, p2, [k1, p1] twice, k1.
7th row: As 5th row.
8th row: As 4th row.
9th row: As 3rd row.
10th row: As 2nd row.
Rep these 10 rows.

Thin Star

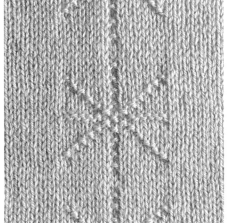

Worked over 13 sts on a background of st st.
1st row (wrong side): Purl.
2nd row: Knit.
3rd row: P6, k1, p6.
4th row: Knit.
5th row: K1, [p5, k1] twice.
6th row: K1, p1, k9, p1, k1.
7th row: P2, [k1, p3] twice, k1, p2.
8th row: K3, p1, k5, p1, k3.
9th row: P4, [k1, p1] twice, k1, p4.
10th row: K5, p1, k1, p1, k5.
Rep the last row twice more.
Work in reverse order from 9th to 2nd row inclusive.
Rep these 20 rows.

Latin Star

Worked over 19 sts on a background of st st.
1st row (wrong side): Purl.
2nd row: Knit.
3rd row: P9, k1, p9.
4th row: K8, p1, k1, p1, k8.
5th row: P1, k1, [p7, k1] twice, p1.
6th row: K2, p1, k5, p1, k1, p1, k5, p1, k2.
7th row: [P1, k1] twice, p5, k1, p5, [k1, p1] twice.
8th row: K2, [p1, k1, p1, k3] twice, p1, k1, p1, k2.
9th row: P3, k1, p1, [k1, p3] twice, k1, p1, k1, p3.
10th row: K4, [p1, k1] 5 times, p1, k4.
11th row: P5, [k1, p1] 4 times, k1, p5.
12th row: K6, p1, k5, p1, k6.
13th row: [P1, k1] 3 times, p2, k1, p1, k1, p2, [k1, p1] 3 times.
14th row: [P1, k1] 3 times, p1, [k2, p1] twice, [k1, p1] 3 times.
Work in reverse order from 13th row to 2nd row inclusive.
Rep these 26 rows.

Flying Wedge

Worked over 18 sts on a background of st st.
1st row (wrong side): Purl.
2nd row: K11, p1, k6.
3rd row: P7, k1, p10.
4th row: K9, p1, k1, p1, k6.
5th row: P7, k1, p1, k1, p8.
6th row: K7, [p1, k1] twice, p1, k6.
7th row: P7, [k1, p1] 5 times, k1.
8th row: [K1, p1] 6 times, k6.
9th row: P5, [k1, p1] 5 times, k1, p2.
10th row: K3, [p1, k1] 5 times, p1, k4.
11th row: P3, [k1, p1] 5 times, k1, p4.
12th row: K5, [p1, k1] 5 times, p1, k2.
13th row: [P1, k1] 6 times, p6.
14th row: K7, [p1, k1] 5 times, p1.
15th row: P7, [k1, p1] twice, k1, p6.
16th row: K7, p1, k1, p1, k8.
17th row: P9, k1, p1, k1, p6.
18th row: K7, p1, k10.
19th row: P11, k1, p6.
20th row: Knit.
Rep these 20 rows.

Rib Patterns

Brioche Rib

Multiple of 2 sts.
Foundation row: Knit.
Commence Pattern
1st row: *K1, K1B; rep from * to last 2 sts, k2.
Rep 1st row throughout.

Staggered Brioche Rib

Multiple of 2 sts + 1.
Foundation row (wrong side): Knit.
Commence Pattern
1st row: K1, *K1B, k1; rep from * to end.
Rep the 1st row 3 times more.
5th row: K2, k1B, *k1, K1B; rep from * to last 2 sts, k2.
Rep the 5th row 3 times more.
Rep the last 8 rows.

Hunters Stitch

Multiple of 11 sts + 4.

1st row (right side): P4, *[KB1, p1] 3 times, KB1, p4; rep from * to end.
2nd row: K4, *p1, [KB1, p1] 3 times, k4; rep from * to end.
Rep these 2 rows.

Rib Stitch

Multiple of 2 sts + 1.
1st row (right side): K1, *yf, sl 1 purlwise, yb, k1; rep from * to end.
2nd row: P1, *k1, p1; rep from * to end.
Rep these 2 rows.

Shadow Rib

Multiple of 3 sts + 2.
1st row (right side): Knit.
2nd row: P2, *KB1, p2; rep from * to end.
Rep these 2 rows.

Blanket Rib

Multiple of 2 sts + 1.
1st row (right side): Knit into front and back of each st (thus doubling the number of sts).
2nd row: K2tog, *p2tog, k2tog; rep from * to end (original number of sts restored).
Rep these 2 rows.

Puff Ribbing Pattern I

Multiple of 6 sts + 3.

Special Abbreviation
K3W = knit 3 sts wrapping yarn twice around needle for each st.

1st row (wrong side): P3, *K3W, p3; rep from * to end.
2nd row: K3, *p3 (dropping extra loops), k3; rep from * to end.
Rep these 2 rows.

Puff Ribbing Pattern II

Multiple of 8 sts + 5.

Special Abbreviation
K3W = knit 3 sts wrapping yarn twice around needle for each st.

1st row (right side): P5, *K3W, p5; rep from * to end.
2nd row: K5, *p3 (dropping extra loops), k5; rep from * to end.
Rep these 2 rows.

Little Bobble Rib

Multiple of 8 sts + 3.

1st row (right side): K3, *p2, [p1, k1] twice into next st then slip 2nd, 3rd and 4th sts of this group over first st (bobble completed), p2, k3; rep from * to end.

2nd row: P3, *k5, p3; rep from * to end.

3rd row: K3, *p5, k3; rep from * to end.

4th row: As 2nd row.

Rep these 4 rows.

Large Bobble Rib

Multiple of 7 sts + 2.

1st row (right side): K2, *p2, k1, p2, k2; rep from * to end.

2nd row: P2, *k2, p1, k2, p2; rep from * to end.

3rd row: K2, *p2, MB, p2, k2; rep from * to end.

4th row: As 2nd row.

Rep these 4 rows.

Chunky Rib Pattern I

Multiple of 8 sts + 6.

1st row (right side): P6, *k2, p6; rep from * to end.

2nd row: K6, *p2, k6; rep from * to end.

Rep the last 2 rows twice more.

7th row: P2, *k2, p2; rep from * to end.

8th row: K2, *p2, k2; rep from * to end.

Rep the last 2 rows twice more.

13th row: P2, k2, *p6, k2; rep from * to last 2 sts, p2.

14th row: K2, p2, *k6, p2; rep from * to last 2 sts, k2.

Rep the last 2 rows twice more.

19th row: As 7th row.

20th row: As 8th row.

Rep the last 2 rows twice more.

Rep these 24 rows.

Chunky Rib Pattern II

Worked as Chunky Rib Pattern I, using reverse side as right side.

Harris Tweed Ribbing

Multiple of 4 sts + 2.

1st row (right side): K2, *p2, k2; rep from * to end.

2nd row: P2, *k2, p2; rep from * to end.

3rd row: Knit.

4th row: Purl.

5th row: As 1st row.

6th row: As 2nd row.

7th row: Purl.

8th row: Knit.

Rep these 8 rows.

Thick and Thin Ribbing

Multiple of 4 sts + 1.

1st row (right side): K1, *p1, k1; rep from * to end.

2nd row: P1, *k1, p1; rep from * to end.

Rep the last 2 rows 3 times more.

9th row: K1, *p3, k1; rep from * to end.

10th row: P1, *k3, p1; rep from * to end.

Rep the last 2 rows 3 times more.

Rep these 16 rows.

Slipped Stitch Ribbing

Multiple of 8 sts + 3.

Note: Slip all sts purlwise.

1st row (right side): P3, *k1 wrapping yarn twice around needle, p3, k1, p3; rep from * to end.

2nd row: K3, *p1, k3, yf, sl 1 dropping extra loop, yb, k3; rep from * to end.

3rd row: P3, *yb, sl 1, yf, p3, k1, p3; rep from * to end.

4th row: K3, *p1, k3, yf, sl 1, yb, k3; rep from * to end.

Rep these 4 rows.

Rib Patterns

Seeded Rib

Multiple of 4 sts + 1.
1st row (right side): P1, *k3, p1; rep from * to end.
2nd row: K2, p1, *k3, p1; rep from * to last 2 sts, k2.
Rep these 2 rows.

Cluster Rib

Multiple of 3 sts + 1.
1st row (right side): P1, *k2, p1; rep from * to end.
2nd row: K1, *yf, k2, slip the yf over the 2 knit sts, k1; rep from * to end.
Rep these 2 rows.

Textured Ribbing

Multiple of 6 sts + 3.
1st row (right side): P3, *k3, p3; rep from * to end.
2nd row: K3, *p1, yb, sl 1 knitwise, yf, p1, k3; rep from * to end.
Rep these 2 rows twice more.
7th row: Knit.

8th row: P4, *yb, sl 1 knitwise, yf, p5; rep from * to last 5 sts, yb, sl 1 knitwise, yf, p4.
Rep these 8 rows.

Sailors Rib

Multiple of 5 sts + 1.
1st row (right side): KB1, *p1, k2, p1, KB1; rep from * to end.
2nd row: P1, *k1, p2, k1, p1; rep from * to end.
3rd row: KB1, *p4, KB1; rep from * to end.
4th row: P1, *k4, p1; rep from * to end.
Rep these 4 rows.

Feather Rib

Multiple of 5 sts + 2.
1st row (right side): P2, *yon, k2tog tbl, k1, p2; rep from * to end.
2nd row: K2, *yf, k2tog tbl, p1, k2; rep from * to end.
Rep these 2 rows.

Rib with Eyelets

Mutiple of 4 sts + 1.
1st row (right side): K1, *p3, k1; rep from * to end.
2nd row: P1, *k3, p1; rep from * to end.
Rep the last 2 rows once more.
5th row: K1, *p2tog, yrn, p1, k1; rep from * to end.
6th row: As 2nd row.
Rep these 6 rows.

Perforated Ribbing

Multiple of 6 sts + 3.
1st row (right side): P1, k1, p1, *yrn, p3tog, yrn, p1, k1, p1; rep from * to end.
2nd row: K1, p1, k1, *p3, k1, p1, k1; rep from * to end.
3rd row: P1, k1, p1, *k3, p1, k1, p1; rep from * to end.
4th row: As 2nd row.
Rep these 4 rows.

Eyelet and Slip Stitch Rib

Multiple of 11 sts + 7.
1st row (right side): P3, yb, sl 1 knitwise, yf, p3, *k1, yf, k2tog, k1, p3, yb, sl 1 knitwise, yf, p3; rep from * to end.
2nd row: K3, p1, k3, *p4, k3, p1, k3; rep from * to end.
3rd row: P3, yb, sl 1 knitwise, yf, p3, *k1, sl 1, k1, psso, yf, k1, p3, yb, sl 1 knitwise, yf, p3; rep from * to end.
4th row: As 2nd row.
Rep these 4 rows.

Double Twisted Rib

Multiple of 6 sts + 2.
1st row (right side): P2, *C2B, C2F, p2; rep from * to end.
2nd row: K2, *p4, k2; rep from * to end.
Rep these 2 rows.

Bobble Twists

Multiple of 8 sts + 6.
1st row (right side): P2, *C2B, p2; rep * to end.
2nd and every alt row: K2, *p2, k2; rep from * to end.
3rd row: P2, k1, MB (make bobble) as follows: [k1, yf, k1, yf, k1] into next st, turn, p5, turn k5, turn p2tog, p1, p2tog, turn, sl 1, k2tog, psso (bobble completed), p2, *C2B, p2, k1, MB, p2; rep from * to end.
5th row: As 1st row.
7th row: P2, C2B, p2, *k1, MB, p2, C2B, p2; rep from * to end.
8th row: As 2nd row.
Rep these 8 rows.

Tracery Rib

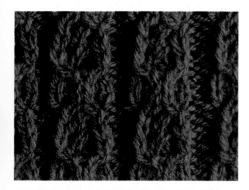

Multiple of 8 sts + 2.
1st row (right slde): P2, *k6, p2; rep from * to end.
2nd row: K2, *p6, k2; rep from * to end.
3rd row: P2, *C3R, C3L, p2; rep from * to end.
4th row: K2, *yf, sl 1 purlwise, p4, sl 1 purlwise, yb, k2; rep from * to end.
5th row: P2, *yb, sl 1, k1, psso, yf, C2F, yf, k2tog, p2; rep from * to end.
6th row: As 4th row.
7th row: As 5th row.
8th row: As 2nd row.
9th row: P2, *C3L, C3R, p2; rep from * to end.
10th row: As 2nd row.
Rep these 10 rows.

Cable and Eyelet Rib I

Multiple of 7 sts + 3.
1st row (right side): P3, *k4, p3; rep from * to end.
2nd row: K1, yf, k2tog, *p4, k1, yf, k2tog; rep from * to end.
3rd row: P3, *C4B, p3; rep from * to end.
4th row: As 2nd row.
5th row: As 1st row.
6th row: As 2nd row.
Rep the last 6 rows.

Cable and Eyelet Rib II

Multiple of 10 sts + 4.
1st row (right side): P1, k2tog, yfrn, *p2, k4, p2, k2tog, yfrn; rep from * to last st, p1.
2nd and every alt row: K1, p2, *k2, p4, k2, p2; rep from * to last st, k1.
3rd row: P1, yon, sl 1, k1, psso, *p2, C4F, p2, yon, sl 1, k1, psso; rep from * to last st, p1.
5th row: As 1st row.
7th row: P1, yon, sl 1, k1, psso, *p2, k4, p2, yon, sl 1, k1, psso; rep from * to last st, p1.
8th row: As 2nd row.
Rep these 8 rows.

Turkish Rib I

(Slanting to the Left)

Multiple of 2 sts.
Special Abbreviation
PR (Purl Reverse) = purl 1 st, return it to left-hand needle, insert right-hand needle through the st beyond and lift this st over the purled st and off the needle. Return st to right-hand needle.
Foundation row (right side): Knit.
1st row: P1, *yrn, PR; rep from * to last st, p1.
2nd row: K1, *sl 1, k1, psso, yf; rep from * to last st, k1.
Rep the last 2 rows.

Turkish Rib II

(Slanting to the Right)

Multiple of 2 sts.
Foundation row (right side): Knit.
1st row: P1, *p2tog, yrn; rep from * to last st, p1.
2nd row: K1, *yf, k2tog; rep from * to last st, k1.
Rep the last 2 rows.

Cable Patterns

Eyelet Cable

Multiple of 8 sts + 1.
Special Abbreviation
C3tog (Cross 3 together) = slip next 2 sts onto cable needle and hold at back of work, knit next st from left-hand needle, then k2tog from cable needle.
1st row (right side): P1, *C3tog, p1, k3, p1; rep from * to end.
2nd row: K1, *p3, k1, p1, yrn, p1, k1; rep from * to end.
3rd row: P1, *k3, p1, C3tog, p1; rep from * to end.
4th row: K1, *p1, yrn, p1, k1, p3, k1; rep from * to end.
Rep these 4 rows.

Medallion Pattern

Multiple of 10 sts + 2.
Note: Sts should only be counted after the 1st, 6th, 7th or 12th rows.
Foundation row (right side): K1, p3, k4, *p6, k4; rep from * to last 4 sts, p3, k1.
Commence Pattern
1st row: K4, p4, *k6, p4; rep from * to last 4 sts, k4.
2nd row: K1, p1, T4B, pick up horizontal thread lying between st just worked and next st and [k1, p1] into it (called M2), T4F, *p2, T4B, M2, T4F; rep from * to last 2 sts, p1, k1.
3rd row: K2, *p2, k2; rep from * to end.
4th row: K1, p1, *k2, p2; rep from * to last 4 sts, k2, p1, k1.
5th row: As 3rd row.
6th row: K2, *sl 1, k1, psso, p6, k2tog, k2; rep from * to end.
7th row: K1, p2, k6, *p4, k6; rep from * to last 3 sts, p2, k1.
8th row: K1, M1, T4F, p2, T4B, *M2, T4F, p2, T4B; rep from * to last st, M1, k1.
9th row: K1, p1, k2, *p2, k2; rep from * to

last 2 sts, p1, k1.
10th row: As 3rd row.
11th row: As 9th row.
12th row: K1, p3, k2tog, k2, sl 1, k1, psso, *p6, k2tog, k2, sl 1, k1, psso; rep from * to last 4 sts, p3, k1.
Rep these 12 rows.

Textured Diagonals

Multiple of 12 sts.
1st row (right side): Knit.
2nd row: P4, k6, *p6, k6; rep from * to last 2 sts, p2.
3rd row: Knit.
4th row: *P6, k6; rep from * to end.
5th row: *K6, C6F; rep from * to end.
6th row: K2, p6, *k6, p6; rep from * to last 4 sts, k4.
7th row: Knit.
8th row: K4, p6, *k6, p6; rep from * to last 2 sts, k2.
9th row: Knit.
10th row: *K6, p6; rep from * to end.
11th row: *C6F, k6; rep from * to end.
12th row: P2, k6, *p6, k6; rep from * to last 4 sts, p4.
Rep these 12 rows.

Loose Woven Cables

Multiple of 6 sts + 2.
1st row (right side): Knit.
2nd row: K1, knit to last st wrapping yarn twice around needle for each st, k1.
3rd row: K1, *C6B (dropping extra loops); rep from * to last st, k1.
Work 2 rows in garter st.

6th row: K4, *knit to last 4 sts, wrapping yarn twice around needle for each st, k4.
7th row: K4, *C6F (dropping extra loops); rep from * to last 4 sts, k4.
8th row: Knit.
Rep these 8 rows.

Zigzag Twists

Multiple of 7 sts + 1.
Special Abbreviations
C6BP or C6FP (Cable 6 Back or Cable 6 Front Purlwise) = slip next 3 sts onto cable needle and hold at back (or front) of work, purl next 3 sts from left-hand needle, then purl sts from cable needle.
1st row (right side): Knit.
2nd row: Purl.
3rd row: K1, *knit next 6 sts wrapping yarn twice round needle for each st, k1; rep from * to end.
4th row: P1, *C6BP dropping extra loops, p1; rep from * to end.
5th row: Knit.
6th row: Purl.
7th row: As 3rd row.
8th row: P1, *C6FP dropping extra loops, p1; rep from * to end.
Rep these 8 rows.

Slip Stitch Twists with Bobbles

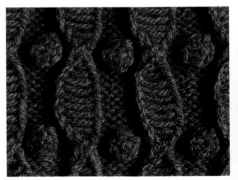

Multiple of 9 sts + 1.
Note: Sts should only be counted after the 11th and 12th rows.
Special Abbreviation
MB (Make Bobble) = [k1, yf, k1, yf, k1] into next st, turn and k5, turn and p5, turn and

k1, sl 1, k2tog, psso, k1, turn and p3tog (bobble completed).

1st row (wrong side): K4, p1, yrn, p1, *k7, p1, yrn, p1; rep from * to last 4 sts, k4.

2nd row: P4, k3, *p7, k3; rep from * to last 4 sts, p4.

3rd row: K4, p3, *k7, p3; rep from * to last 4 sts, k4.

Rep the last 2 rows 3 times more then the 2nd row again.

11th row: K4, p1, slip next st off left-hand needle and allow it to drop down 10 rows to the made loop, p1, *k7, p1, slip next st off needle, p1; rep from * to last 4 sts, k4.

12th row: P4, C2F, *p3, MB, p3, C2F; rep from * to last 4 sts, p4.

Rep these 12 rows.

Forked Cable

Multiple of 8 sts + 2.

1st row (wrong side): Purl.

2nd row: P3, k4, *p4, k4; rep from * to last 3 sts, p3.

Rep the last 2 rows twice more then the 1st row again.

8th row: K3, p4, *k4, p4; rep from * to last 3 sts, k3.

9th row: Purl.

10th row: K1 *C4F, C4B; rep from * to last st, k1.

Rep these 10 rows.

Turtle Check

Multiple of 12 sts + 2.

Special Abbreviations

T4LF (Twist 4 Left) = slip next st onto cable needle and hold at front of work, purl 3 sts from left-hand needle, then knit st from cable needle.

T4RB (Twist 4 Right) = slip next 3 sts onto cable needle and hold at back of work, knit next st from left-hand needle, then purl sts from cable needle.

1st row (right side): K4, p6, *k6, p6; rep from * to last 4 sts, k4.

2nd row: P4, k6, *p6, k6; rep from * to last 4 sts, p4.

3rd row: K3, T4LF, T4RB, *k4, T4LF, T4RB; rep from * to last 3 sts, k3.

4th row: P3, k3, p2, k3, *p4, k3, p2, k3; rep from * to last 3 sts, p3.

5th row: K2, *T4LF, k2, T4RB, k2; rep from * to end.

6th row: P2, *k3, p4, k3, p2; rep from * to end.

7th row: K1, *T4LF, k4, T4RB; rep from * to last st, k1.

8th row: K4, p6, *k6, p6; rep from * to last 4 sts, k4.

9th row: As 2nd row.

Rep the last 2 rows once more then the 8th row again.

13th row: K1, *T4RB, k4, T4LF; rep from * to last st, k1.

14th row: As 6th row.

15th row: K2, *T4RB, k2, T4LF, k2; rep from * to end.

16th row: As 4th row.

17th row: K3, T4RB, T4LF, *k4, T4RB, T4LF; rep from * to last 3 sts, k3.

18th row: As 2nd row.

19th row: As 1st row.

20th row: As 2nd row.

Rep these 20 rows.

Twisted Pyramids

Multiple of 6 sts + 2.

1st row (wrong side): Purl.

2nd row: P1, *T2F, k2, T2B; rep from * to last st, p1.

3rd row: K2, *p4, k2; rep from * to end.

4th row: P2, *k4, p2; rep from * to end.

5th row: As 3rd row.

6th row: P2, *T2F, T2B, p2; rep from * to end.

7th row: K3, p2, *k4, p2; rep from * to last 3 sts, k3.

8th row: K3, C2L, *k4, C2L; rep from * to last 3 sts, k3.

9th row: Purl.

10th row: K2, *T2B, T2F, k2; rep from * to end.

11th row: P3, k2, *p4, k2; rep from * to last 3 sts, p3.

12th row: K3, p2, *k4, p2; rep from * to last 3 sts, k3.

13th row: As 11th row.

14th row: K1, *T2B, p2, T2F; rep from * to last st, k1.

15th row: P2, *k4, p2; rep from * to end.

16th row: C2L, *k4, C2L; rep from * to end.

Rep these 16 rows.

Twisted Arches

Multiple of 8 sts + 2.

1st row (right side): P2, *k6, p2; rep from * to end.

2nd row: K2, *p6, k2; rep from * to end.

Rep the last 2 rows once more.

5th row: P2, *C3L, C3R, p2; rep from * to end.

6th row: As 2nd row.

7th row: K4, p2, *k6, p2; rep from * to last 4 sts, k4.

8th row: P4, k2, *p6, k2; rep from * to last 4 sts, p4.

Rep the last 2 rows once more.

11th row: K1, *C3R, p2, C3L; rep from * to last st, k1.

12th row: As 8th row.

Rep these 12 rows.

Small Twist Pattern

Multiple of 8 sts + 6.

1st row (right side): Knit.

2nd and every alt row: Purl.

3rd row: K1, C4F, *k4, C4F; rep from * to last st, k1.

5th row: Knit.

7th row: K5, C4F, *k4, C4F; rep from * to last 5 sts, k5.

8th row: Purl.

Rep these 8 rows.

Cable Patterns

Doughnut Pattern

Multiple of 16 sts + 10.
Work 3 rows in st st, starting purl (1st row is wrong side).
4th row: K9, C4F, C4B, *k8, C4F, C4B; rep from * to last 9 sts, k9.
Work 3 rows in st st, starting purl.
8th row: K1, C4B, C4F, *k8, C4B, C4F; rep from * to last st, k1.
Work 3 rows in st st, starting purl.
12th row: K1, C4F, C4B, *k8, C4F, C4B; rep from * to last st, k1.
Work 3 rows in st st, starting purl.
16th row: K9, C4B, C4F, *k8, C4B, C4F; rep from * to last 9 sts, k9.
Rep these 16 rows.

Large Lattice Diamonds

Multiple of 12 sts.
1st row (right side): K2, p8, *C4F, p8; rep from * to last 2 sts, k2.
2nd row: P2, k8, *p4, k8; rep from * to last 2 sts, p2.
3rd row: K2, p8, *k4, p8; rep from * to last 2 sts, k2.

4th row: As 2nd row.
5th row: As 1st row.
6th row: As 2nd row.
7th row: *T3F, p6, T3B; rep from * to end.
8th row: K1, p2, k6, p2, *k2, p2, k6, p2; rep from * to last st, k1.
9th row: P1, T3F, p4, T3B, *p2, T3F, p4, T3B; rep from * to last st, p1.
10th row: K2, p2, *k4, p2; rep from * to last 2 sts, k2.
11th row: P2, T3F, p2, T3B, *p4, T3F, p2, T3B; rep from * to last 2 sts, p2.
12th row: K3, p2, k2, p2, *k6, p2, k2, p2; rep from * to last 3 sts, k3.
13th row: P3, T3F, T3B, *p6, T3F, T3B; rep from * to last 3 sts, p3.
14th row: K4, p4, *k8, p4; rep from * to last 4 sts, k4.
15th row: P4, C4F, *p8, C4F; rep from * to last 4 sts, p4.
16th row: As 14th row.
17th row: P4, k4, *p8, k4; rep from * to last 4 sts, p4.
18th row: As 14th row.
19th row: As 15th row.
20th row: As 14th row.
21st row: P3, T3B, T3F, *p6, T3B, T3F; rep from * to last 3 sts, p3.
22nd row: As 12th row.
23rd row: P2, T3B, p2, T3F, *p4, T3B, p2, T3F; rep from * to last 2 sts, p2.
24th row: As 10th row.
25th row: P1, T3B, p4, T3F, *p2, T3B, p4, T3F; rep from * to last st, p1.
26th row: As 8th row.
27th row: *T3B, p6, T3F; rep from * to end.
28th row: As 2nd row.
Rep these 28 rows.

Woven Lattice Pattern

Multiple of 6 sts + 2.
1st row (wrong side): K3, p4, *k2, p4; rep from * to last st, k1.
2nd row: P1, C4F, *p2, C4F; rep from * to last 3 sts, p3.
3rd row: As 1st row.
4th row: P3, *k2, T4B; rep from * to last 5 sts, k4, p1.
5th row: K1, p4, *k2, p4; rep from * to last 3 sts, k3.
6th row: P3, C4B, *p2, C4B; rep from * to last st, p1.

7th row: As 5th row.
8th row: P1, k4, *T4F, k2; rep from * to last 3 sts, p3.
Rep these 8 rows.

All-Over Lattice Stitch

Multiple of 12 sts + 2.
Work 3 rows in st st, starting purl (1st row is wrong side).
4th row: K1, *C4B, k4, C4F; rep from * to last st, k1.
Work 3 rows in st st, starting purl.
8th row: K3, C4F, C4B, *k4, C4F, C4B; rep from * to last 3 sts, k3.
Rep these 8 rows.

Woven Cables in Relief

Multiple of 15 sts + 2.
1st row (right side): Knit.
2nd row: Purl.
3rd row: K1, C10F, *k5, C10F; rep from * to last 6 sts, k6.
Work 5 rows in st st, starting purl.
9th row: K6, C10B, *k5, C10B; rep from * to last st, k1.
Work 3 rows in st st, starting purl.
Rep these 12 rows.

Large Honeycomb

Multiple of 12 sts + 2.

1st row (right side): K4, p6, *k6, p6; rep from * to last 4 sts, k4.

2nd row: P4, k6, *p6, k6; rep from * to last 4 sts, p4.

Rep the last 2 rows 3 times more.

9th row: K1, *T6F, T6B; rep from * to last st, k1.

10th row: As 1st row.

11th row: As 2nd row.

Rep the last 2 rows 3 times more, then the 10th row again.

19th row: K1, *T6B, T6F; rep from * to last st, k1.

20th row: As 2nd row.

Rep these 20 rows.

Hourglass Pattern I

Multiple of 10 sts + 6.

Special Abbreviation

C4FP (Cable 4 Front Purlwise) = slip next 2 sts onto a cable needle and hold at front of work, purl next 2 sts from left-hand needle, then purl sts on cable needle.

1st row (right side): K6, *p4, k6; rep from * to end.

2nd row: P6, *k4, p6; rep from * to end.

Rep the last 2 rows once more.

5th row: K6, *C4FP, k6; rep from * to end.

6th row: As 2nd row.

Rep the last 2 rows once more.

9th row: As 1st row.

10th row: As 2nd row.

11th row: K1, p4, *k6, p4; rep from * to last st, k1.

12th row: P1, k4, *p6, k4; rep from * to last st, p1.

Rep the last 2 rows once more.

15th row: K1, C4FP, *k6, C4FP; rep from * to last st, k1.

16th row: As 12th row.

Rep the last 2 rows once more.

19th row: As 11th row.

20th row: As 12th row.

Rep these 20 rows.

Hourglass Pattern II

Worked as Hourglass Pattern I, using reverse side as right side.

Ridge and Cable Stripes

Multiple of 10 sts + 8.

Work 5 rows in st st, starting purl (1st row is wrong side).

6th row: K7, C4B, *k6, C4B; rep from * to last 7 sts, k7.

7th row: K7, p4, *k6, p4; rep from * to last 7 sts, k7.

8th row: P7, k4, *p6, k4; rep from * to last 7 sts, p7.

9th row: As 7th row.

10th row: P7, C4B, *p6, C4B; rep from * to last 7 sts, p7.

11th row: As 7th row.

12th row: As 8th row.

13th row: As 7th row.

14th row: As 6th row.

Work 5 rows in st st, starting purl.

20th row: K2, C4F, *k6, C4F; rep from * to last 2 sts, k2.

21st row: K2, p4, *k6, p4; rep from * to last 2 sts, k2.

22nd row: P2, k4, *p6, k4; rep from * to last 2 sts, p2.

23rd row: As 21st row.

24th row: P2, C4F, *p6, C4F; rep from * to last 2 sts, p2.

25th row: As 21st row.

26th row: As 22nd row.

27th row: As 21st row.

28th row: As 20th row.

Rep these 28 rows.

Little Cable Check

Multiple of 20 sts + 2.

Note: Sts should not be counted after 1st, 5th, 9th and 13th rows.

Special Abbreviation

C3tog (Cross 3tog) = slip next 2 sts onto cable needle and hold at back of work, knit next st from left-hand needle then k2tog tbl from cable needle.

1st row (right side): P2, C3tog, p2, [C3R, p2] twice, *[C3tog, p2] twice, [C3R, p2] twice; rep from * to last 5 sts, C3tog, p2.

2nd row: K2, p1, yrn, p1, k2, [p3, k2] twice, *[p1, yrn, p1, k2] twice, [p3, k2] twice; rep from * to last 4 sts, p1, yrn, p1, k2.

3rd row: P2, *k3, p2; rep from * to end.

4th row: K2, *p3, k2; rep from * to end.

5th row: P2, C3tog, p2, [k3, p2] twice, *[C3tog, p2] twice, [k3, p2] twice; rep from * to last 5 sts, C3tog, p2.

6th row: As 2nd row.

7th row: As 3rd row.

8th row: As 4th row.

9th row: P2, C3R, p2, [C3tog, p2] twice, *[C3R, p2] twice, [C3tog, p2] twice; rep from * to last 5 sts, C3R, p2.

10th row: K2, p3, k2, [p1, yrn, p1, k2] twice, *[p3, k2] twice, [p1, yrn, p1, k2] twice; rep from * to last 5 sts, p3, k2.

11th row: As 3rd row.

12th row: As 4th row.

13th row: P2, k3, p2, [C3tog, p2] twice, *[k3, p2] twice, [C3tog, p2] twice; rep from * to last 5 sts, k3, p2.

14th row: As 10th row.

15th row: As 3rd row.

16th row: As 4th row.

Rep these 16 rows.

Cable Patterns

Crosses and Stripes

Multiple of 12 sts + 2.
Work 6 rows in garter st (1st row is right side).
7th row: K2, *p2, k2; rep from * to end.
8th row: P2, *k2, p2; rep from * to end.
Rep the last 2 rows once more.
11th row: K2, *p2, slip next 4 sts onto cable needle and hold at back of work, knit next 2 sts from left-hand needle then slip the 2 purl sts from cable needle back to left-hand needle, purl these 2 sts (keeping cable needle at back of work), then knit 2 sts from cable needle, p2, k2; rep from * to end.
12th row: As 8th row.
13th row: As 7th row.
14th row: As 8th row.
Rep these 14 rows.

Criss Cross Pattern Stitch

Multiple of 12 sts + 6.
1st row (right side): K6, *p2, k2, p2, k6; rep from * to end.
2nd row: P6, *k2, p2, k2, p6; rep from * to end.
Rep the last 2 rows once more.
5th row: C6F, *p2, k2, p2, C6F; rep from * to end.
6th row: As 2nd row.
7th row: As 1st row.
8th row: As 2nd row.
9th row: P2, k2, p2, *k6, p2, k2, p2; rep from * to end.
10th row: K2, p2, k2, *p6, k2, p2, k2; rep from * to end.
Rep the last 2 rows once more.
13th row: P2, k2, p2, *C6F, p2, k2, p2; rep from * to end.
14th row: As 10th row.
15th row: As 9th row.

Squares and Twists

16th row: As 10th row.
Rep these 16 rows.

Multiple of 10 sts + 4.
1st row (wrong side): P4, *k2, p2, k2, p4; rep from * to end.
2nd row: K4, *p2, C2F, p2, k4; rep from * to end.
Rep the last 2 rows once more.
5th row: K1, p2, *k2, p4, k2, p2; rep from * to last st, k1.
6th row: P1, C2F, *p2, k4, p2, C2F; rep from * to last st, p1.
Rep the last 2 rows once more.
Rep these 8 rows.

Honeycomb Trellis

Multiple of 6 sts + 2.
Special Abbreviations
T3FL = slip next st onto cable needle and hold at front of work, p2, then k1 from cable needle.
T3BR = slip next 2 sts onto cable needle and hold at back of work, k1, then p2 from cable needle.
1st row (right side): K2, *p4, k2; rep from * to end.
2nd row: P2, *k4, p2; rep from * to end.
3rd row: K1, *T3FL, T3BR; rep from * to last st, k1.
4th row: K3, p2, *k4, p2; rep from * to last 3 sts, k3.
5th row: P3, k2, *p4, k2; rep from * to last 3 sts, p3.
6th row: As 4th row.
7th row: K1, *T3BR, T3FL; rep from * to last st, k1.
8th row: As 2nd row.
Rep these 8 rows.

Twist Motif

Multiple of 16 sts + 2.
Work 4 rows in st st, starting knit (1st row is right side).
5th row: K7, C2F, C2B, *k12, C2F, C2B; rep from * to last 7 sts, k7.
6th row: Purl.
7th row: K7, C2B, C2F, *k12, C2B, C2F; rep from * to last 7 sts, k7.
Work 7 rows in st st, starting purl.
15th row: K1, *C2B, k12, C2F; rep from * to last st, k1.
16th row: Purl.
17th row: K1, *C2F, k12, C2B; rep from * to last st, k1.
Work 3 rows in st st, starting purl.
Rep these 20 rows.

Diagonal Twists

Multiple of 6 sts.
1st row (wrong side): *K5, p1; rep from * to end.
2nd row: *T2F, p4; rep from * to end.
3rd row: K4, p1, *k5, p1; rep from * to last st, k1.
4th row: P1, T2F, *p4, T2F; rep from * to last 3 sts, p3.
5th row: K3, p1, *k5, p1; rep from * to last 2 sts, k2.
6th row: P2, T2F, *p4, T2F; rep from * to last 2 sts, p2.
7th row: K2, p1, *k5, p1; rep from * to last 3 sts, k3.
8th row: P3, T2F, *p4, T2F; rep from * to last st, p1.
9th row: K1, p1, *k5, p1; rep from * to last 4 sts, k4.
10th row: *P4, T2F; rep from * to end.
11th row: *P1, k5; rep from * to end.

12th row: P5, T2F, *p4, T2F; rep from * to last 5 sts, p5.
Rep these 12 rows.

Twisted Diagonals

Multiple of 6 sts.
1st and every alt row (wrong side): Purl.
2nd row: *K4, C2F; rep from * to end.
4th row: K3, C2F, *k4, C2F; rep from * to last st, k1.
6th row: K2, C2F, *k4, C2F; rep from * to last 2 sts, k2.
8th row: K1, C2F, *k4, C2F; rep from * to last 3 sts, k3.
10th row: *C2F, k4; rep from * to end.
12th row: K5, C2F, *k4, C2F; rep from * to last 5 sts, k5.
Rep these 12 rows.

Arrowheads

Multiple of 10 sts.
1st row (right side): Knit.
2nd row: Purl.
3rd row: *T2F, k6, T2B; rep from * to end.
4th row: K1, p8, *k2, p8; rep from * to last st, k1.
5th row: P1, T2F, k4, T2B, *p2, T2F, k4, T2B; rep from * to last st, p1.
6th row: K2, p6, *k4, p6; rep from * to last 2 sts, k2.
7th row: P2, T2F, k2, T2B, *p4, T2F, k2, T2B; rep from * to last 2 sts, p2.
8th row: K3, p4, *k6, p4; rep from * to last 3 sts, k3.
9th row: P3, T2F, T2B, *p6, T2F, T2B; rep from * to last 3 sts, p3.
10th row: K4, p2, *k8, p2; rep from * to last 4 sts, k4.
Rep these 10 rows.

Lozenge Pattern

Multiple of 12 sts + 8.
Special Abbreviation
T4 (Twist 4) = slip next 3 sts onto cable needle and hold at back of work, knit next st from left-hand needle, slip the 2 purl sts from cable needle back to left-hand needle, bring remaining st on cable needle to front of work, purl next 2 sts from left-hand needle, then knit st from cable needle.
1st row (right side): P2, *k1, p2; rep from * to end.
2nd row: K2, *p1, k2; rep from * to end.
3rd row: P2, [k1, p2] twice, *T4, p2, [k1, p2] twice; rep from * to end.
4th row: As 2nd row.
Rep the last 4 rows 3 times more, then first 2 rows again.
19th row: P2, T4, p2, *[k1, p2] twice, T4, p2; rep from * to end.
20th row: As 2nd row.
21st row: As 1st row.
22nd row: As 2nd row.
Rep the last 4 rows twice more, then 19th and 20th rows again.
Rep these 32 rows.

Wheat Pattern

Multiple of 10 sts + 1.
1st row (wrong side): P1, *k2, p5, k2, p1; rep from * to end.
2nd row: KB1, *p2, C2B, k1, C2F, p2, KB1; rep from * to end.
Rep the last 2 rows 4 times more.
11th row: P3, k2, p1, k2, *p5, k2, p1, k2; rep from * to last 3 sts, p3.
12th row: K1, *C2F, p2, KB1, p2, C2B, k1; rep from * to end.
Rep the last 2 rows 4 times more.
Rep these 20 rows.

Little Wave

Multiple of 7 sts + 4.
1st row (right side): Knit.
2nd row: P4, *k2, p5; rep from * to end.
3rd row: K4, *C2B, k5; rep from * to end.
4th row: P4, *k1, p1, k1, p4; rep from * to end.
5th row: *K5, C2B; rep from * to last 4 sts, k4.
6th row: *P5, k2; rep from * to last 4 sts, p4.
7th row: Knit.
8th row: As 6th row.
9th row: *K5, C2F; rep from * to last 4 sts, k4.
10th row: As 4th row.
11th row: K4, *C2F, k5; rep from * to end.
12th row: As 2nd row.
Rep these 12 rows.

Openwork and Twist Pattern

Multiple of 15 sts + 12.
Special Abbreviation
T4LR (Twist 4 Left and Right) = slip next 3 sts onto cable needle and hold at back of work, knit next st from left-hand needle then slip the first st on cable needle back to left-hand needle, p2 from cable needle then k1 from left-hand needle.
1st row (right side): P1, T4LR, p2, T4LR, p1, *k1, yf, sl 1, k1, psso, p1, T4LR, p2, T4LR, p1; rep from * to end.
2nd row: K1, p1, [k2, p1] 3 times, k1, *p3, k1, p1, [k2, p1] 3 times, k1; rep from * to end.
3rd row: P1, k1, p2, T4LR, p2, k1, p1, *k2tog, yf, k1, p1, k1, p2, T4LR, p2, k1, p1; rep from * to end.
4th row: As 2nd row.
Rep these 4 rows.

Cable Patterns

Textured Lozenge Stitch

Multiple of 6 sts + 2.

1st row (wrong side): Purl.
2nd row: P1, *T2F, k2, T2B; rep from * to last st, p1.
3rd row: K2, *p4, k2; rep from * to end.
4th row: P2, *T2F, T2B, p2; rep from * to end.
5th row: K3, p2, *k4, p2; rep from * to last 3 sts, k3.
6th row: K3, C2L, *k4, C2L; rep from * to last 3 sts, k3.
7th row: Purl.
8th row: K2, *T2B, T2F, k2; rep from * to end.
9th row: P3, k2, *p4, k2; rep from * to last 3 sts, p3.
10th row: K1, *T2B, p2, T2F; rep from * to last st, k1.
11th row: P2, *k4, p2; rep from * to end.
12th row: C2L, *k4, C2L; rep from * to end.
Rep these 12 rows.

Stocking Stitch Hearts

Multiple of 14 sts + 4.

1st row (wrong side): Knit.
2nd row: Purl.
3rd row: K8, p2, *k12, p2; rep from * to last 8 sts, k8.
4th row: P7, C2F, C2B, *p10, C2F, C2B; rep from * to last 7 sts, p7.
5th row: K7, p4, *k10, p4; rep from * to last 7 sts, k7.
6th row: P6, C2F, k2, C2B, *p8, C2F, k2, C2B; rep from * to last 6 sts, p6.
7th row: K6, p6, *k8, p6; rep from * to last 6 sts, k6.
8th row: P5, C2F, k4, C2B, *p6, C2F, k4, C2B; rep from * to last 5 sts, p5.
9th row: K5, p8, *k6, p8; rep from * to last 5 sts, k5.
10th row: P4, *C2F, k6, C2B, p4; rep from * to end.
11th row: K4, *p10, k4; rep from * to end.
12th row: P4, *k3, T2B, T2F, k3, p4; rep from * to end.
13th row: K4, *p4, k2, p4, k4; rep from * to end.
14th row: P4, *T2F, T2B, p2, T2F, T2B, p4; rep from * to end.
15th row: K5, p2, k4, p2, *k6, p2, k4, p2; rep from * to last 5 sts, k5.
16th row: P5, M1, k2tog tbl, p4, k2tog, M1, *p6, M1, k2tog tbl, p4, k2tog, M1; rep from * to last 5 sts, p5.
17th row: Knit.
18th row: Purl.
Rep these 18 rows.

Rosebud Garden

Multiple of 14 sts + 5.
Note: Count each M5 and sts resulting from M5 on following rows as 1 st.

1st row (wrong side): K7, [p1, k1] twice, p1, *k9, [p1, k1] twice, p1; rep from * to last 7 sts, k7.
2nd row: P7, [k1, p1] twice, k1, *p9, [k1, p1] twice, k1; rep from * to last 7 sts, p7. Rep the last 2 rows once more then the 1st row again.
6th row: P6, T2B, p1, k1, p1, T2F, *p7, T2B, p1, k1, p1, T2F; rep from * to last 6 sts, p6.
7th row: K6, [p1, k2] twice, p1, *k7, [p1, k2] twice, p1; rep from * to last 6 sts, k6.
8th row: P5, *T2B, p2, k1, p2, T2F, p5; rep from * to end.
9th row: K5, *[p1, k3] twice, p1, k5; rep from * to end.
10th row: P5, *M5 as follows: [k1, yf, k1, yf, k1] into next st, p3, k1, p3, M5, p5; rep from * to end.
11th row: K5, *p5, k3, p1, k3, p5, k5; rep from * to end.
12th row: P5, *k5, p3, k1, p3, k5, p5; rep from * to end.
13th row: As 11th row.
14th row: P5, *k5, p3, M5, p3, k5, p5; rep from * to end.
15th row: K5, *[p5, k3] twice, p5, k5; rep from * to end.
16th row: P5, *D5 as follows: k2tog tbl, k3tog, pass k2tog st over k3tog st, p3, k5, p3, D5, p5; rep from * to end.
17th row: K9, p5, *k13, p5; rep from * to last 9 sts, k9.
18th row: P9, k5, *p13, k5; rep from * to last 9 sts, p9.
19th row: As 17th row.
20th row: P9, D5, *p13, D5; rep from * to last 9 sts, p9.
21st row: K2, p1, k1, p1, k9, *[p1, k1] twice, p1, k9; rep from * to last 5 sts, p1, k1, p1, k2.
22nd row: P2, k1, p1, k1, p9, *[k1, p1] twice, k1, p9; rep from * to last 5 sts, k1, p1, k1, p2.

Rep the last 2 rows once more then the 21st row again.

26th row: P2, k1, *p1, T2F, p7, T2B, p1, k1; rep from * to last 2 sts, p2.
27th row: [K2, p1] twice, k7, *[p1, k2] twice, p1, k7; rep from * to last 6 sts, [p1, k2] twice.
28th row: P2, k1, *p2, T2F, p5, T2B, p2, k1; rep from * to last 2 sts, p2.
29th row: K2, p1, k3, p1, k5, *[p1, k3] twice, p1, k5; rep from * to last 7 sts, p1, k3, p1, k2.
30th row: P2, k1, *p3, M5, p5, M5, p3, k1; rep from * to last 2 sts, p2.
31st row: K2, p1, *k3, p5, k5, p5, k3, p1; rep from * to last 2 sts, k2.
32nd row: P2, k1, *p3, k5, p5, k5, p3, k1; rep from * to last 3 sts, p2.
33rd row: As 31st row.
34th row: P2, M5, *p3, k5, p5, k5, p3, M5; rep from * to last 2 sts, p2.
35th row: K2, p5, *k3, p5, k5, p5, k3, p5; rep from * to last 2 sts, k2.
36th row: P2, k5, *p3, D5, p5, D5, p3, k5; rep from * to last 2 sts, p2.
37th row: K2, p5, *k13, p5; rep from * to last 2 sts, k2.
38th row: P2, k5, *p13, k5; rep from * to last 2 sts, p2.
39th row: As 37th row.
40th row: P2, D5, *p13, D5; rep from * to last 2 sts, p2.
Rep these 40 rows.

Knot Cable

Worked over 6 sts on a background of reverse st st.

Special Abbreviation

C6LR (Cross 6 Left and Right) = slip next 2 sts onto cable needle and hold at back of work, slip next 2 sts onto 2nd cable needle and hold at front of work, knit next 2 sts from left-hand needle then knit the 2 sts from 2nd cable needle, then knit the 2 sts from 1st cable needle.

1st row (right side): Knit.
2nd row: Purl.
3rd row: C6LR.
4th row: Purl.
5th row: Knit.
Rep the last 2 rows once more.
8th row: Purl.
Rep these 8 rows.

9-Stitch Cable with Bobbles

Worked over 9 sts on a background of reverse st st.

1st row (right side): Knit.
2nd row: Purl.
Rep the last 2 rows once more.
5th row: C9F.
6th row: Purl.
7th row: K4, [k1, yf, k1, yf, k1] into next st, turn and k5, turn and p5, turn and sl 1, k1,

psso, k1, k2tog, turn and p3tog (1 bobble completed), k4.
8th row: Purl.
Rep 1st and 2nd rows twice more.
Rep these 12 rows.

5-Stitch Cable with Bobbles

Worked over 5 sts on a background of reverse st st.

Special Abbreviation

MK (Make Knot) = [K1, p1, k1, p1, k1] into next st, then pass 2nd, 3rd, 4th and 5th sts over 1st (knot completed).

1st row (right side): C5.
2nd and every alt row: Purl.
3rd row: Knit.
5th row: K2, MK, k2.
7th row: Knit.
8th row: Purl.
Rep these 8 rows.

Sloping Cable

Worked over 10 sts on a background of reverse st st.

Note: Increases should be made by knitting into front and back of next st.

1st row (wrong side): K1, p8, k1.
2nd row: P1, yb, sl 1, k1, psso, k4, inc in next st, k1, p1.
Rep the last 2 rows 3 times more then the first row again.
10th row: P1, C8F, p1.

11th row: As 1st row.
12th row: P1, inc in next st, k5, k2tog, p1.
Rep the last 2 rows 3 times more then the first row again.
20th row: P1, C8B, p1.
Rep these 20 rows.

Double Twisted Cable

Worked over 8 sts on a background of reverse st st.

1st row: Knit.
2nd and every alt row: Purl.
3rd row: [C4B] twice.
5th row: Knit.
7th row: As 3rd row.
9th row: Knit.
11th row: As 3rd row.
12th row: Purl.
Rep 1st and 2nd rows 5 times more.
Rep these 22 rows.

8-Stitch Plait

Worked over 8 sts on a background of reverse st st.

1st and every alt row (wrong side): Purl.
2nd row: K2, C4B, k2.
4th row: C4B, k4.
6th row: K2, C4F, k2.
8th row: K4, C4F.
Rep these 8 rows.

Cable Panels

Alternating Plait

Worked over 8 sts on a background of reverse st st.

1st and every alt row (wrong side): Purl.
2nd row: K4, C4F.
4th row: Knit.
6th row: As 2nd row.
8th row: C4B, k4.
10th row: Knit.
12th row: As 8th row.
Rep these 12 rows.

Wandering Cable

Worked over 12 sts on a background of reverse st st.

Note: Increases to be made by purling into front and back of next st.

1st row (wrong side): K2, p4, k6.
2nd row: P6, k4, p2.
3rd row: As 1st row.

4th row: P6, C4F, p2.
5th row: As 1st row.
6th row: P4, p2tog, k4, inc in next st, p1.
7th row: K3, p4, k5.
8th row: P5, C4F, p3.
9th row: As 7th row.
10th row: P3, p2tog, k4, inc in next st, p2.
11th row: K4, p4, k4.
12th row: P4, C4F, p4.
13th row: As 11th row.
14th row: P2, p2tog, k4, inc in next st, p3.
15th row: K5, p4, k3.
16th row: P3, C4F, p5.
17th row: As 15th row.
18th row: P1, p2tog, k4, inc in next st, p4.
19th row: K6, p4, k2.
20th row: P2, C4F, p6.
21st row: As 19th row.
22nd row: P2, k4, p6.
23rd row: As 19th row.
24th row: P2, C4B, p6.
25th row: As 19th row.
26th row: P1, inc in next st, k4, p2tog, p4.
27th row: As 15th row.
28th row: P3, C4B, p5.
29th row: As 15th row.
30th row: P2, inc in next st, k4, p2tog, p3.
31st row: As 11th row.
32nd row: P4, C4B, p4.
33rd row: As 11th row.
34th row: P3, inc in next st, k4, p2tog, p2.
35th row: As 7th row.
36th row: P5, C4B, p3.
37th row: As 7th row.
38th row: P4, inc in next st, k4, p2tog, p1.
39th row: As 1st row.
40th row: P6, C4B, p2.
Rep these 40 rows.

Small Moss Stitch Cable

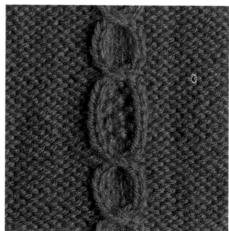

Worked over 5 sts on a background of reverse st st.
1st row (wrong side): [P1, k1] twice, p1.
2nd row: K2, p1, k2.
Rep the last 2 rows once more then the 1st row again.

6th row: Slip next st onto cable needle and hold at front of work, slip next 3 sts onto 2nd cable needle and hold at back of work, knit next st from left-hand needle, knit the 3 sts from 2nd cable needle, then knit st from 1st cable needle.
Work 5 rows in st st, starting purl.
12th row: As 6th row.
Work 1st and 2nd rows twice more.
Rep these 16 rows.

Twisted Eyelet Cable

Worked over 8 sts on a background of reverse st st.

1st row (right side): Knit.
2nd and every alt row: Purl.
3rd row: K2, yf, slip next 2 sts onto cable needle and hold at front of work, k2tog from left-hand needle, then k2tog from cable needle, yf, k2.
5th row: Knit.
7th row: C3F, k2, C3B.
9th row: K1, C3F, C3B, k1.
10th row: Purl.
Rep these 10 rows.

12-Stitch Braid Cable

Worked over 12 sts on a background of reverse st st.

1st row (right side): C4F, k4, C4B.
2nd row: Purl.
3rd row: K2, C4F, C4B, k2.
4th row: Purl.
5th row: K4, C4B, k4.
6th row: Purl.
Rep these 6 rows.

Tight Braid Cable

Worked over 10 sts on a background of reverse st st.
1st row (wrong side): Purl.
2nd row: K2, [C4F] twice.
3rd row: Purl.
4th row: [C4B] twice, k2.
Rep these 4 rows.

Noughts and Crosses Cable

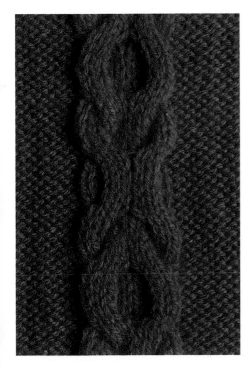

Worked over 12 sts on a background of reverse st st.

Work 4 rows in st st, starting knit.
5th row: C6B, C6F.
6th row: Purl.
Rep these 6 rows once more.
Work 4 rows in st st, starting knit.
17th row: C6F, C6B.
18th row: Purl.
Rep the last 6 rows once more.
Rep these 24 rows.

Lace Cable Pattern I

Worked over 8 sts on a background of reversed st st.
1st row (right side): K2, yf, sl 1, k1, psso, k4.
2nd and every alt row: Purl.
3rd row: K3, yf, sl 1, k1, psso, k3.
5th row: K4, yf, sl 1, k1, psso, k2.
7th row: K5, yf, sl 1, k1, psso, k1.
9th row: C6B, yf, sl 1, k1, psso.
10th row: Purl.
Rep these 10 rows.

Lace Cable Pattern II

Worked over 8 sts on a background of reverse st st.
1st and every alt row (wrong side): K1, p6, k1.
2nd row: P1, k6, p1.
4th row: P1, C6B, p1.
6th row: As 2nd row.
8th row: P1, k1, yf, k2tog, k3, p1.
10th row: P1, sl 1, k1, psso, yf, k4, p1.
12th row: As 8th row.
14th row: As 2nd row.
16th row: As 4th row.
18th row: As 2nd row.
20th row: P1, k3, sl 1, k1, psso, yf, k1, p1.
22nd row: P1, k4, yf, k2tog, p1.
24th row: As 20th row.
Rep these 24 rows.

Old Scottish Stitch

Worked over 12 sts on a background of reverse st st.
1st row (right side): Knit.
2nd and every alt row to 14th row: Purl.
3rd row: C8B, k4.
5th row: Knit.
7th row: K4, C8F.
9th row: Knit.
11th row: As 3rd row.
13th row: Knit.
15th row: K3, yf, sl 1, k1, psso, k4, yf, sl 1, k1, psso, k1.
16th row: P3, yrn, p2tog, p4, yrn, p2tog, p1.
Rep the last 2 rows 3 times more then 15th row again.
24th row: Purl.
Rep these 24 rows.

Cable Panels

Braid Twist

Worked over 6 sts on a background of reverse st st.

1st row (wrong side): K1, p5.
2nd row: K3, C2F, p1.
3rd row: As 1st row.
4th row: C2B, C2F, C2B.
5th row: P5, k1.
6th row: P1, C2B, k3.
7th row: As 5th row.
8th row: C2F, C2B, C2F.
Rep these 8 rows.

Cross and Diamond Twist

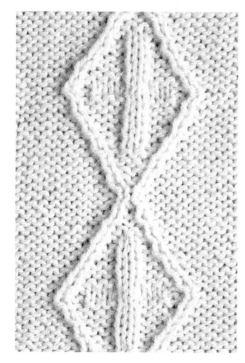

Worked over 14 sts on a background of reversed st st.

1st row (wrong side): K6, p2, k6.
2nd row: P5, T2B, T2F, p5.
3rd row: K5, p1, k2, p1, k5.
4th row: P4, T2B, p2, T2F, p4.
5th row: K4, [p1, k4] twice.
6th row: P3, T2B, p1, k2, p1, T2F, p3.
7th row: K3, p1, k2, p2, k2, p1, k3.
8th row: P2, T2B, p2, k2, p2, T2F, p2.

9th row: K2, p1, k3, p2, k3, p1, k2.
10th row: P1, T2B, p3, k2, p3, T2F, p1.
11th row: K1, p1, k4, p2, k4, p1, k1.
12th row: T2B, p1, k8, p1, T2F.
13th row: P1, k2, p8, k2, p1.
14th row: T2F, p4, k2, p4, T2B.
15th row: As 11th row.
16th row: P1, T2F, p3, k2, p3, T2B, p1.
17th row: As 9th row.
18th row: P2, T2F, p2, k2, p2, T2B, p2.
19th row: As 7th row.
20th row: P3, T2F, p4, T2B, p3.
21st row: As 5th row.
22nd row: P4, T2F, p2, T2B, p4.
23rd row: As 3rd row.
24th row: P5, T2F, T2B, p5.
Rep these 24 rows.

Triangular Twists

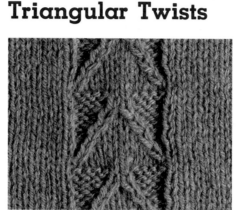

Worked over 10 sts on a background of st st.

1st row (right side): Knit.
2nd row: Purl.
3rd row: T2F, k6, T2B.
4th row: K1, p8, k1.
5th row: P1, T2F, k4, T2B, p1.
6th row: K2, p6, k2.
7th row: P2, T2F, k2, T2B, p2.
8th row: K3, p4, k3.
9th row: P3, T2F, T2B, p3.
10th row: K4, p2, k4.
Rep these 10 rows.

Tree Twist

Worked over 12 sts on a background of reverse st st.

Honeycomb Diamond Twist

Worked over 12 sts on a background of st st.

1st and every alt row (wrong side): Purl.
2nd row: K4, C2F, C2B, k4.
4th row: K2, [C2F, C2B] twice, k2.
6th row: [C2F, C2B] 3 times.
8th row: [C2B, C2F] 3 times.
10th row: K2, [C2B, C2F] twice, k2.
12th row: K4, C2B, C2F, k4.
Rep these 12 rows.

Long Lozenge Twists

1st row (wrong side): K5, p2, k5.
2nd row: P5, k2, p5.
Rep these 2 rows once more then the 1st row again.
6th row: P4, C2R, C2L, p4.
7th row: K3, p1, k1, p2, k1, p1, k3.
8th row: P2, T2B, C2R, C2L, T2F, p2.
9th row: K1, p1, k2, p4, k2, p1, k1.
10th row: T2B, p1, T2B, k2, T2F, p1, T2F.
11th row: P1, k2, p1, k1, p2, k1, p1, k2, p1.
12th row: P3, k1, p1, k2, p1, k1, p3.
13th row: As 7th row.
14th row: As 2nd row.
Rep these 14 rows.

Worked over 16 sts on a background of reverse st st.

Special Abbreviation

T4 (Twist 4) = slip next 3 sts onto cable needle and hold at back of work, knit next st from left-hand needle, then slip the 2 purl sts from cable needle back to left-hand needle, bring remaining st on cable needle to front of work, purl next 2 sts from left-hand needle, then knit st from cable needle.

1st row (right side): K1, [p2, k1] 5 times.
2nd row: P1, [k2, p1] 5 times.
3rd row: [K1, p2] twice, T4, [p2, k1] twice.
4th row: As 2nd row.
5th row: As 1st row.
6th row: As 2nd row.
Rep the last 4 rows 3 times more.
19th row: T4, p2, [k1, p2] twice, T4.
20th row: As 2nd row.
21st row: As 1st row.
22nd row: As 2nd row.
Rep the last 4 rows twice more.
31st row: As 19th row.
32nd row: As 2nd row.
Rep these 32 rows.

Diamond Twists

Worked over 14 sts on a background of reverse st st.

Special Abbreviation

T3BR (Twist 3 Back Right) = slip next 3 sts onto cable needle and hold at back of work, knit next st from left-hand needle, then slip the 2 purl sts from cable needle back onto left-hand needle and purl them, then knit remaining st on cable needle.

1st row (right side): P5, C2R, C2L, p5.

2nd row: K5, p4, k5.
3rd row: P4, T2B, k2, T2F, p4.
4th row: K4, p1, k1, p2, k1, p1, k4.
5th row: P3, [T2B] twice, [T2F] twice, p3.
6th row: K3, p1, k1, p1, k2, p1, k1, p1, k3.
7th row: P2, T2B, p1, k1, p2, k1, p1, T2F, p2.
8th row: K2, [p1, k2] 4 times.
9th row: P1, T2B, p2, T3BR, p2, T2F, p1.
10th row: K1, p1, k3, p1, k2, p1, k3, p1, k1.
11th row: T2B, p3, k1, p2, k1, p3, T2F.
12th row: P1, k4, p1, k2, p1, k4, p1.
13th row: T2F, p3, k1, p2, k1, p3, T2B.
14th row: As 10th row.
15th row: P1, T2F, p2, T3BR, p2, T2B, p1.
16th row: As 8th row.
17th row: P2, T2F, p1, k1, p2, k1, p1, T2B, p2.
18th row: As 6th row.
19th row: P3, [T2F] twice, [T2B] twice, p3.
20th row: As 4th row.
21st row: P4, T2F, k2, T2B, p4.
22nd row: As 2nd row.
23rd row: P5, T2F, T2B, p5.
24th row: K6, p2, k6.
Rep these 24 rows.

Big Arrow Twist

Worked over 14 sts on a background of reverse st st.
1st row (right side): T2F, k1, p1, C2L, k2, C2R, p1, k1, T2B.
2nd row: K1, p2, k1, p6, k1, p2, k1.
3rd row: P1, T2F, p1, k1, T2F, T2B, k1, p1, T2B, p1.
4th row: K2, [p1, k1] twice, p2, [k1, p1] twice, k2.
5th row: P2, T2F, k1, p1, C2L, p1, k1, T2B, p2.
6th row: K3, p2, [k1, p2] twice, k3.
7th row: P3, T2F, p1, k2, p1, T2B, p3.
8th row: K4, p1, k1, p2, k1, p1, k4.
9th row: P4, T2F, k2, T2B, p4.
10th row: K5, p4, k5.
11th row: P5, T2F, T2B, p5.
12th row: K6, p2, k6.
13th row: C2L, p4, C2L, p4, C2R.
14th row: P2, [k4, p2] twice.

15th row: K1, T2F, p3, k2, p3, T2B, k1.
16th row: P1, k1, p1, k3, p2, k3, p1, k1, p1.
17th row: K1, p1, C2L, p2, C2L, p2, C2R, p1, k1.
18th row: P1, k1, [p2, k2] twice, p2, k1, p1.
19th row: K1, p1, k1, T2F, p1, k2, p1, T2B, k1, p1, k1.
20th row: [P1, k1] 3 times, p2, [k1, p1] 3 times.
Rep these 20 rows.

Ripple Twist

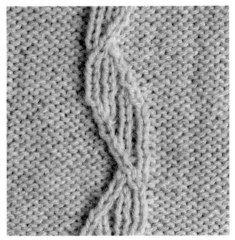

Worked over 9 sts on a background of reverse st st.
1st row (right side): P5, T2B, k1, p1.
2nd row: [K1, p1] twice, k5.
3rd row: P4, C2R, p1, k1, p1.
4th row: K1, p1, k1, p2, k4.
5th row: P3, T2B, [k1, p1] twice.
6th row: [K1, p1] 3 times, k3.
7th row: P2, C2R, [p1, k1] twice, p1.
8th row: [K1, p1] twice, k1, p2, k2.
9th row: P1, T2B, k1, p1, k1, T2B, p1.
10th row: K2, p2, [k1, p1] twice, k1.
11th row: [P1, k1] twice, p1, T2B, p2.
12th row: K3, [p1, k1] 3 times.
13th row: [P1, k1] twice, T2B, p3.
14th row: K4, p2, k1, p1, k1.
15th row: P1, C2L, T2B, p4.
16th row: K5, p3, k1.
17th row: P1, k1, T2F, p5.
18th row: K5, [p1, k1] twice.
19th row: P1, k1, p1, C2L, p4.
20th row: As 14th row.
21st row: [P1, k1] twice, T2F, p3.
22nd row: As 12th row.
23rd row: [P1, k1] twice, p1, C2L, p2.
24th row: As 10th row.
25th row: P1, T2F, k1, p1, k1, T2F, p1.
26th row: As 8th row.
27th row: P2, T2F, [p1, k1] twice, p1.
28th row: As 6th row.
29th row: P3, T2F, [k1, p1] twice.
30th row: As 4th row.
31st row: P4, T2F, C2R, p1.
32nd row: K1, p3, k5.
Rep these 32 rows.

Cable Panels

Climbing Vine

Worked over 14 sts on a background of reverse st st.

Special Abbreviations
C2BP or C2FP (Cross 2 Back or Cross 2 Front Purlwise) = slip next st onto cable needle and hold a back (or front) of work, purl next st from left-hand needle, then purl st from cable needle.

1st row (wrong side): P3, k3, p4, C2BP, k2.
2nd row: P1, C2F, k1, T2B, k2, p3, T2F, k1.
3rd row: P2, k4, p2, k1, p3, C2BP.
4th row: K3, T2B, p1, k1, C2B, p3, T2F.
5th row: K4, C2FP, p2, k2, p4.
6th row: K2, T2B, p2, k1, [C2B] twice, p3.
7th row: K2, C2FP, p4, k3, p3.
8th row: K1, T2B, p3, k2, T2F, k1, C2B, p1.
9th row: C2FP, p3, k1, p2, k4, p2.
10th row: T2B, p3, C2F, k1, p1, T2F, k3.
11th row: P4, k2, p2, C2BP, k4.
12th row: P3, [C2F] twice, k1, p2, T2F, k2.
Rep these 12 rows.

Arch Twists

Worked over 8 sts on a background of reverse st st.
Work 6 rows in st st, starting knit (right side).
7th row: T2F, k4, T2B.

8th row: K1, p6, k1.
9th row: P1, T2F, k2, T2B, p1.
10th row: K2, p4, k2.
11th row: P2, T2F, T2B, p2.
12th row: K3, p2, k3.
Rep these 12 rows.

Corn Panel

Worked over 18 sts on a background of reverse st st.
1st row (right side): P5, C2B, p1, C2B, p1, C2F, p5.
2nd row: K5, p2, [k1, p2] twice, k5.
3rd row: P4, C2B, k1, p1, C2B, p1, k1, C2F, p4.
4th row: K4, p3, k1, p2, k1, p3, k4.
5th row: P3, [C2B] twice, p1, C2B, p1, [C2F] twice, p3.
6th row: K3, p4, k1, p2, k1, p4, k3.
7th row: P2, [C2B] twice, k1, p1, C2B, p1, k1, [C2F] twice, p2.
8th row: K2, p5, k1, p2, k1, p5, k2.
9th row: P1, [C2B] 3 times, p1, C2B, p1, [C2F] 3 times, p1.
10th row: K1, p6, k1, p2, k1, p6, k1.
11th row: [C2B] 3 times, k1, p1, C2B, p1, k1, [C2F] 3 times.
12th row: P7, k1, p2, k1, p7.
13th row: As 9th row.
14th row: As 10th row.
15th row: As 7th row.
16th row: As 8th row.
17th row: As 5th row.
18th row: As 6th row.
19th row: As 3rd row.
20th row: As 4th row.
21st row: As 1st row.
22nd row: As 2nd row.
23rd row: P6, k1, p1, C2B, p1, k1, p6.
24th row: K6, p1, k1, p2, k1, p1, k6.

25th row: P8, C2B, p8.
26th row: K8, p2, k8.
27th row: Purl.
28th row: Knit.
Rep these 28 rows.

Branched Grapevine Panel

Worked over 13 sts on a background of reverse st st.
1st and every alt row (wrong side): Purl.
2nd row: K2, C2B, k2, C2F, k5.
4th row: K3, C2B, C2F, k6.
6th row: K4, C2B, k4, MB (make bobble) as follows: [k1, yf, k1, yf, k1] into next st, turn and k5, turn and p5, turn and k1, sl 1, k2tog, psso, k1, turn and p3tog (bobble completed), k2.
8th row: K5, C2B, k2, C2F, k2.
10th row: K6, C2B, C2F, k3.
12th row: K2, MB, k4, C2F, k4.
Rep these 12 rows.

Diamond and Bobble Twist

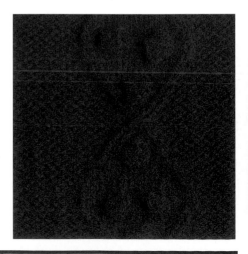

Work over 13 sts on a background of reverse st st.

1st row (right side): P5, C3R, p5.
2nd row: K5, p3, k5.
3rd row: P4, C2R, k1, C2L, p4.
4th row: K4, p5, k4.
5th row: P3, C2R, k1, MB, k1, C2L, p3.
6th row: K3, p7, k3.
7th row: P2, C2R, k5, C2L, p2.
8th row: K2, p9, k2.
9th row: P1, C2R, k7, C2L, p1.
10th row: K1, p11, k1.
11th row: P1, k3, MB, k3, MB, k3, p1.
12th row: As 10th row.
13th row: P1, T2F, k7, T2B, p1.
14th row: As 8th row.
15th row: P2, T2F, k5, T2B, p2.
16th row: As 6th row.
17th row: P3, T2F, k1, MB, k1, T2B, p3.
18th row: As 4th row.
19th row: P4, T2F, k1, T2B, p4.
20th row: As 2nd row.
Rep these 20 rows.

Arrow and Bobble

Worked over 14 sts on a background of reverse st st.

1st row (right side): P1, k1, p10, k1, p1.
2nd row: K1, p1, k10, p1, k1.
3rd row: P1, T2F, p8, T2B, p1.
4th row: K2, p1, k8, p1, k2.
5th row: P2, T2F, p6, T2B, p2.
6th row: K3, p1, k6, p1, k3.
7th row: P3, T2F, p4, T2B, p3.
8th row: [K4, p1] twice, k4.
9th row: P4, T2F, p2, T2B, p4.
10th row: K5, p1, k2, p1, k5.
11th row: P5, T2F, T2B, p5.
12th row: K6, p2, k6.
13th row: P6, C2L, p6.
14th row: As 12th row.

15th row: P6, made bobble thus: k1, p1, k1, into each of next 2 sts, turn, p6, turn, k6, turn, p6, turn, [k3tog] twice, p6.
16th row: Knit.
Rep these 16 rows.

Raised Diamonds

Worked over 18 sts on a background of st st.
1st row (right side): K7, T2B, T2F, k7.
2nd row: P8, k2, p8.
3rd row: K6, T2B, p2, T2F, k6.
4th row: P7, k4, p7.
5th row: K5, [T2B] twice, [T2F] twice, k5.
6th row: P6, k1, p1, k2, p1, k1, p6.
7th row: K4, [T2B] twice, p2, [T2F] twice, k4.
8th row: P5, k1, p1, k4, p1, k1, p5.
9th row: K3, [T2B] 3 times, [T2F] 3 times, k3.
10th row: P4, [k1, p1] twice, k2, [p1, k1] twice, p4.
11th row: K2, [T2B] 3 times, p2, [T2F] 3 times, k2.
12th row: P3, [k1, p1] twice, k4, [p1, k1] twice, p3.
13th row: K1, [T2B] 4 times, [T2F] 4 times, k1.
14th row: P2, [k1, p1] 3 times, k2, [p1, k1] 3 times, p2.
15th row: [T2B] 4 times, p2, [T2F] 4 times.
16th row: [P1, k1] 3 times, p1, k4, [p1, k1] 3 times, p1.
17th row: C2L, [T2F] 3 times, p2, [T2B] 3 times, C2R.
18th row: As 14th row.
19th row: K1, C2L, [T2F] 3 times, [T2B] 3 times, C2R, k1.
20th row: As 12th row.
21st row: K2, C2L, [T2F] twice, p2, [T2B] twice, C2R, k2.
22nd row: As 10th row.
23rd row: K3, C2L, [T2F] twice, [T2B] twice, C2R, k3.
24th row: As 8th row.

25th row: K4, C2L, T2F, p2, T2B, C2R, k4.
26th row: As 6th row.
27th row: K5, C2L, T2F, T2B, C2R, k5.
28th row: As 4th row.
29th row: K6, C2L, p2, C2R, k6.
30th row: As 2nd row.
31st row: K7, C2L, C2R, k7.
32nd row: Purl.
Rep these 32 rows.

Twist and Wave

Worked over 18 sts on a background of reversed st st.

1st row (right side): P5, k8, p5.
2nd row: K5, p8, k5.
3rd row: As 1st row.
4th row: K5, [p2, k1] twice, p2, k5.
5th row: P4, T3B, C2R, C2L, T3F, p4.
6th row: K4, p2, k1, p4, k1, p2, k4.
7th row: P3, T3B, p1, T2F, T2B, p1, T3F, p3.
8th row: [K3, p2] 3 times, k3.
9th row: P2, T3B, p2, C2R, C2L, p2, T3F, p2.
10th row: K2, p2, k3, p4, k3, p2, k2.
11th row: P1, T3B, p3, T2F, T2B, p3, T3F, p1.
12th row: K1, [p2, k5] twice, p2, k1.
13th row: T3B, p4, C2R, C2L, p4, T3F.
14th row: P2, k5, p4, k5, p2.
15th row: T3F, p4, T2F, T2B, p4, T3B.
16th row: As 12th row.
17th row: P1, T3F, p3, C2R, C2L, p3, T3B, p1.
18th row: As 10th row.
19th row: P2, T3F, p2, T2F, T2B, p2, T3B, p2.
20th row: As 8th row.
21st row: P3, T3F, p1, C2R, C2L, p1, T3B, p3.
22nd row: As 6th row.
23rd row: P4, T3F, T2F, T2B, T3B, p4.
24th row: As 2nd row.
Rep these 24 rows.

Cable Panels

Twist and Cable

Worked over 16 sts on a background of reverse st st.

1st row (wrong side): K4, p8, k4.
2nd row: P3, T2B, k6, T2F, p3.
3rd row: K3, p1, k1, p6, k1, p1, k3.
4th row: P2, T2B, p1, k6, p1, T2F, p2.
5th row: K2, p1, k2, p6, k2, p1, k2.
6th row: P1, T2B, p2, C6F, p2, T2F, p1.
7th row: K1, p1, k3, p6, k3, p1, k1.
8th row: T2B, p3, k6, p3, T2F.
9th row: P1, k4, p6, k4, p1.
10th row: T2F, p3, k6, p3, T2B.
11th row: As 7th row.
12th row: P1, T2F, p2, C6F, p2, T2B, p1.
13th row: As 5th row.
14th row: P2, T2F, p1, k6, p1, T2B, p2.
15th row: As 3rd row.
16th row: P3, T2B, k6, T2F, p3.
Rep these 16 rows.

Cable and Twist Ripple

Worked over 9 sts on a background of reverse st st.
1st row (right side): T2F, T3B, p1, T3B.
2nd row: K1, p2, k2, p3, k1.
3rd row: P1, T3B, p1, C3B, p1.
4th row: K1, p3, k2, p2, k1.
5th row: T3B, p1, T3B, T2F.
6th row: P1, [k2, p2] twice.

7th row: [K2, p2] twice, k1.
8th row: As 6th row.
9th row: T3F, p1, T3F, T2B.
10th row: As 4th row.
11th row: P1, C3F, p1, T3F, p1.
12th row: As 2nd row.
13th row: T2B, T3F, p1, T3F.
14th row: [P2, k2] twice, p1.
15th row: K1, [p2, k2] twice.
16th row: As 14th row.
Rep these 16 rows.

Cable Gate

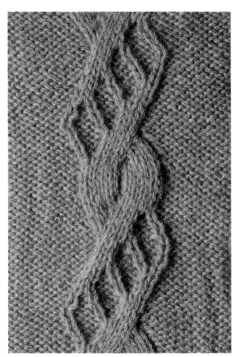

Worked over 16 sts on a background of reverse st st.

Note: Increases should be made by purling into front and back of next st.

Special Abbreviations
T4FL (Twist 4 Front Left) = slip next 3 sts onto cable needle and hold at front of work, purl next st from left-hand needle, then knit sts from cable needle.

C4FL (Cross 4 Front Left) = slip next 3 sts onto cable needle and hold at front of work, knit next st from left-hand needle, then knit sts from cable needle.

C5LI (Cross 5 Left Increase) = slip next 4 sts onto cable needle and hold at front of work, knit into front and back of next st on left-hand needle, then knit sts from cable needle.

1st row (wrong side): K2, [p5, k2] twice.
2nd row: P2, [k5, p2] twice.
3rd row: As 1st row.
4th row: P1, inc in next st, k4, sl 1, k1, psso, k2tog, k4, inc in next st, p1.
5th row: K3, p10, k3.
6th row: P2, T2B, C5L, k2tog, k2, inc in next st, p2.

7th row: K4, p7, k2, p1, k2.
8th row: P1, T2B, p2, C5L, k2tog, inc in next st, p3.
9th row: K5, p5, k4, p1, k1.
10th row: T2B, p3, T2B, T4FL, p5.
11th row: K5, p3, k2, p1, k4, p1.
12th row: T2F, p2, T2B, p2, T4FL, p4.
13th row: K4, p3, k4, p1, k2, p1, k1.
14th row: P1, T2F, T2B, p3, T2B, T3F, p3.
15th row: K3, p2, k2, p1, k4, p2, k2.
16th row: P2, T3F, p2, T2B, p2, T3F, p2.
17th row: K2, p2, k4, p1, k2, p2, k3.
18th row: P3, T3F, T2B, p3, T2B, T2F, p1.
19th row: K1, p1, k2, p1, k4, p3, k4.
20th row: P4, T4FL, p2, T2B, p2, T2F.
21st row: P1, k4, p1, k2, p3, k5.
22nd row: P5, C4FL, T2B, p3, T2B.
23rd row: K1, p1, k4, p5, k5.
24th row: P3, p2tog, k1, C5LI, p2, T2B, p1.
25th row: K2, p1, k2, p7, k4.
26th row: P2, p2tog, k3, C5LI, T2B, p2.
27th row: As 5th row.
28th row: P1, p2tog, k5, purl into front and back of loop lying between st just worked and next st, k5, p2tog, p1.
Rep these 28 rows.

Diamond Lattice Panel

Worked over 18 sts on a background of reverse st st.

Special Abbreviations
T4BR (Twist 4 Back Right) = slip next st onto cable needle and hold at back of work, knit next 3 sts from left-hand needle, then purl st from cable needle.

T4FL (Twist 4 Front Left) = slip next 3 sts onto cable needle and hold at front of work, purl next st from left-hand needle, then knit sts from cable needle.

C2FP or C2BP (Cross 2 Front Purlwise or Cross 2 Back Purlwise) = slip next st onto cable needle and hold at front (or back) of work, purl next st from left-hand needle then purl st from cable needle.

1st row (wrong side): K6, p6, k6.
2nd row: P6, C6B, p6.
3rd row: As 1st row.
4th row: P5, T4BR, T4FL, p5.
5th row: K5, p3, k2, p3, k5.
6th row: P4, T4BR, p2, T4FL, p4.
7th row: [K4, p3] twice, k4.
8th row: P3, T3B, k1, p4, k1, T3F, p3.
9th row: K3, p2, k1, p1, k4, p1, k1, p2, k3.
10th row: P2, T3B, p1, T2F, p2, T2B, p1, T3F, p2.
11th row: K2, p2, k3, p1, k2, p1, k3, p2, k2.
12th row: P1, T2B, k1, p3, T2F, T2B, p3, k1, T2F, p1.
13th row: [K1, p1] twice, k4, C2FP, k4, [p1, k1] twice.
14th row: T2B, p1, T2F, p2, T2B, T2F, p2, T2B, p1, T2F.
15th row: P1, k3, [p1, k2] 3 times, p1, k3, p1.
16th row: K1, p3, T2F, T2B, p2, T2F, T2B, p3, k1.
17th row: P1, [k4, C2BP] twice, k4, p1.
18th row: K1, p3, T2F, T2B, p2, T2B, T2F, p3, k1.
19th row: As 15th row.
20th row: T2F, p1, T2B, p2, T2F, T2B, p2, T2F, p1, T2B.
21st row: As 13th row.
22nd row: P1, T2F, k1, p3, T2B, T2F, p3, k1, T2B, p1.
23rd row: As 11th row.
24th row: P2, T3F, p1, T2B, p2, T2F, p1, T3B, p2.
25th row: As 9th row.
26th row: P3, T3F, k1, p4, k1, T3B, p3.
27th row: As 7th row.
28th row: P4, T4F, p2, T4B, p4.
29th row: As 5th row.
30th row: P5, T4F, T4B, p5.
Rep these 30 rows.

Chalice Cable

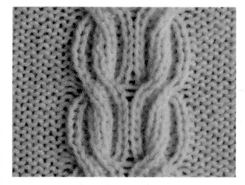

Worked over 16 sts on a background of reverse st st.
1st row (right side): K1, [p2, k2] 3 times, p2, k1.
2nd row: P1, k2, [p2, k2] 3 times, p1.

Rep the last 2 rows twice more.
7th row: Slip next 4 sts onto cable needle and hold at back of work, k1, p2, k1 from left-hand needle, then k1, p2, k1 from cable needle, slip next 4 sts onto cable needle and hold at front of work, k1, p2, k1 from left-hand needle, then k1, p2, k1 from cable needle.
8th row: As 2nd row.
9th row: As 1st row.
10th row: As 2nd row.
Rep these 10 rows.

Candle Cable

Worked over 18 sts on a background of reverse st st.
1st row (wrong side): [K1, p1] twice, k3, p4, k3, [p1, k1] twice.
2nd row: P1, T2F, k1, p3, C4F, p3, k1, T2B, p1.
3rd row: K7, p4, k7.
4th row: P6, T3B, T3F, p6.
5th row: K6, p2, k2, p2, k6.
6th row: P5, T3B, p2, T3F, p5.
7th row: K5, p8, k5.
8th row: P4, C3B, C2R, C2L, C3F, p4.
9th row: K4, p10, k4.
10th row: P3, C3B, C2R, k2, C2L, C3F, p3.
11th row: K3, p12, k3.
12th row: P2, C3B, C2R, k4, C2L, C3F, p2.
13th row: K2, p14, k2.
14th row: P1, T2B, k1, T3F, k4, T3B, k1, T2F, p1.
15th row: K1, [p1, k1] twice, p8, [k1, p1] twice, k1.
16th row: T2B, p1, k1, p1, T3F, k2, T3B, p1, k1, p1, T2F.
17th row: [P1, k2] twice, p6, [k2, p1] twice.
18th row: T2F, p1, k1, p2, T3F, T3B, p2, k1, p1, T2B.
Rep these 18 rows.

Banjo Cable

Worked over 8 sts on a background of reverse st st.
1st row (wrong side): K2, p4, k2.
2nd row: P2, k4, p2.
3rd row: K2, p1, sl 2 purlwise, p1, k2.
4th row: Slip next 3 sts onto cable needle and hold at back of work, knit next st from left-hand needle, then p1, k1, p1 from cable needle, slip next st onto cable needle and hold at front of work, k1, p1, k1 from left-hand needle, then k1 from cable needle.
5th row: [P1, k1] 3 times, p2.
6th row: [K1, p1] 3 times, k2.
Rep the last 2 rows twice more.
11th row: Yf, sl 1 purlwise, yb, [k1, p1] 3 times, sl 1 purlwise, yb.
12th row: Slip next st onto cable needle and hold at front of work, p2, k1 from left-hand needle, then k1 from cable needle, slip next 3 sts onto cable needle and hold at back of work, knit next st from left-hand needle then k1, p2 from cable needle.
13th row: As 1st row.
14th row: As 2nd row.
Rep the last 2 rows once more.
Rep these 16 rows.

Cable Arrows

Worked over 8 sts on a background of reverse st st.
1st row (right side): Knit.
2nd row: Purl.
3rd row: P1, T3B, T3F, p1.
4th row: K1, p2, k2, p2, k1.
5th row: T3B, p2, T3F.
6th row: P2, k4, p2.
Rep these 6 rows.

Cable Panels

Cable and Box Panel

Worked over 8 sts on a background of reverse st st.

1st row (right side): Knit.
2nd row: Purl.
3rd row: C8F.
Work 4 rows in st st, starting purl.
8th row: P2, k4, p2.
9th row: K2, p4, k2.
Rep the last 2 rows twice more.
Work 3 rows in st st, starting purl.
Rep these 16 rows.

Garter and Stocking Stitch Cable

Worked over 8 sts on a background of reverse st st.

1st row (right side): Knit.
2nd row: P4, k4.

Rep the last 2 rows twice more.
7th row: C8B.
8th row: K4, p4.
9th row: Knit.
Rep the last 2 rows 4 times more, then the 8th row again.
19th row: C8B.
20th row: As 2nd row.
21st row: Knit.
Rep the last 2 rows once more then the 20th row again.
Rep these 24 rows.

Cable with Moss Stitch and Rib

Worked over 15 sts on a background of reverse st st.

Special Abbreviations
T4BR (Twist 4 Back Right) = slip next 2 sts onto cable needle and hold at back of work, k2 from left-hand needle, then k1, p1 from cable needle.
T4FL (Twist 4 Front Left) = slip next 2 sts onto cable needle and hold at front of work, p1, k1 from left-hand needle, then knit sts from cable needle.

1st row (right side): K3, p1, [k1, p1] twice, k5, p2.
2nd row: K2, p4, k1, [p1, k1] 3 times, p2.
3rd row: T3F, [p1, k1] 3 times, C4F, p2.
4th row: K2, p4, k1, [p1, k1] twice, p3, k1.
5th row: P1, T3F, k1, p1, k1, T4BR, C3F, p1.
6th row: [K1, p3] twice, k1, p1, k1, p2, k2.
7th row: P2, T3F, T4BR, k1, p1, k1, T3F.
8th row: P2, k1, [p1, k1] twice, p5, k3.
9th row: P3, T4BR, [k1, p1] 3 times, k2.
10th row: P2, k1, [p1, k1] 3 times, p3, k3.

11th row: P1, T4BR, k1, [p1, k1] 3 times, T3B.
12th row: K1, p3, k1, [p1, k1] 3 times, p3, k1.
13th row: T3B, k1, [p1, k1] 3 times, T4B, p1.
14th row: K3, p3, k1, [p1, k1] 3 times, p2.
15th row: K2, [p1, k1] 3 times, C4B, p3.
16th row: K3, p5, k1, [p1, k1] twice, p2.
17th row: T3F, k1, p1, k1, T4BR, C3F, p2.
18th row: K2, p2, k1, p1, k1, [p3, k1] twice.
19th row: P1, T3F, T4BR, k1, p1, k1, T3F, p1.
20th row: K1, p3, k1, [p1, k1] twice, p4, k2.
21st row: P2, C4B, [k1, p1] 3 times, C3F.
22nd row: P2, k1, [p1, k1] 3 times, p4, k2.
23rd row: P2, k5, p1, [k1, p1] twice, k3.
24th row: As 22nd row.
25th row: P2, C4B, [k1, p1] 3 times, T3B.
26th row: As 20th row.
27th row: P1, C3B, T4FL, k1, p1, k1, T3B, p1.
28th row: As 18th row.
29th row: T3B, k1, p1, k1, T4FL, T3B, p2.
30th row: As 16th row.
31st row: K2, [p1, k1] 3 times, T4FL, p3.
32nd row: As 14th row.
33rd row: T3F, k1, [p1, k1] 3 times, T4FL, p1.
34th row: As 12th row.
35th row: P1, T4F, k1, [p1, k1] 3 times, T3F.
36th row: As 10th row.
37th row: P3, T4F, [k1, p1] 3 times, k2.
38th row: As 8th row.
39th row: P2, C3B, T4FL, k1, p1, k1, T3B.
40th row: As 6th row.
41st row: P1, T3B, k1, p1, k1, T4FL, T3B, p1.
42nd row: As 4th row.
43rd row: T3B, [p1, k1] 3 times, C4F, p2.
44th row: As 2nd row.
Rep these 44 rows.

Cable Circles

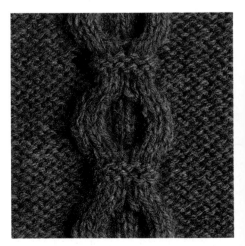

Worked over 12 sts on a background of reverse st st.

1st row (right side): Purl.
2nd row: Knit.

3rd row: P3, k6, p3.
4th row: K3, p6, k3.
5th row: C6B, C6F.
Work 5 rows in st st, starting purl.
11th row: T6F, T6B.
12th row: K3, p6, k3.
Rep these 12 rows.

Knotted Cable

Worked over 6 sts on a background of reverse st st.
1st row (right side): K2, p2, k2.
2nd and every alt row: P2, k2, p2.
3rd row: C6.
5th, 7th and 9th rows: K2, p2, k2.
10th row: As 2nd row.
Rep these 10 rows.

Double Chain

Worked over 18 sts on a background of reverse st st.
1st row (right side): P3, k3, [p1, k1] twice, p1, k4, p3.
2nd row: K3, p3, [k1, p1] twice, k1, p4, k3.
Rep the last 2 rows once more.
5th row: P3, slip next 3 sts onto cable needle and hold at back of work, k1, p1, k1 from left-hand needle, then k3 from cable needle, slip next 3 sts onto cable needle and hold at front of work, knit the next 3 sts from left-hand needle, then p1, k1, p1 from cable needle, p3.
6th row: K3, p1, k1, p7, k1, p1, k4.
7th row: P3, k1, p1, k7, p1, k1, p4.
Rep the last 2 rows 3 times more then work 6th row again.
15th row: P3, slip next 3 sts onto cable needle and leave at front of work, knit next 3 sts from left-hand needle, then p1, k1, p1 from cable needle, slip next 3 sts onto cable needle and leave at back of work, k1, p1, k1 from left-hand needle, then k3 from cable needle, p3.
16th row: As 2nd row.
17th row: As 1st row.
Rep the last 2 rows 3 times more then work 16th row again.
Rep these 24 rows.

Cable Rope

Worked over 8 sts on a background of reverse st st.

Special Abbreviations
T4BR (Twist 4 Back) = slip next st onto cable needle and hold back of work, knit next 3 sts from left-hand needle, then purl st from cable needle.
T4FL (Twist 4 Front) = slip next 3 sts onto cable needle and hold at front of work, purl next st from left-hand needle then knit sts from cable needle.

1st row (wrong side): K1, p6, k1.
2nd row: P1, k6, p1.
3rd row: As 1st row.
4th row: P1, C6B, p1.
5th row: As 1st row.
6th row: T4BR, T4FL.
7th row: P3, k2, p3.
8th row: K3, p2, k3.
Rep the last 2 rows 5 times more then the 7th row again.
20th row: T4FL, T4BR.
Rep the first 4 rows once more, then 1st and 2nd rows again.
Rep these 26 rows.

Triple Cable Rope

Worked over 14 sts on a background of reverse st st.
1st row (right side): P2, [k2, p2] 3 times.
2nd row: K2, [p2, k2] 3 times.
Rep these 2 rows twice more.
7th row: P2, T3F, p1, k2, p1, T3B, p2.
8th row: K3, p2, [k1, p2] twice, k3.
9th row: P3, T3F, k2, T3B, p3.
10th row: K4, p6, k4.
11th row: P4, T3F, T3B, p4.
12th row: K5, p4, k5.
13th row: P5, C4F, p5.
14th row: As 12th row.
15th row: P4, C3B, C3F, p4.
16th row: As 10th row.
17th row: P3, T3B, k2, T3F, p3.
18th row: As 8th row.
19th row: P2, T3B, p1, k2, p1, T3F, p2.
20th row: As 2nd row.
Rep 1st and 2nd rows twice more.
Rep these 24 rows.

Cable Panels

Cabled Arrows

Worked over 14 sts on a background of reverse st st.

1st row (right side): K4, p2, k2, p2, k4.
2nd row: P4, k2, p2, k2, p4.
Rep these 2 rows 3 times more.
9th row: C4F, p2, k2, p2, C4B.
10th row: As 2nd row.
11th row: K2, C4F, k2, C4B, k2.
12th row: Purl.
13th row: K4, p1, T2F, T2B, p1, k4.
14th row: As 2nd row.
15th row: As 1st row.
16th row: As 2nd row.
Rep these 16 rows.

Ribbed Cable Rope

Worked over 8 sts on a background of reverse st st.

Special Abbreviations
T6L (Twist 6 Left) = slip next 3 sts onto cable needle and hold at front of work, k1, p1, k1 from left-hand needle, then k1, p1, k1 from cable needle.
T4BR (Twist 4 Back Right) = slip 1 st onto cable needle and hold at back of work, k1, p1, k1 from left-hand needle, then p1 from cable needle.
T4FL (Twist 4 Front Left) = slip next 3 sts onto cable needle and hold at front of work, p1 from left-hand needle, then k1, p1, k1 from cable needle.

1st row (right side): P1, T6L, p1.
2nd row: K1, p1, k1, p2, k1, p1, k1.
3rd row: P1, k1, p1, k2, p1, k1, p1.
4th row: As 2nd row.
5th row: As 1st row.
6th row: As 2nd row.
7th row: T4BR, T4FL.
8th row: As 3rd row.
9th row: As 2nd row.
Rep the last 2 rows 3 times more, then the 3rd row again.
17th row: T4FL, T4BR.
18th row: As 2nd row.
Rep these 18 rows.

Big Wavy Cable Pattern

Worked over 16 sts on a background of reverse st st.
1st row (right side): P2, k4, p4, k4, p2.
2nd row: K2, p4, k4, p4, k2.
3rd row: P2, C4F, p4, C4B, p2.
4th row: As 2nd row.

Rep the last 4 rows once more.
9th row: [T4B, T4F] twice.
10th row: P2, k4, p4, k4, p2.
11th row: K2, p4, k4, p4, k2.
12th row: As 10th row.
13th row: [T4F, T4B] twice.
14th row: As 2nd row.
15th row: P2, C4B, p4, C4F, p2.
16th row: As 2nd row.
17th row: As 1st row.
18th row: As 2nd row.
Rep the last 4 rows once more, then first 2 rows again.
25th row: As 9th row.
26th row: As 10th row.
27th row: As 11th row.
28th row: As 10th row.
29th row: As 13th row.
30th row: As 2nd row.
31st row: As 3rd row.
32nd row: As 2nd row.
Rep these 32 rows.

Ornamental Lantern Cable

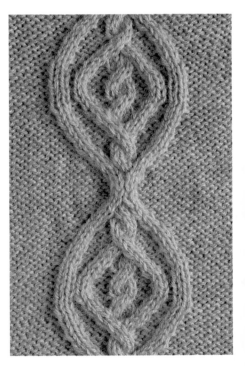

Worked over 22 sts on a background of reverse st st.
1st row (wrong side): K9, p4, k9.
2nd row: P9, k4, p9.
3rd row: As 1st row.
4th row: P7, C4B, C4F, p7.
5th row: K7, p8, k7.
6th row: P5, T4B, C4F, T4F, p5.
7th row: K5, p2, k2, p4, k2, p2, k5.
8th row: P3, T4B, p2, k4, p2, T4F, p3.
9th row: K3, p2, k4, p4, k4, p2, k3.
10th row: P2, T3B, p4, C4F, p4, T3F, p2.
11th row: K2, p2, k5, p4, k5, p2, k2.

12th row: P1, T3B, p3, C4B, C4F, p3, T3F, p1.
13th row: K1, p2, k4, p8, k4, p2, k1.
14th row: T3B, p2, T4B, k4, T4F, p2, T3F.
15th row: P2, k3, p2, k2, p4, k2, p2, k3, p2.
16th row: K2, p1, T4B, p2, C4B, p2, T4F, p1, k2.
17th row: P2, k1, p2, k4, p4, k4, p2, k1, p2.
18th row: K2, p1, k2, p4, k4, p4, k2, p1, k2.
19th row: As 17th row.
20th row: K2, p1, T4F, p2, C4B, p2, T4B, p1, k2.
21st row: As 15th row.
22nd row: T3F, p2, T4F, k4, T4B, p2, T3B.
23rd row: As 13th row.
24th row: P1, T3F, p3, T4F, T4B, p3, T3B, p1.
25th row: As 11th row.
26th row: P2, T3F, p4, C4F, p4, T3B, p2.
27th row: As 9th row.
28th row: P3, T4F, p2, k4, p2, T4B, p3.
29th row: As 7th row.
30th row: P5, T4F, C4F, T4B, p5.
31st row: As 5th row.
32nd row: P7, T4F, T4B, p7.
Rep these 32 rows.

Wavy Cable Pattern

Worked over 14 sts on a background of reverse st st.

1st row (wrong side): K5, p4, k5.
2nd row: P5, C4B, p5.
3rd row: As 1st row.
4th row: P4, T3B, T3F, p4.
5th row: K4, p2, k2, p2, k4.
6th row: P2, T4B, p2, T4F, p2.
7th row: K2, p2, k6, p2, k2.

8th row: P2, T4F, p2, T4B, p2.
9th row: As 5th row.
10th row: P4, T3F, T3B, p4.
11th and 13th rows: As 1st row.
12th row: As 2nd row.
14th row: P5, k4, p5.
15th row: As 1st row.
16th row: As 2nd row.
17th row: As 1st row.
18th row: As 14th row.
Rep these 18 rows.

Moss and Bobble Cable

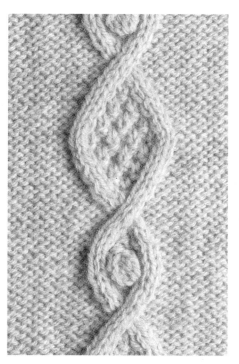

Worked over 13 sts on a background of reverse st st.

1st row (wrong side): K4, p2, k1, p2, k4.
2nd row: P3, T3B, k1, T3F, p3.
3rd row: K3, p2, k1, p1, k1, p2, k3.
4th row: P2, T3B, k1, p1, k1, T3F, p2.
5th row: K2, p2, [k1, p1] twice, k1, p2, k2.
6th row: P1, T3B, [k1, p1] twice, k1, T3F, p1.
7th row: K1, p2, [k1, p1] 3 times, k1, p2, k1.
8th row: T3B, [k1, p1] 3 times, k1, T3F.
9th row: P2, [k1, p1] 4 times, k1, p2.
10th row: T3F, [p1, k1] 3 times, p1, T3B.
11th row: K1, p2, [k1, p1] 3 times, k1, p2, k1.
12th row: P1, T3F, [p1, k1] twice, p1, T3B, p1.
13th row: As 5th row.
14th row: P2, T3F, p1, k1, p1, T3B, p2.
15th row: As 3rd row.
16th row: P3, T3F, p1, T3B, p3.
17th row: As 1st row.
18th row: P4, C5B, p4.
19th row: As 1st row.
20th row: P3, T3B, p1, T3F, p3.

21st row: [K3, p2] twice, k3.
22nd row: P2, T3B, p3, T3F, p2.
23rd row: K2, p2, k5, p2, k2.
24th row: P2, k2, p2, make bobble (MB) as follows: [k1, yf, k1, yf, k1] into next st, turn, p5, turn, k5, turn, p2tog, p1, p2tog, turn, sl 1, k2tog, psso (bobble completed), p2, k2, p2.
25th row: As 23rd row.
26th row: P2, T3F, p3, T3B, p2.
27th row: As 21st row.
28th row: P3, T3F, p1, T3B, p3.
29th row: As 1st row.
30th row: As 18th row.
Rep these 30 rows.

Elongated Cable Plait

Worked over 12 sts on a background of reverse st st.

1st row (wrong side): K3, p6, k3.
2nd row: P3, k2, C4B, p3.
3rd row: As 1st row.
4th row: P3, C4F, k2, p3.
Rep the last 4 rows once more, then the 1st row again.
10th row: P2, T3B, k2, T3F, p2.
11th row: K2, p2, [k1, p2] twice, k2.
12th row: P1, T3B, p1, k2, p1, T3F, p1.
13th row: K1, [p2, k2] twice, p2, k1.
14th row: T3B, p2, k2, p2, T3F.
15th row: [P2, k3] twice, p2.
16th row: T3F, p2, k2, p2, T3B.
17th row: As 13th row.
18th row: P1, T3F, p1, k2, p1, T3B, p1.
19th row: As 15th row.
20th row: P2, T3F, k2, T3B, p2.
Rep first 4 rows once more.
Rep these 24 rows.

Cable Panels

Broken Cross Panel

Worked over 18 sts on a background of reverse st st.
1st row (right side): K6, p2, k2, p2, k6.
2nd row: P6, k2, p2, k2, p6.
Rep the last 2 rows once more.
5th row: C6F, p2, k2, p2, C6F.
6th row: As 2nd row.
7th row: As 1st row.
8th row: As 2nd row.
9th row: P2, k2, p2, k6, p2, k2, p2.
10th row: K2, p2, k2, p6, k2, p2, k2.
Rep the last 2 rows once more.
13th row: P2, k2, p2, C6F, p2, k2, p2.
14th row: As 10th row.
15th row: As 9th row.
16th row: As 10th row.
Rep these 16 rows.

Enclosed Cables

Worked over 14 sts on a background of reverse st st.
1st row (right side): P1, k2, p2, C4F, p2, k2, p1.
2nd row: K1, p2, k2, p4, k2, p2, k1.
3rd row: P1, k2, p2, k4, p2, k2, p1.
4th row: As 2nd row.
Rep the last 4 rows once more, then the 1st and 2nd rows again.
11th row: P1, [T3F, T3B] twice, p1.
12th row: K2, [p4, k2] twice.
13th row: P2, [C4F, p2] twice.
14th row: As 12th row.
15th row: P1, [T3B, T3F] twice, p1.
16th row: As 2nd row.
17th row: As 1st row.
18th row: As 2nd row.
19th row: As 3rd row.
20th row: As 2nd row.
Rep these 20 rows.

Plaited Lattice Panel

Worked over 23 sts on a background of reverse st st.
1st row (right side): K3, [p1, k3] 5 times.
2nd row: P3, [k1, p3] 5 times.
Rep the last 2 rows twice more.
7th row: [K3, p1] twice, C7B, [p1, k3] twice.
8th and every alt row: As 2nd row.
9th row: As 1st row.
11th row: K3, p1, [C7F, p1] twice, k3.
13th row: As 1st row.
15th row: [C7B, p1] twice, C7B.
17th row: As 1st row.
19th row: As 11th row.
21st row: As 1st row.
23rd row: As 7th row.
25th row: As 1st row.

27th row: As 1st row.
28th row: As 2nd row.
Rep these 28 rows.

Bunched Cable

Worked over 16 sts on a background of reverse st st.
1st row (right side): K4, p3, k2, p3, k4.
2nd row: P4, k3, p2, k3, p4.
Rep the last 2 rows 4 times more.
11th row: C8F, C8B.
12th row: Purl.
Rep these 12 rows.

Fancy Cross and Cable Panel

Worked over 24 sts on a background of reverse st st.
1st row (wrong side): [K2, p2] 3 times, [p2, k2] 3 times.
2nd row: P2, C2R, p2, T4F, C4F, T4B, p2, C2R, p2.

3rd row: K2, p2, k4, p8, k4, p2, k2.
4th row: P2, k2, p4, [C4B] twice, p4, k2, p2.
5th row: As 3rd row.
6th row: P2, C2R, p2, T4B, C4F, T4F, p2, C2R, p2.
7th row: [K2, p2] twice, k2, p4, [k2, p2] twice, k2.
8th row: P2, [k2, p2] twice, k4, p2, [k2, p2] twice.
9th row: K2, [p4, k4] twice, p4, k2.
10th row: P2, [k4, p4] twice, k4, p2.
11th row: As 9th row.
12th row: P2, k4, p4, C4F, p4, k4, p2.
13th row: As 9th row.
14th row: As 10th row.
15th row: As 9th row.
16th row: P2, k2, T4F, p2, k4, p2, T4B, k2, p2.
Rep these 16 rows.

Twisted Rope Panel

Worked over 22 sts on a background of reverse st st.
1st row (right side): K2, p2, [k6, p2] twice, k2.
2nd row: P2, k2, [p6, k2] twice, p2.
3rd row: K2, p2, C6F, p2, C6B, p2, k2.
4th row: As 2nd row.
5th row: As 1st row.
6th row: As 2nd row.
Rep these 6 rows twice more.
19th row: K6, [p2, k2] twice, p2, k6.
20th row: P6, [k2, p2] twice, k2, p6.
21st row: C6B, [p2, k2] twice, p2, C6F.
22nd row: As 20th row.
23rd row: As 19th row.
24th row: As 20th row.
Rep the last 6 rows twice more.
Rep these 36 rows.

Lattice Cable

Worked across 24 sts on a background of reverse st st.
1st row (right side): K2, p8, C4B, p8, k2.
2nd row: P2, k8, p4, k8, p2.
3rd row: T4F, p4, T4B, T4F, p4, T4B.
4th row: K2, [p2, k4] 3 times, p2, k2.
5th row: P2, T4F, T4B, p4, T4F, T4B, p2.
6th row: K4, p4, k8, p4, k4.
7th row: P4, C4B, p8, C4F, p4.
8th row: As 6th row.
9th row: P2, T4B, T4F, p4, T4B, T4F, p2.
10th row: As 4th row.
11th row: T4B, p4, T4F, T4B, p4, T4F.
12th row: As 2nd row.
Rep these 12 rows.

Criss-Cross Cable Panel

Worked over 12 sts on a background of reverse st st.
1st row (wrong side): K1, p4, k2, p4, k1.
2nd row: [T3B, T3F] twice.
3rd row: P2, k2, p4, k2, p2.
4th row: [T3F, T3B] twice.

5th row: As 1st row.
6th row: P1, k4, p2, k4, p1.
7th row: As 1st row.
8th row: P1, C4B, p2, C4F, p1.
9th row: As 1st row.
10th row: As 2nd row.
11th row: As 3rd row.
12th row: K2, p2, C4F, p2, k2.
13th row: As 3rd row.
14th row: As 4th row.
15th row: As 1st row.
16th row: P1, C4F, p2, C4B, p1.
17th row: As 1st row.
18th row: As 6th row.
Rep these 18 rows.

Criss-Cross Cable with Twists

Worked over 16 sts on a background of reverse st st.
1st row (right side): P2, C4F, p4, C4F, p2.
2nd row: K2, p4, k4, p4, k2.
3rd row: P2, k4, p4, k4, p2.
4th row: As 2nd row.
5th row: As 1st row.
6th row: As 2nd row.
7th row: [T4B, T4F] twice.
8th row: As 3rd row.
9th row: K2, p4, C4F, p4, k2.
10th row: As 3rd row.
11th row: As 2nd row.
12th row: As 3rd row.
13th row: As 9th row.
Rep the last 4 rows twice more.
22nd row: As 3rd row.
23rd row: [T4F, T4B] twice.
24th row: As 2nd row.
Rep these 24 rows.

All-over Lace Patterns

Purse Stitch

Multiple of 2 sts.
1st row: P1, *yrn, p2tog; rep from * to last st, p1.
Rep this row.

Simple Garter Stitch Lace

Multiple of 4 sts + 2.
1st row: K2, *yfrn, p2tog, k2; rep from * to end.
Rep this row.

Lacy Openwork

Multiple of 4 sts + 1.
1st row: K1, *yfrn, p3tog, yon, k1; rep from * to end.
2nd row: P2tog, yon, k1, yfrn, *p3tog, yon, k1, yfrn; rep from * to last 2 sts, p2tog.
Rep these 2 rows.

Feather Openwork

Multiple of 5 sts + 2.
1st row (right side): K1, *k2tog, yf, k1, yf, sl 1, k1, psso; rep from * to last st, k1.
2nd row: Purl.
Rep these 2 rows.

Chevron and Feather

Multiple of 13 sts + 1.
1st row (right side): *K1, yf, k4, k2tog, sl 1, k1, psso, k4, yf; rep from * to last st, k1.
2nd row: Purl.
Rep these 2 rows.

Alternating Feather Openwork

Multiple of 6 sts + 1.

Gate and Ladder Pattern

1st row (right side): K1, *k2tog, yf, k1, yf, sl 1, k1, psso, k1; rep from * to end.
2nd row: Purl.
Rep these 2 rows 5 times more.
13th row: K1, *yf, sl 1, k1, psso, k1, k2tog, yf, k1; rep from * to end.
14th row: Purl.
Rep the last 2 rows 5 times more.
Rep these 24 rows.

Multiple of 9 sts + 3.
Foundation row (wrong side): Purl.
Commence Pattern
1st row: K1, k2tog, k3, [yf] twice, k3, *k3tog, k3, [yf] twice, k3; rep from * to last 3 sts, k2tog, k1.
2nd row: P6, k1, *p8, k1; rep from * to last 5 sts, p5.
Rep the last 2 rows.

Ridge and Hole Pattern

Multiple of 2 sts + 1.
Note: Stitches should only be counted after the 1st, 3rd or 4th rows of this pattern.
1st row (right side): Purl.
2nd row: *P2tog; rep from * to last st, p1.
3rd row: P1, *purl through horizontal strand of yarn lying between stitch just worked and next st, p1; rep from * to end.
4th row: P1, *yrn, p2tog; rep from * to end.
Rep these 4 rows.

Filet Net

Multiple of 3 sts.

1st row (right side): K2, *sl 2, pass 1st slipped st over 2nd and off needle, sl 1, pass 2nd slipped st over 3rd and off needle, slip the 3rd slipped st back onto left-hand needle, [yf] twice (to make 2 sts), knit the 3rd slipped st in usual way; rep from * to last st, k1 (original number of sts retained).

2nd row: K3, *p1, k2; rep from * to end.
Rep these 2 rows.

Cell Stitch

Multiple of 4 sts + 3.

1st row (right side): K2, *yf, sl 1, k2tog, psso, yf, k1; rep from * to last st, k1.

2nd row: Purl.

3rd row: K1, k2tog, yf, k1, *yf, sl 1, k2tog, psso, yf, k1; rep from * to last 3 sts, yf, sl 1, k1, psso, k1.

4th row: Purl.
Rep these 4 rows.

Diagonal Openwork

Multiple of 4 sts + 2.

1st row (right side): *K1, yf, sl 1, k2tog, psso, yf; rep from * to last 2 sts, k2.

2nd and every alt row: Purl.

3rd row: K2, *yf, sl 1, k2tog, psso, yf, k1; rep from * to end.

5th row: K2tog, yf, k1, yf, *sl 1, k2tog, psso, yf, k1, yf; rep from * to last 3 sts, sl 1, k1, psso, k1.

7th row: K1, k2tog, yf, k1, yf, *sl 1, k2tog, psso, yf, k1, yf; rep from * to last 2 sts, sl 1, k1, psso.

8th row: Purl.
Rep these 8 rows.

Grand Eyelets

Multiple of 4 sts.

Note: Sts should not be counted after the 1st row.

1st row: P2, *yrn, p4tog; rep from * to last 2 sts, p2.

2nd row: K3, [k1, p1, k1] into next st, *k1, [k1, p1, k1] into next st; rep from * to last 2 sts, k2.

3rd row: Knit.
Rep these 3 rows.

Little Fountain Pattern

Multiple of 4 sts + 1.

Note: Sts should only be counted after the 3rd and 4th rows.

1st row (right side): K1, *yf, k3, yf, k1; rep from * to end.

2nd row: Purl.

3rd row: K2, sl 1, k2tog, psso, *k3, sl 1, k2tog, psso; rep from * to last 2 sts, k2.

4th row: Purl.
Rep these 4 rows.

Bead Stitch

Multiple of 7 sts.

1st row (right side): K1, k2tog, yf, k1, yf, sl 1, k1, psso, *k2, k2tog, yf, k1, yf, sl 1, k1, psso; rep from * to last st, k1.

2nd row: *P2tog tbl, yrn, p3, yrn, p2tog; rep from * to end.

3rd row: K1, yf, sl 1, k1, psso, k1, k2tog, yf, *k2, yf, sl 1, k1, psso, k1, k2tog, yf; rep from * to last st, k1.

4th row: P2, yrn, p3tog, yrn, *p4, yrn, p3tog, yrn; rep from * to last 2 sts, p2.
Rep these 4 rows.

Lacy Lattice Stitch

Multiple of 6 sts + 1.

1st row (right side): K1, *yfrn, p1, p3tog, p1, yon, k1; rep from * to end.

2nd and every alt row: Purl.

3rd row: K2, yf, sl 1, k2tog, psso, yf, *k3, yf, sl 1, k2tog, psso, yf; rep from * to last 2 sts, k2.

5th row: P2tog, p1, yon, k1, yfrn, p1, *p3tog, p1, yon, k1, yfrn, p1; rep from * to last 2 sts, p2tog.

7th row: K2tog, yf, k3, yf, *sl 1, k2tog, psso, yf, k3, yf; rep from * to last 2 sts, sl 1, k1, psso.

8th row: Purl.
Rep these 8 rows.

All-over Lace Patterns

Little Shell Pattern

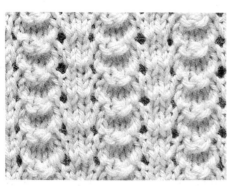

Multiple of 7 sts + 2.
1st row (right side): Knit.
2nd row: Purl.
3rd row: K2, *yfrn, p1, p3tog, p1, yon, k2; rep from * to end.
4th row: Purl.
Rep these 4 rows.

Pillar Openwork

Multiple of 3 sts + 2.
1st row (right side): K1, *yf, sl 1 purlwise, k2, psso the k2; rep from * to last st, k1.
2nd row: Purl.
Rep these 2 rows.

Twisted Openwork Pattern I

Multiple of 4 sts + 1.
1st row (right side): P1, *k3, p1; rep from * to end.

2nd row: K1, *p3, k1; rep from * to end.
3rd row: As 1st row.
4th row: K1, *yfrn, p3tog, yon, k1; rep from * to end.
5th row: K2, p1, *k3, p1; rep from * to last 2 sts, k2.
6th row: P2, k1, *p3, k1; rep from * to last 2 sts, p2.
7th row: As 5th row.
8th row: P2tog, yon, k1, yfrn, *p3tog, yon, k1, yfrn; rep from * to last 2 sts, p2tog.
Rep these 8 rows.

Twisted Openwork Pattern II

Worked as Twisted Openwork Pattern I, using reverse side as right side.

Little Flowers

Multiple of 6 sts + 3.
1st row (right side): Knit.
2nd and every alt row: Purl.
3rd row: Knit.
5th row: *K4, yf, sl 1, k1, psso; rep from * to last 3 sts, k3.
7th row: K2, k2tog, yf, k1, yf, sl 1, k1, psso, *k1, k2tog, yf, k1, yf, sl 1, k1, psso; rep from * to last 2 sts, k2.
9th and 11th rows: Knit.
13th row: K1, yf, sl 1, k1, psso, *k4, yf, sl 1, k1, psso; rep from * to end.
15th row: K2, yf, sl 1, k1, psso, k1, k2tog, yf, *k1, yf, sl 1, k1, psso, k1, k2tog, yf; rep from * to last 2 sts, k2.

16th row: Purl.
Rep these 16 rows.

Eyelet V-Stitch

Multiple of 12 sts + 1.
1st row (right side): Knit.
2nd and every alt row: Purl.
3rd row: K4, yf, sl 1, k1, psso, k1, k2tog, yf, *k7, yf, sl 1, k1, psso, k1, k2tog, yf; rep from * to last 4 sts, k4.
5th row: K5, yf, sl 1, k2tog, psso, yf, *k9, yf, sl 1, k2tog, psso, yf; rep from * to last 5 sts, k5.
7th row: Knit.
9th row: K1, *k2tog, yf, k7, yf, sl 1, k1, psso, k1; rep from * to end.
11th row: K2tog, yf, k9, *yf, sl 1, k2tog, psso, yf, k9; rep from * to last 2 sts, yf, sl 1, k1, psso.
12th row: Purl.
Rep these 12 rows.

Pine Cone Pattern

Multiple of 10 sts + 1.
1st row (right side): Knit.
2nd and every alt row: Purl.
3rd row: K3, k2tog, yf, k1, yf, sl 1, k1, psso, *k5, k2tog, yf, k1, yf, sl 1, k1, psso; rep from * to last 3 sts, k3.
5th row: K2, k2tog, yf, k3, yf, sl 1, k1, psso, *k3, k2tog, yf, k3, yf, sl 1, k1, psso; rep from * to last 2 sts, k2.
7th and 9th rows: As 3rd row.
11th row: Knit.
13th row: K1, *yf, sl 1, k1, psso, k5, k2tog, yf, k1; rep from * to end.
15th row: K2, yf, sl 1, k1, psso, k3, k2tog,

yf, *k3, yf, sl 1, k1, psso, k3, k2tog, yf; rep from * to last 2 sts, k2.
17th and 19th rows: As 13th row.
20th row: Purl.
Rep these 20 rows.

Raindrops

Multiple of 6 sts + 5.
1st row (right side): P5, *yrn, p2tog, p4; rep from * to end.
2nd row: K5, *p1, k5; rep from * to end.
3rd row: P5, *k1, p5; rep from * to end.
Rep the last 2 rows once more then the 2nd row again.
7th row: P2, yrn, p2tog, *p4, yrn, p2tog; rep from * to last st, p1.
8th row: K2, p1, *k5, p1; rep from * to last 2 sts, k2.
9th row: P2, k1, *p5, k1; rep from * to last 2 sts, p2.
Rep the last 2 rows once more then the 8th row again.
Rep these 12 rows.

Snowflakes I

Multiple of 8 sts + 7.
1st and every alt row (wrong side): Purl.
2nd row: K5, sl 1, k1, psso, yf, k1, yf, k2tog, *k3, sl 1, k1, psso, yf, k1, yf, k2tog; rep from * to last 5 ,sts, k5.
4th row: K6, yf, sl 2, k1, p2sso, yf, *k5, yf, sl 2, k1, p2sso, yf; rep from * to last 6 sts, k6.
6th row: As 2nd row.
8th row: K1, sl 1, k1, psso, yf, k1, yf, k2tog, *k3, sl 1, k1, psso, yf, k1, yf, k2tog; rep from * to last st, k1.
10th row: K2, yf, sl 2, k1, p2sso, yf, *k5,

Snowflakes II

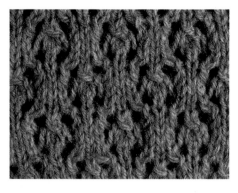

Multiple of 6 sts + 1.
Note: Sts should not be counted after 3rd, 4th, 9th and 10th rows.
1st row (right side): K1, *yf, sl 1, k1, psso, k1, k2tog, yf, k1; rep from * to end.
2nd and every alt row: Purl.
3rd row: K2, yf, *k3, yf; rep from * to last 2 sts, k2.
5th row: K2tog, yf, sl 1, k1, psso, k1, k2tog, yf, *sl 1, k2tog, psso, yf, sl 1, k1, psso, k1, k2tog, yf; rep from * to last 2 sts, sl 1, k1, psso.
7th row: K1, *k2tog, yf, k1, yf, sl 1, k1, psso, k1; rep from * to end.
9th row: As 3rd row.
11th row: K1, *k2tog, yf, sl 1, k2tog, psso, yf, sl 1, k1, psso, k1; rep from * to end.
12th row: Purl.
Rep these 12 rows.

Eyelet Diamonds

Multiple of 16 sts + 11.
1st row (right side): K10, yf, sl 1, k1, psso, k3, k2tog, yf, *k9, yf, sl 1, k1, psso, k3, k2tog, yf; rep from * to last 10 sts, k10.
2nd and every alt row: Purl.
3rd row: K3, k2tog, yf, k1, yf, sl 1, k1, psso, *k3, yf, sl 1, k1, psso, k1, k2tog, yf, k3, k2tog, yf, k1, yf, sl 1, k1, psso; rep from * to last 3 sts, k3.
5th row: K2, k2tog, yf, k3, yf, sl 1, k1, psso,

yf, sl 2, k1, p2sso, yf; rep from * to last 2 sts, k2.
12th row: As 8th row.
Rep these 12 rows.

*k3, yf, sl 1, k2tog, psso, yf, k3, k2tog, yf, k3, yf, sl 1, k1, psso; rep from * to last 2 sts, k2.
7th row: K1, k2tog, yf, k5, yf, sl 1, k1, psso, *k7, k2tog, yf, k5, yf, sl 1, k1, psso; rep from * to last st, k1.
9th row: K2, yf, sl 1, k1, psso, k3, k2tog, yf, *k9, yf, sl 1, k1, psso, k3, k2tog, yf; rep from * to last 2 sts, k2.
11th row: K3, yf, sl 1, k1, psso, k1, k2tog, yf, k3, *k2tog, yf, k1, yf, sl 1, k1, psso, k3, yf, sl 1, k1, psso, k1, k2tog, yf, k3; rep from * to end.
13th row: K4, yf, sl 1, k2tog, psso, yf, *k3, k2tog, yf, k3, yf, sl 1, k1, psso, k3, yf, sl 1, k2tog, psso, yf; rep from * to last 4 sts, k4.
15th row: K9, k2tog, yf, k5, yf, sl 1, k1, psso, *k7, k2tog, yf, k5, yf, sl 1, k1, psso; rep from * to last 9 sts, k9.
16th row: Purl.
Rep these 16 rows.

Swinging Triangles

Multiple of 12 sts + 1.
1st and every alt row (wrong side): Purl.
2nd row: *K10, sl 1, k1, psso, yf; rep from * to last st, k1.
4th row: K9, sl 1, k1, psso, yf, *k10, sl 1, k1, psso, yf; rep from * to last 2 sts, k2.
6th row: *K8, [sl 1, k1, psso, yf] twice; rep from * to last st, k1.
8th row: K7, [sl 1, k1, psso, yf] twice, *k8, [sl 1, k1, psso, yf] twice; rep from * to last 2 sts, k2.
10th row: *K6, [sl 1, k1, psso, yf] 3 times; rep from * to last st, k1.
12th row: K5, [sl 1, k1, psso, yf] 3 times, *k6, [sl 1, k1, psso, yf] 3 times; rep from * to last 2 sts, k2.
14th row: *K4, [sl 1, k1, psso, yf] 4 times; rep from * to last st, k1.
16th row: K1, *yf, k2tog, k10; rep from * to end.
18th row: K2, yf, k2tog, *k10, yf, k2tog; rep from * to last 9 sts, k9.
20th row: K1, *[yf, k2tog] twice, k8; rep from * to end.
22nd row: K2, [yf, k2tog] twice, *k8, [yf, k2tog] twice; rep from * to last 7 sts, k7.
24th row: K1, *[yf, k2tog] 3 times, k6; rep from * to end.
26th row: K2, [yf, k2tog] 3 times, *k6, [yf, k2tog] 3 times; rep from * to last 5 sts, k5.
28th row: K1, *[yf, k2tog] 4 times, k4; rep from * to end.
Rep these 28 rows.

All-over Lace Patterns

Zigzag Eyelets

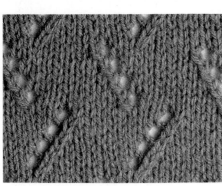

Multiple of 9 sts.

1st row (right side): K4, *yf, sl 1, k1, psso, k7; rep from * to last 5 sts, yf, sl 1, k1, psso, k3.

2nd and every alt row: Purl.

3rd row: K5, *yf, sl 1, k1, psso, k7; rep from * to last 4 sts, yf, sl 1, k1, psso, k2.

5th row: K6, *yf, sl 1, k1, psso, k7; rep from * to last 3 sts, yf, sl 1, k1, psso, k1.

7th row: *K7, yf, sl 1, k1, psso; rep from * to end.

9th row: K3, *k2tog, yf, k7; rep from * to last 6 sts, k2tog, yf, k4.

11th row: K2, *k2tog, yf, k7; rep from * to last 7 sts, k2tog, yf, k5.

13th row: K1, *k2tog, yf, k7; rep from * to last 8 sts, k2tog, yf, k6.

15th row: *K2tog, yf, k7; rep from * to end.

16th row: Purl.

Rep these 16 rows.

Rhombus Lace

Multiple of 8 sts + 2.

1st row (right side): K1, [k2tog, yf] twice, *k4, [k2tog, yf] twice; rep from * to last 5 sts, k5.

2nd and every alt row: Purl.

3rd row: [K2tog, yf] twice, *k4, [k2tog, yf] twice; rep from * to last 6 sts, k6.

5th row: K1, k2tog, yf, k4, *[k2tog, yf] twice, k4; rep from * to last 3 sts, k2tog, yf, k1.

7th row: K3, [k2tog, yf] twice, *k4, [k2tog, yf] twice; rep from * to last 3 sts, k3.

9th row: K2, *[k2tog, yf] twice, k4; rep from * to end.

11th row: As 1st row.

13th row: K5, [k2tog, yf] twice, *k4, [k2tog, yf] twice; rep from * to last st, k1.

15th row: *K4, [k2tog, yf] twice; rep from * to last 2 sts, k2.

17th row: As 7th row.

19th row: As 5th row.

21st row: K2tog, yf, k4, *[k2tog, yf] twice, k4; rep from * to last 4 sts, k2tog, yf, k2.

23rd row: As 13th row.

24th row: Purl.

Rep these 24 rows.

Diagonal Ridges

Multiple of 5 sts + 2.

1st row (right side): K2tog, yf, *k3, k2tog, yf; rep from * to last 5 sts, k5.

2nd row: P2, *k3, p2; rep from * to end.

3rd row: K4, k2tog, yf, *k3, k2tog, yf; rep from * to last st, k1.

4th row: K1, *p2, k3; rep from * to last st, p1.

5th row: *K3, k2tog, yf; rep from * to last 2 sts, k2.

6th row: K2, *p2, k3; rep from * to end.

7th row: K2, *k2tog, yf, k3; rep from * to end.

8th row: *K3, p2; rep from * to last 2 sts, k2.

9th row: K1, k2tog, yf, *k3, k2tog, yf; rep from * to last 4 sts, k4.

10th row: P1, *k3, p2; rep from * to last st, k1.

Rep these 10 rows.

Lacy Diagonals

Mutliple of 10 sts + 2.

1st row (right side): K7, sl 1, k1, psso, yf, k2tog, yf, *k6, sl 1, k1, psso, yf, k2tog, yf; rep from * to last st, k1.

2nd and every alt row: Purl.

3rd row: *K6, sl 1, k1, psso, yf, k2tog, yf; rep from * to last 2 sts, k2.

5th row: K5, sl 1, k1, psso, yf, k2tog, yf, *k6, sl 1, k1, psso, yf, k2tog, yf; rep from * to last 3 sts, k3.

7th row: K4, sl 1, k1, psso, yf, k2tog, yf, *k6, sl 1, k1, psso, yf, k2tog, yf; rep from * to last 4 sts, k4.

9th row: K3, sl 1, k1, psso, yf, k2tog, yf, *k6, sl 1, k1, psso, yf, k2tog, yf; rep from * to last 5 sts, k5.

11th row: K2, *sl 1, k1, psso, yf, k2tog, yf, k6; rep from * to end.

13th row: K1, sl 1, k1, psso, yf, k2tog, yf, *k6, sl 1, k1, psso, yf, k2tog, yf; rep from * to last 7 sts, k7.

15th row: Sl 1, k1, psso, yf, k2tog, yf, *k6, sl 1, k1, psso, yf, k2tog, yf; rep from * to last 8 sts, k8.

17th row: K1, *k2tog, yf, k6, sl 1, k1, psso, yf; rep from * to last st, k1.

19th row: *K2tog, yf, k6, sl 1, k1, psso, yf; rep from * to last 2 sts, k2.

20th row: Purl.

Rep these 20 rows.

Fish Hooks

Multiple of 8 sts + 1.

1st and every alt row (wrong side): Purl.

2nd row: Knit.

4th row: K2, sl 1, k1, psso, yf, k1, yf, k2tog, *k3, sl 1, k1, psso, yf, k1, yf, k2tog; rep from * to last 2 sts, k2.

6th row: K1, *sl 1, k1, psso, yf, k3, yf, k2tog, k1; rep from * to end.

8th row: K4, sl 1, k1, psso, yf, *k6, sl 1, k1, psso, yf; rep from * to last 3 sts, k3.

10th row: K3, sl 1, k1, psso, yf, *k6, sl 1, k1, psso, yf; rep from * to last 4 sts, k4.

12th row: K2, sl 1, k1, psso, yf, *k6, sl 1, k1, psso, yf; rep from * to last 5 sts, k5.

14th row: K1, *sl 1, k1, psso, yf, k6; rep from * to end.

16th row: Knit.

18th row: As 4th row.

20th row: As 6th row.

22nd row: K3, yf, k2tog, *k6, yf, k2tog; rep from * to last 4 sts, k4.

24th row: K4, yf, k2tog, *k6, yf, k2tog; rep from * to last 3 sts, k3.

26th row: K5, yf, k2tog, *k6, yf, k2tog; rep from * to last 2 sts, k2.

28th row: *K6, yf, k2tog; rep from * to last st, k1.

Rep these 28 rows.

Cogwheel Eyelets

Multiple of 8 sts + 1.

1st row (right side): K2, k2tog, yf, k1, yf, sl 1, k1, psso, *k3, k2tog, yf, k1, yf, sl 1, k1, psso; rep from * to last 2 sts, k2.

2nd and every alt row: Purl.

3rd row: K1, *k2tog, yf, k3, yf, sl 1, k1, psso, k1; rep from * to end.

5th row: K2tog, yf, k5, *yf, sl 1, k2tog, psso, yf, k5; rep from * to last 2 sts, yf, sl 1, k1, psso.

7th row: Sl 1, k1, psso, yf, k5, *yf, sl 2tog knitwise, k1, p2sso, yf, k5; rep from * to last 2 sts, yf, k2tog.

9th row: As 7th row.

11th row: K2, yf, sl 1, k1, psso, k1, k2tog, yf, *k3, yf, sl 1, k1, psso, k1, k2tog, yf; rep from * to last 2 sts, k2.

13th row: K3, yf, sl 1, k2tog, psso, yf, *k5, yf, sl 1, k2tog, psso, yf; rep from * to last 3 sts, k3.

15th row: K1, *yf, sl 1, k1, psso, k3, k2tog, yf, k1; rep from * to end.

17th row: As 11th row.

19th row: As 13th row.

21st row: K3, yf, sl 2tog knitwise, k1, p2sso, yf, *k5, yf, sl 2tog knitwise, k1, p2sso, yf; rep from * to last 3 sts, k3.

23rd row: As 21st row.

25th row: As 3rd row.

27th row: As 5th row.

28th row: Purl.

Rep these 28 rows.

Diamond Trellis

Multiple of 16 sts + 1.

1st row (right side): K2tog, yf, k12, *[k2tog, yf] twice, k12; rep from * to last 3 sts, k2tog, yf, k1.

2nd and every alt row: Purl.

Inverted Hearts

Multiple of 14 sts + 1.

1st row (right side): P2tog, yon, k11, *yfrn, p3tog, yon, k11; rep from * to last 2 sts, yfrn, p2tog.

2nd row: K1, *p13, k1; rep from * to end.

3rd row: K2, yf, sl 1, k1, psso, k9, *[k2tog, yf] twice, k1, yf, sl 1, k1, psso, k9; rep from * to last 4 sts, k2tog, yf, k2.

5th row: K1, *[yf, sl 1, k1, psso] twice, k7, [k2tog, yf] twice, k1; rep from * to end.

7th row: K2, [yf, sl 1, k1, psso] twice, k5, [k2tog, yf] twice, *k3, [yf, sl 1, k1, psso] twice, k5, [k2tog, yf] twice; rep from * to last 2 sts, k2.

9th row: K3, [yf, sl 1, k1, psso] twice, k3, [k2tog, yf] twice, *k5, [yf, sl 1, k1, psso] twice, k3, [k2tog, yf] twice; rep from * to last 3 sts, k3.

11th row: K4, [yf, sl 1, k1, psso] twice, k1, [k2tog, yf] twice, *k7, [yf, sl 1, k1, psso] twice, k1, [k2tog, yf] twice; rep from * to last 4 sts, k4.

13th row: K5, yf, sl 1, k1, psso, yf, k3tog, yf, k2tog, yf, *k9, yf, sl 1, k1, psso, yf, k3tog, yf, k2tog, yf; rep from * to last 5 sts, k5.

15th row: K6, yf, k3tog, yf, k2tog, yf, *k11, yf, k3tog, yf, k2tog, yf; rep from * to last 6 sts, k6.

17th row: K6, [k2tog, yf] twice, *k12, [k2tog, yf] twice; rep from * to last 7 sts, k7.

19th row: K5, [k2tog, yf] twice, k1, yf, sl 1, k1, psso, *k9, [k2tog, yf] twice, k1, yf, sl 1, k1, psso; rep from * to last 5 sts, k5.

21st row: K4, [k2tog, yf] twice, k1, [yf, sl 1, k1, psso] twice, *k7, [k2tog, yf] twice, k1, [yf, sl 1, k1, psso] twice; rep from * to last 4 sts, k4.

23rd row: K3, [k2tog, yf] twice, k3, [yf, sl 1, k1, psso] twice, *k5, [k2tog, yf] twice, k3, [yf, sl 1, k1, psso] twice; rep from * to last 3 sts, k3.

25th row: K2, [k2tog, yf] twice, k5, [yf, sl 1, k1, psso] twice, *k3, [k2tog, yf] twice, k5, [yf, sl 1, k1, psso] twice; rep from * to last 2 sts, k2.

27th row: *K1, [k2tog, yf] twice, k7, [yf, sl 1, k1, psso] twice; rep from * to last st, k1.

29th row: [K2tog, yf] twice, k9, *yf, sl 1, k1, psso, yf, k3tog, yf, k2tog, yf, k9; rep from * to last 4 sts, [yf, sl 1, k1, psso] twice.

31st row: K1, k2tog, yf, k11, *yf, k3tog, yf, k2tog, yf, k11; rep from * to last 3 sts, yf, k2tog, k1.

32nd row: Purl.

Rep these 32 rows.

3rd row: P2, yon, sl 1, k1, psso, k7, *k2tog, yfrn, p3, yon, sl 1, k1, psso, k7; rep from * to last 4 sts, k2tog, yfrn, p2.

4th row: K2, p11, *k3, p11; rep from * to last 2 sts, k2.

5th row: P3, yon, sl 1, k1, psso, k5, k2tog, yfrn, *p5, yon, sl 1, k1, psso, k5, k2tog, yfrn; rep from * to last 3 sts, p3.

6th row: K3, p9, *k5, p9; rep from * to last 3 sts, k3.

7th row: P4, yon, sl 1, k1, psso, k3, k2tog, yfrn, *p7, yon, sl 1, k1, psso, k3, k2tog, yfrn; rep from * to last 4 sts, p4.

8th row: K4, p7, *k7, p7; rep from * to last 4 sts, k4.

9th row: P2, p2tog, yon, k1, yf, sl 1, k1, psso, k1, k2tog, yf, k1, yfrn, p2tog, *p3, p2tog, yon, k1, yf, sl 1, k1, psso, k1, k2tog, yf, k1, yfrn, p2tog; rep from * to last 2 sts, p2.

10th row: As 6th row.

11th row: P1, *p2tog, yon, k3, yf, sl 1, k2tog, psso, yf, k3, yfrn, p2tog, p1; rep from * to end.

12th row: As 4th row.

Rep these 12 rows.

Eyelet Boxes

Multiple of 14 sts + 11.

1st row (right side): K2, p7, *k3, yf, sl 1, k1, psso, k2, p7; rep from * to last 2 sts, k2.

2nd, 4th, 6th, 8th and 10th rows: P2, k7, *p7, k7; rep from * to last 2 sts, p2.

3rd row: K2, p7, *k1, k2tog, yf, k1, yf, sl 1, k1, psso, k1, p7; rep from * to last 2 sts, k2.

5th row: K2, p7, *k2tog, yf, k3, yf, sl 1, k1, psso, p7; rep from * to last 2 sts, k2.

7th row: K2, p7, *k2, yf, sl 1, k2tog, psso, yf, k2, p7; rep from * to last 2 sts, k2.

9th row: As 1st row.

11th row: P2, k3, yf, sl 1, k1, psso, k2, *p7, k3, yf, sl 1, k1, psso, k2; rep from * to last 2 sts, p2.

12th, 14th, 16th and 18th rows: K2, p7, *k7, p7; rep from * to last 2 sts, k2.

13th row: P2, k1, k2tog, yf, k1, yf, sl 1, k1, psso, k1, *p7, k1, k2tog, yf, k1, yf, sl 1, k1, psso, k1; rep from * to last 2 sts, p2.

15th row: P2, k2tog, yf, k3, yf, sl 1, k1, psso, *p7, k2tog, yf, k3, yf, sl 1, k1, psso; rep from * to last 2 sts, p2.

17th row: P2, k2, yf, sl 1, k2tog, psso, yf, k2, *p7, k2, yf, sl 1, k2tog, psso, yf, k2; rep from * to last 2 sts, p2.

19th row: As 11th row.

20th row: K2, p7, *k7, p7; rep from * to last 2 sts, k2.

Rep these 20 rows.

All-over Lace Patterns

Shadow Triangles

Multiple of 10 sts + 3.

1st row (right side): K2, yf, sl 1, k1, psso, k5, k2tog, yf, *k1, yf, sl 1, k1, psso, k5, k2tog, yf; rep from * to last 2 sts, k2.

2nd row: P4, k5, *p5, k5; rep from * to last 4 sts, p4.

3rd row: K3, *yf, sl 1, k1, psso, k3, k2tog, yf, k3; rep from * to end.

4th row: P5, k3, *p7, k3; rep from * to last 5 sts, p5.

5th row: K4, yf, sl 1, k1, psso, k1, k2tog, yf, *k5, yf, sl 1, k1, psso, k1, k2tog, yf; rep from * to last 4 sts, k4.

6th row: P6, k1, *p9, k1; rep from * to last 6 sts, p6.

7th row: K5, yf, sl 1, k2tog, psso, yf, *k7, yf, sl 1, k2tog, psso, yf; rep from * to last 5 sts, k5.

8th row: Purl.

9th row: K4, k2tog, yf, k1, yf, sl 1, k1, psso, *k5, k2tog, yf, k1, yf, sl 1, k1, psso; rep from * to last 4 sts, k4.

10th row: K4, p5, *k5, p5; rep from * to last 4 sts, k4.

11th row: K3, *k2tog, yf, k3, yf, sl 1, k1, psso, k3; rep from * to end.

12th row: K3, *p7, k3; rep from * to end.

13th row: K2, k2tog, yf, k5, yf, sl 1, k1, psso, *k1, k2tog, yf, k5, yf, sl 1, k1, psso; rep from * to last 2 sts, k2.

14th row: P1, k1, *p9, k1; rep from * to last st, p1.

15th row: K1, k2tog, yf, k7, *yf, sl 1, k2tog, psso, yf, k7; rep from * to last 3 sts, yf, sl 1, k1, psso, k1.

16th row: Purl.
Rep these 16 rows.

Little and Large Diamonds

Multiple 12 sts + 1.

1st row (right side): K1, *yf, sl 1, k1, psso, k7, k2tog, yf, k1; rep from * to end.

2nd and every alt row: Purl.

3rd row: K2, yf, sl 1, k1, psso, k5, *k2tog, yf, k3, yf, sl 1, k1, psso, k5; rep from * to last 4 sts, k2tog, yf, k2.

5th row: K3, yf, sl 1, k1, psso, k3, *k2tog, yf, k5, yf, sl 1, k1, psso, k3; rep from * to last 5 sts, k2tog, yf, k3.

7th row: *K1, k2tog, yf, k1, yf, sl 1, k1, psso; rep from * to last st, k1.

9th row: K2tog, yf, k3, *yf, sl 1, k2tog, psso, yf, k3; rep from * to last 2 sts, yf, sl 1, k1, psso.

11th row: K4, k2tog, yf, k1, yf, sl 1, k1, psso, *k7, k2tog, yf, k1, yf, sl 1, k1, psso; rep from * to last 4 sts, k4.

13th row: K3, k2tog, yf, k3, yf, sl 1, k1, psso, *k5, k2tog, yf, k3, yf, sl 1, k1, psso; rep from * to last 3 sts, k3.

15th row: K2, k2tog, yf, k5, yf, sl 1, k1, psso, *k3, k2tog, yf, k5, yf, sl 1, k1, psso; rep from * to last 2 sts, k2.

17th row: As 7th row.

19th row: As 9th row.

20th row: Purl.
Rep these 20 rows.

Eyelet Pyramids

Multiple of 12 sts + 3.

1st row (right side): P2, k11, *p1, k11; rep from * to last 2 sts, p2.

2nd row: K2, p11, *k1, p11; rep from * to last 2 sts, k2.

3rd row: *P3, k2, [yf, sl 1, k1, psso] 3 times, k1; rep from * to last 3 sts, p3.

4th row: K3, *p9, k3; rep from * to end.

5th row: P4, k2, [yf, sl 1, k1, psso] twice, k1, *p5, k2, [yf, sl 1, k1, psso] twice, k1; rep from * to last 4 sts, p4.

6th row: K4, p7, *k5, p7; rep from * to last 4 sts, k4.

7th row: P5, k2, yf, sl 1, k1, psso, k1, *p7, k2, yf, sl 1, k1, psso, k1; rep from * to last 5 sts, p5.

8th row: K5, p5, *k7, p5; rep from * to last 5 sts, k5.

9th row: P6, k3, *p9, k3; rep from * to last 6 sts, p6.

10th row: K6, p3, *k9, p3; rep from * to last 6 sts, k6.

11th row: P7, k1, *p11, k1; rep from * to last 7 sts, p7.

12th row: K7, p1, *k11, p1; rep from * to last 7 sts, k7.

13th row: As 12th row.

14th row: As 11th row.

15th row: K1, [yf, sl 1, k1, psso] twice, k1, p3, *k2, [yf, sl 1, k1, psso] 3 times, k1, p3; rep from * to last 6 sts, k2, yf, sl 1, k1, psso, k2.

16th row: As 9th row.

17th row: K2, yf, sl 1, k1, psso, k1, p5, *k2, [yf, sl 1, k1, psso] twice, k1, p5; rep from * to last 5 sts, k2, yf, sl 1, k1, psso, k1.

18th row: P5, k5, *p7, k5; rep from * to last 5 sts, p5.

19th row: K1, yf, sl 1, k1, psso, k1, p7, *k2, yf, sl 1, k1, psso, k1, p7; rep from * to last 4 sts, k2, yf, sl 1, k1, psso.

20th row: P4, k7, *p5, k7; rep from * to last 4 sts, p4.

21st row: As 4th row.

22nd row: P3, *k9, p3; rep from * to end.

23rd row: As 2nd row.

24th row: As 1st row.
Rep these 24 rows.

Feather and Fan

Multiple of 18 sts + 2.

1st row (right side): Knit.

2nd row: Purl.

3rd row: K1, *[k2tog] 3 times, [yf, k1] 6 times, [k2tog] 3 times; rep from * to last st, k1.

4th row: Knit.
Rep these 4 rows.

2-Coloured Feather and Fan

Worked as Feather and Fan.
Work 4 rows in colour A and 4 rows in colour B throughout.

Ears of Corn

Multiple of 12 sts + 2.

1st row (right side): Knit.

2nd row: Purl.

3rd row: K4, k2tog, k1, yf, *k9, k2tog, k1, yf; rep from * to last 7 sts, k7.

4th row: P8, yrn, p1, p2tog, *p9, yrn, p1, p2tog; rep from * to last 3 sts, p3.

5th row: K2, *k2tog, k1, yf, k9; rep from * to end.

6th row: P10, yrn, p1, p2tog, *p9, yrn, p1, p2tog; rep from * to last st, p1.

Work 2 rows in st st, starting knit.

9th row: K7, yf, k1, sl 1, k1, psso, *k9, yf, k1, sl 1, k1, psso; rep from * to last 4 sts, k4.

10th row: P3, p2tog tbl, p1, yrn, *p9, p2tog tbl, p1, yrn; rep from * to last 8 sts, p8.

11th row: *K9, yf, k1, sl 1, k1, psso; rep from * to last 2 sts, k2.

12th row: P1, p2tog tbl, p1, yrn, *p9, p2tog tbl, p1, yrn; rep from * to last 10 sts, p10.

Rep these 12 rows.

Creeping Vines

Multiple of 22 sts + 3.

1st row (right side): K4, k2tog, k3, [yf, k2tog] twice, *yf, k13, k2tog, k3, [yf, k2tog] twice; rep from * to last 12 sts, yf, k12.

2nd and every alt row: Purl.

3rd row: K3, *k2tog, k3, yf, k1, yf, [sl 1, k1, psso, yf] twice, k3, sl 1, k1, psso, k7; rep from * to end.

5th row: K2, k2tog, [k3, yf] twice, [sl 1, k1, psso, yf] twice, k3, sl 1, k1, psso, *k5, k2tog, [k3, yf] twice, [sl 1, k1, psso, yf] twice, k3, sl 1, k1, psso; rep from * to last 6 sts, k6.

7th row: K1, k2tog, k3, yf, k5, yf, [sl 1, k1, psso, yf] twice, k3, sl 1, k1, psso, *k3, k2tog, k3, yf, k5, yf, [sl 1, k1, psso, yf] twice, k3, sl 1, k1, psso; rep from * to last 5 sts, k5.

9th row: K12, yf, [sl 1, k1, psso, yf] twice, k3, sl 1, k1, psso, *k13, yf, [sl 1, k1, psso, yf] twice, k3, sl 1, k1, psso; rep from * to last 4 sts, k4.

11th row: K7, k2tog, k3, [yf, k2tog] twice, yf, k1, yf, k3, sl 1, k1, psso; rep from * to last 3 sts, k3.

13th row: K6, k2tog, k3, [yf, k2tog] twice, [yf, k3] twice, sl 1, k1, psso, *k5, k2tog, k3, [yf, k2tog] twice, [yf, k3] twice, sl 1, k1, psso; rep from * to last 2 sts, k2.

15th row: K5, k2tog, k3, [yf, k2tog] twice, yf, k5, yf, k3, sl 1, k1, psso, *k3, k2tog, k3, [yf, k2tog] twice, yf, k5, yf, k3, sl 1, k1, psso; rep from * to last st, k1.

16th row: Purl.

Rep these 16 rows.

Horseshoe Print

Multiple of 10 sts + 1.

1st row (wrong side): Purl.

2nd row: K1, *yf, k3, sl 1, k2tog, psso, k3, yf, k1; rep from * to end.

3rd row: Purl.

4th row: P1, *k1, yf, k2, sl 1, k2tog, psso, k2, yf, k1, p1; rep from * to end.

5th row: K1, *p9, k1; rep from * to end.

6th row: P1, *k2, yf, k1, sl 1, k2tog, psso, k1, yf, k2, p1; rep from * to end.

7th row: As 5th row.

8th row: P1, *k3, yf, sl 1, k2tog, psso, yf, k3, p1; rep from * to end.

Rep these 8 rows.

Fancy Horseshoe Print

Multiple of 10 sts + 1.

Wave Pattern

1st row (right side): K1, *yf, k3, sl 1, k2tog, psso, k3, yf, k1; rep from * to end.

2nd and every alt row: Purl.

3rd row: K2, yf, k2, sl 1, k2tog, psso, k2, *yf, k3, yf, k2, sl 1, k2tog, psso, k2; rep from * to last 2 sts, yf, k2.

5th row: K2tog, [yf, k1] twice, *sl 1, k2tog, psso, [k1, yf] twice, sl 1, k2tog, psso, [yf, k1] twice; rep from * to last 7 sts, sl 1, k2tog, psso, [k1, yf] twice, sl 1, k1, psso.

6th row: Purl.

Rep these 6 rows.

Wave Pattern

Multiple of 14 sts + 3.

1st row (right side): K2, yf, k5, k3tog, k5, yf, *k1, yf, k5, k3tog, k5, yf; rep from * to last 2 sts, k2.

2nd row: Purl.

3rd row: Knit.

4th row: As 1st row.

Rep the last 4 rows once more, then the first 3 rows again.

12th, 13th and 15th rows: Purl.

14th and 16th rows: Knit.

Rep these 16 rows.

Flickering Flames

Multiple of 10 sts + 1.

1st row (right side): K1, *yf, k3, sl 1, k2tog, psso, k3, yf, k1; rep from * to end.

2nd row: Purl.

Rep the last 2 rows 3 times more.

9th row: K2tog, k3, yf, k1, yf, k3, *sl 1, k2tog, psso, k3, yf, k1, yf, k3; rep from * to last 2 sts, sl 1, k1, psso.

10th row: Purl.

Rep the last 2 rows 3 times more.

Rep these 16 rows.

All-over Lace Patterns

Tracery Pattern

Multiple of 12 sts + 1.

1st row (right side): K1, *yf, k2tog, yf, sl 1, k1, psso, k3, k2tog, yf, k3; rep from * to end.

2nd and every alt row: P1, *yrn, p2tog, p10; rep from * to end.

3rd row: K1, *yf, k2tog, yf, k1, sl 1, k1, psso, k1, k2tog, k1, yf, k3; rep from * to end.

5th row: K1, *yf, k2tog, k1, k2tog, yf, k1, yf, sl 1, k1, psso, k4; rep from * to end.

7th row: K1, *yf, [k2tog] twice, k1, [yf, k1] twice, sl 1, k1, psso, k3; rep from * to end.

8th row: As 2nd row.

Rep these 8 rows.

Chalice Pattern

Multiple of 10 sts + 3.

1st row (right side): K2, yf, k1, sl 1, k1, psso, k3, k2tog, k1, *[yf, k1] twice, sl 1, k1, psso, k3, k2tog, k1; rep from * to last 2 sts, yf, k2.

2nd and every alt row: Purl.

3rd row: K3, *yf, k1, sl 1, k1, psso, k1, k2tog, k1, yf, k3; rep from * to end.

5th row: K4, yf, k1, sl 1, k2tog, psso, k1, yf, *k5, yf, k1, sl 1, k2tog, psso, k1, yf; rep from * to last 4 sts, k4.

7th row: K2, k2tog, k1, yf, k3, yf, k1, sl 1, k1, psso, *k1, k2tog, k1, yf, k3, yf, k1, sl 1, k1, psso; rep from * to last 2 sts, k2.

9th row: K1, sl 1, k1, psso, k2, yf, k3, yf, k2, *sl 1, k2tog, psso, k2, yf, k3, yf, k2; rep from * to last 3 sts, k2tog, k1.

11th row: K3, *k2tog, k1, [yf, k1] twice, sl 1, k1, psso, k3; rep from * to end.

13th row: K2, k2tog, k1, yf, k3, yf, k1, sl 1, k1, psso, *k1, k2tog, k1, yf, k3, yf, k1, sl 1, k1, psso; rep from * to last 2 sts, k2.

15th row: K1, sl 1, k1, psso, k1, yf, k5, yf, k1, *sl 1, k2tog, psso, k1, yf, k5, yf, k1; rep from * to last 3 sts, k2tog, k1.

17th row: K3, *yf, k1, sl 1, k1, psso, k1,

k2tog, k1, yf, k3; rep from * to end.

19th row: K3, *yf, k2, sl 1, k2tog, psso, k2, yf, k3; rep from * to end.

20th row: Purl.

Rep these 20 rows.

Clover Pattern

Multiple of 12 sts + 1.

1st row (right side): K2tog, k4, yf, k1, yf, k4, *sl 1, k2tog, psso, k4, yf, k1, yf, k4; rep from * to last 2 sts, sl 1, k1, psso.

2nd and every alt row: Purl.

3rd row: K2tog, k3, [yf, k3] twice, *sl 1, k2tog, psso, k3, [yf, k3] twice; rep from * to last 2 sts, sl 1, k1, psso.

5th row: K2tog, k2, yf, k5, yf, k2, *sl 1, k2tog, psso, k2, yf, k5, yf, k2; rep from * to last 2 sts, sl 1, k1, psso.

7th row: K1, *yf, k4, sl 1, k2tog, psso, k4, yf, k1; rep from * to end.

9th row: K2, yf, k3, sl 1, k2tog, psso, k3, *[yf, k3] twice, sl 1, k2tog, psso, k3; rep from * to last 2 sts, yf, k2.

11th row: K3, yf, k2, sl 1, k2tog, psso, k2, *yf, k5, yf, k2, sl 1, k2tog, psso, k2; rep from * to last 3 sts, yf, k3.

12th row: Purl.

Rep these 12 rows.

Goblet Lace

Multiple of 10 sts + 1.

1st row (right side): K1, *yf, sl 1, k1, psso, k2tog, yf, k1; rep from * to end.

2nd and every alt row: Purl.

Rep the last 2 rows twice more.

7th row: K1, *yf, sl 1, k1, psso, k5, k2tog, yf, k1; rep from * to end.

9th row: K2, yf, sl 1, k1, psso, k3, k2tog, yf, *k3, yf, sl 1, k1, psso, k3, k2tog, yf; rep from * to last 2 sts, k2.

11th row: K3, yf, sl 1, k1, psso, k1, k2tog, yf, *k5, yf, sl 1, k1, psso, k1, k2tog, yf; rep from * to last 3 sts, k3.

13th row: K4, yf, sl 1, k2tog, psso, yf, *k7, yf, sl 1, k2tog, psso, yf; rep from * to last 4 sts, k4.

14th row: Purl.

Rep these 14 rows.

Triangles and Lace

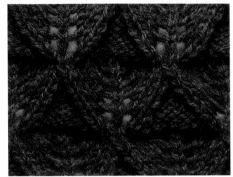

Multiple of 12 sts + 1.

1st row (right side): K1, *yf, sl 1, k1, psso, p7, k2tog, yf, k1; rep from * to end.

2nd row: P3, k7, *p5, k7; rep from * to last 3 sts, p3.

3rd row: K1, *yf, k1, sl 1, k1, psso, p5, k2tog, k1, yf, k1; rep from * to end.

4th row: P4, k5, *p7, k5; rep from * to last 4 sts, p4.

5th row: K1, *yf, k2, sl 1, k1, psso, p3, k2tog, k2, yf, k1; rep from * to end.

6th row: P5, k3, *p9, k3; rep from * to last 5 sts, p5.

7th row: K1, *yf, k3, sl 1, k1, psso, p1, k2tog, k3, yf, k1; rep from * to end.

8th row: P6, k1, *p11, k1; rep from * to last 6 sts, p6.

9th row: K1, *yf, k4, sl 1, k2tog, psso, k4, yf, k1; rep from * to end.

10th row: Purl.

11th row: P4, k2tog, yf, k1, yf, sl 1, k1, psso, *p7, k2tog, yf, k1, yf, sl 1, k1, psso; rep from * to last 4 sts, p4.

12th row: K4, p5, *k7, p5; rep from * to last 4 sts, k4.

13th row: P3, k2tog, k1, [yf, k1] twice, sl 1, k1, psso, *p5, k2tog, k1, [yf, k1] twice, sl 1, k1, psso; rep from * to last 3 sts, p3.

14th row: K3, p7, *k5, p7; rep from * to last 3 sts, k3.

15th row: P2, k2tog, k2, yf, k1, yf, k2, sl 1, k1, psso, *p3, k2tog, k2, yf, k1, yf, k2, sl 1, k1, psso; rep from * to last 2 sts, p2.

16th row: K2, p9, *k3, p9; rep from * to last 2 sts, k2.

17th row: P1, *k2tog, k3, yf, k1, yf, k3, sl 1, k1, psso, p1; rep from * to end.

18th row: K1, *p11, k1; rep from * to end.

19th row: K2tog, k4, yf, k1, yf, k4, *sl 1, k2tog, psso, k4, yf, k1, yf, k4; rep from * to last 2 sts, sl 1, k1, psso.

20th row: Purl.

Rep these 20 rows.

Plumes

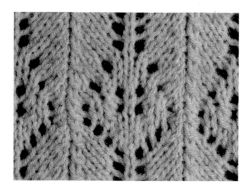

Multiple of 11 sts + 2.

1st row (right side): K1, *k2tog, k3, yf, k1, yf, k3, sl 1, k1, psso; rep from * to last st, k1.

2nd and every alt row: Purl.

3rd and 5th rows: As 1st row.

7th row: K1, *k2tog, k2, yf, k3, yf, k2, sl 1, k1, psso; rep from * to last st, k1.

9th row: K1, *k2tog, k1, yf, k5, yf, k1, sl 1, k1, psso; rep from * to last st, k1.

11th row: K1, *[k2tog, yf, k1] twice, yf, sl 1, k1, psso, k1, yf, sl 1, k1, psso; rep from * to last st, k1.

13th row: As 11th row.

15th row: As 9th row.

17th row: As 7th row.

18th row: Purl.

Rep these 18 rows.

Obstacles

Multiple of 14 sts + 1.

1st row (right side): P2, k2tog, k3, yf, k1, yf, k3, sl 1, k1, psso, *p3, k2tog, k3, yf, k1, yf, k3, sl 1, k1, psso; rep from * to last 2 sts, p2.

2nd, 4th, 6th and 8th rows: K2, p11, *k3, p11; rep from * to last 2 sts, k2.

3rd row: P2, k2tog, k2, yf, k3, yf, k2, sl 1, k1, psso, *p3, k2tog, k2, yf, k3, yf, k2, sl 1, k1, psso; rep from * to last 2 sts, p2.

5th row: P2, k2tog, k1, yf, k5, yf, k1, sl 1, k1, psso, *p3, k2tog, k1, yf, k5, yf, k1, sl 1, k1, psso; rep from * to last 2 sts, p2.

7th row: P2, k2tog, yf, k7, yf, sl 1, k1, psso, *p3, k2tog, yf, k7, yf, sl 1, k1, psso; rep from * to last 2 sts, p2.

9th row: K1, *yf, k3, sl 1, k1, psso, p3, k2tog, k3, yf, k1; rep from * to end.

10th, 12th, and 14th rows: P6, k3, *p11, k3; rep from * to last 6 sts, p6.

11th row: K2, yf, k2, sl 1, k1, psso, p3, k2tog, k2, *yf, k3, yf, k2, sl 1, k1, psso, p3, k2tog, k2; rep from * to last 2 sts, yf, k2.

13th row: K3, yf, k1, sl 1, k1, psso, p3, k2tog, k1, *yf, k5, yf, k1, sl 1, k1, psso, p3, k2tog, k1; rep from * to last 3 sts, yf, k3.

15th row: K4, yf, sl 1, k1, psso, p3, k2tog, *yf, k7, yf, sl 1, k1, psso, p3, k2tog; rep from * to last 4 sts, yf, k4.

16th row: P6, k3, *p11, k3; rep from * to last 6 sts, p6.

Rep these 16 rows.

Filigree Lace

Multiple of 16 sts + 2.

1st Foundation row (right side): K6, k2tog, yf, k2, yf, sl 1, k1, psso, *k10, k2tog, yf, k2, yf, sl 1, k1, psso; rep from * to last 6 sts, k6.

2nd Foundation row: P5, p2tog tbl, yrn, p4, yrn, p2tog, *p8, p2tog tbl, yrn, p4, yrn, p2tog; rep from * to last 5 sts, p5.

3rd Foundation row: K4, k2tog, yf, k6, yf, sl 1, k1, psso, *k6, k2tog, yf, k6, yf, sl 1, k1, psso; rep from * to last 4 sts, k4.

4th Foundation row: P3, p2tog tbl, yrn, p4, yrn, p2tog, p2, yrn, p2tog, *p4, p2tog tbl, yrn, p4, yrn, p2tog, p2, yrn, p2tog; rep from * to last 3 sts, p3.

Commence Pattern

1st row: K2, *k2tog, yf, k5, yf, sl 1, k1, psso, k3, yf, sl 1, k1, psso, k2; rep from * to end.

2nd row: P1, *p2tog tbl, yrn, p6, yrn, p2tog, p4, yrn, p2tog; rep from * to last st, p1.

3rd row: K1, sl 1 purlwise, k1, yf, sl 1, k1, psso, k4, yf, sl 1, k1, psso, k2, k2tog, yf, k1, *[sl 1 purlwise] twice, k1, yf, sl 1, k1, psso, k4, yf, sl 1, k1, psso, k2, k2tog, yf, k1; rep from * to last 2 sts, sl 1 purlwise, k1.

4th row: P4, yrn, p2tog, p3, yrn, p2tog, p1, p2tog tbl, *yrn, p6, yrn, p2tog, p3, yrn, p2tog, p1, p2tog tbl; rep from * to last 4 sts, yrn, p4.

5th row: K1, yf, sl 1, k1, psso, k2, yf, sl 1, k1, psso, k4, k2tog, *yf, k4, yf, sl 1, k1, psso, k2, yf, sl 1, k1, psso, k4, k2tog; rep from * to last 5 sts, yf, k5.

6th row: P1, yrn, p2tog, p3, yrn, p2tog, p2, p2tog tbl, *yrn, p5, yrn, p2tog, p3, yrn, p2tog, p2, p2tog tbl; rep from * to last 6 sts, yrn, p6.

7th row: K1, yf, sl 1, k1, psso, k4, yf, sl 1, k1, psso, k2tog, *yf, k6, yf, sl 1, k1, psso, k4, yf, sl 1, k1, psso, k2tog; rep from * to last 7 sts, yf, k7.

8th row: P1, yrn, p2tog, p2, p2tog tbl, yrn, p1, [sl 1 purlwise] twice, p1, yrn, p2tog, *p4, yrn, p2tog, p2, p2tog tbl, yrn, p1, [sl 1 purlwise] twice, p1, yrn, p2tog; rep from * to last 5 sts, p5.

9th row: K1, yf, sl 1, k1, psso, k1, k2tog, yf, k2, C2R, k2, yf, sl 1, k1, psso, *k3, yf, sl 1, k1, psso, k1, k2tog, yf, k2, C2R, k2, yf, sl 1, k1, psso; rep from * to last 4 sts, k4.

10th row: P3, p2tog tbl, yrn, p4, yrn, p2tog, p2, yrn, p2tog, *p4, p2tog tbl, yrn, p4, yrn, p2tog, p2, yrn, p2tog; rep from * to last 3 sts, p3.

Rep the last 10 rows.

Oriel Lace

Multiple of 12 sts + 1.

1st row (right side): P1, *yb, sl 1, k1, psso, k3, yfrn, p1, yon, k3, k2tog, p1; rep from * to end.

2nd row: K1, *p5, k1; rep from * to end.

Rep the last 2 rows twice more.

7th row: P1, *yon, k3, k2tog, p1, yb, sl 1, k1, psso, k3, yfrn, p1; rep from * to end.

8th row: As 2nd row.

9th row: P2, yon, k2, k2tog, p1, yb, sl 1, k1, psso, k2, *yfrn, p3, yon, k2, k2tog, p1, yb, sl 1, k1, psso, k2; rep from * to last 2 sts, yfrn, p2.

10th row: K2, p4, k1, p4, *k3, p4, k1, p4; rep from * to last 2 sts, k2.

11th row: P3, yon, k1, k2tog, p1, yb, sl 1, k1, psso, k1, *yfrn, p5, yon, k1, k2tog, p1, yb, sl 1, k1, psso, k1; rep from * to last 3 sts, yfrn, p3.

12th row: K3, p3, k1, p3, *k5, p3, k1, p3; rep from * to last 3 sts, k3.

13th row: P4, yon, k2tog, p1, yb, sl 1, k1, psso, *yfrn, p7, yon, k2tog, p1, yb, sl 1, k1, psso; rep from * to last 4 sts, yfrn, p4.

14th row: K4, p2, k1, p2, *k7, p2, k1, p2; rep from * to last 4 sts, k4.

15th row: As 7th row.

16th row: As 2nd row.

Rep the last 2 rows twice more.

21st row: P1, *yb, sl 1, k1, psso, k3, yfrn, p1, yon, k3, k2tog, p1; rep from * to end.

22nd row: As 2nd row.

23rd row: P1, *yb, sl 1, k1, psso, k2, yfrn, p3, yon, k2, k2tog, p1; rep from * to end.

24th row: K1, *p4, k3, p4, k1; rep from * to end.

25th row: P1, *yb, sl 1, k1, psso, k1, yfrn, p5, yon, k1, k2tog, p1; rep from * to end.

26th row: K1, *p3, k5, p3, k1; rep from * to end.

27th row: P1, *yb, sl 1, k1, psso, yfrn, p7, yon, k2tog, p1; rep from * to end.

28th row: K1, *p2, k7, p2, k1; rep from * to end.

Rep these 28 rows.

All-over Lace Patterns

Peacock Plumes

Multiple of 16 sts + 1.
1st and 3rd rows (wrong side): Purl.
2nd row: Knit.
4th row: [K1, yf] 3 times, [sl 1, k1, psso] twice, sl 2, k1, p2sso, [k2tog] twice, *yf, [k1, yf] 5 times, [sl 1, k1, psso] twice, sl 2, k1, p2sso, [k2tog] twice; rep from * to last 3 sts, [yf, k1] 3 times.
Rep the last 4 rows 3 times more.
17th and 19th rows: Purl.
18th row: Knit.
20th row: [K2tog] 3 times, [yf, k1] 5 times, *yf, [sl 1, k1, psso] twice, sl 2, k1, p2sso, [k2tog] twice, [yf, k1] 5 times; rep from * to last 6 sts, yf, [sl 1, k1, psso] 3 times.
Rep the last 4 rows 3 times more.
Rep these 32 rows.

Ornamental Arrow Pattern

Multiple of 12 sts + 1.
1st row (right side): K1, *sl 1, k1, psso, k3, yf, k1, yf, k3, k2tog, k1; rep from * to end.
2nd row: P1, *p2tog, p2, yrn, p3, yrn, p2, p2tog tbl, p1; rep from * to end.
3rd row: K1, *sl 1, k1, psso, k1, yf, k5, yf, k1, k2tog, k1; rep from * to end.
4th row: P1, *yrn, p2tog, p7, p2tog tbl, yrn, p1; rep from * to end.
5th row: K1, *yf, k3, k2tog, k1, sl 1, k1, psso, k3, yf, k1; rep from * to end.
6th row: P2, yrn, p2, p2tog tbl, p1, p2tog, p2, yrn, *p3, yrn, p2, p2tog tbl, p1, p2tog, p2, yrn; rep from * to last 2 sts, p2.
7th row: K3, yf, k1, k2tog, k1, sl 1, k1, psso, k1, yf, *k5, yf, k1, k2tog, k1, sl 1, k1, psso, k1, yf; rep from * to last 3 sts, k3.
8th row: P4, p2tog tbl, yrn, p1, yrn, p2tog,

*p7, p2tog tbl, yrn, p1, yrn, p2tog; rep from * to last 4 sts, p4.
Rep these 8 rows.

Fish-scale Pattern

Multiple of 12 sts.
1st row (right side): *Sl 1, k1, psso, k3, yfrn, p2, yon, k3, k2tog; rep from * to end.
2nd row: *P2tog, p2, yon, k4, yfrn, p2, p2tog tbl; rep from * to end.
3rd row: *Sl 1, k1, psso, k1, yfrn, p6, yon, k1, k2tog; rep from * to end.
4th row: *P2tog, yon, k8, yfrn, p2tog tbl; rep from * to end.
5th row: P1, yon, k3, k2tog, sl 1, k1, psso, k3, yfrn, *p2, yon, k3, k2tog, sl 1, k1, psso, k3, yfrn; rep from * to last st, p1.
6th row: K2, yfrn, p2, p2tog tbl, p2tog, p2, yon, *k4, yfrn, p2, p2tog tbl, p2tog, p2, yon; rep from * to last 2 sts, k2.
7th row: P3, yon, k1, k2tog, sl 1, k1, psso, k1, yfrn, *p6, yon, k1, k2tog, sl 1, k1, psso, k1, yfrn; rep from * to last 3 sts, p3.
8th row: K4, yfrn, p2tog tbl, p2tog, yon, *k8, yfrn, p2tog tbl, p2tog, yon; rep from * to last 4 sts, k4.
Rep these 8 rows.

Lattice Twist with Eyelets

Multiple of 8 sts + 3.
1st row (right side): K3, *k2tog, yf, k1, yf, sl 1, k1, psso, k3; rep from * to end.
2nd and every alt row: Purl.
3rd row: K2, C2F, k3, C2B, *k1, C2F, k3, C2B; rep from * to last 2 sts, k2.

5th row: K1, C2F, k5, *C3R, k5; rep from * to last 3 sts, C2B, k1.
7th row: K2, yf, sl 1, k1, psso, k3, k2tog, yf, *k1, yf, sl 1, k1, psso, k3, k2tog, yf; rep from * to last 2 sts, k2.
9th row: K3, *C2B, k1, C2F, k3; rep from * to end.
11th row: K4, C3R, *k5, C3R; rep from * to last 4 sts, k4.
12th row: Purl.
Rep these 12 rows.

Filigree Cables Pattern

Multiple of 12 sts + 8.
1st row (right side): P2, *k2, yf, k2tog, p2; rep from * to end.
2nd row: K2, *p2, yrn, p2tog, k2; rep from * to end.
Rep the last 2 rows twice more.
7th row: P2, k2, yf, k2tog, p2, *C4F, p2, k2, yf, k2tog, p2; rep from * to end.
8th row: As 2nd row.
Rep the 1st and 2nd rows 3 times more.
15th row: P2, C4F, p2, *k2, yf, k2tog, p2, C4F, p2; rep from * to end.
16th row: As 2nd row.
Rep these 16 rows.

Cable and Lace Check

Multiple of 12 sts + 8.

1st row (wrong side): K2, p2tog, yrn, p2, k2, *p4, k2, p2tog, yrn, p2, k2; rep from * to end.

2nd row: P2, k2tog, yf, k2, p2, *k4, p2, k2tog, yf, k2, p2; rep from * to end.

3rd row: As 1st row.

4th row: P2, k2tog, yf, k2, p2, *C4B, p2, k2tog, yf, k2, p2; rep from * to end.

5th, 6th and 7th rows: As 1st, 2nd and 3rd rows.

8th row: P2, *C4B, p2; rep from * to end.

9th row: K2, p4, k2, *p2tog, yrn, p2, k2, p4, k2; rep from * to end.

10th row: P2, k4, p2, *k2tog, yf, k2, p2, k4, p2; rep from * to end.

11th row: As 9th row.

12th row: P2, C4B, p2, *k2tog, yf, k2, p2, C4B, p2; rep from * to end.

13th, 14th and 15th rows: As 9th, 10th and 11th rows.

16th row: As 8th row.

Rep these 16 rows.

Meandering Cables with Eyelets

Multiple of 16 sts + 10.

Note: Sts should only be counted after the 1st, 14th, 15th and 28th rows.

1st row (wrong side): K2, *p6, k2; rep from * to end.

2nd row: P2, [k2tog, yf] twice, k2tog, *p2, k6, p2, [k2tog, yf] twice, k2tog; rep from * to last 2 sts, p2.

3rd row: K2, p5, k2, *p6, k2, p5, k2; rep from * to end.

4th row: P2, k1, [yf, k2tog] twice, p2, *C6F, p2, k1, [yf, k2tog] twice, p2; rep from * to end.

5th row: As 3rd row.

6th row: P2, k1, [yf, k2tog] twice, p2, *k6, p2, k1, [yf, k2tog] twice, p2; rep from * to end.

Rep the last 2 rows twice more, then 5th row again.

12th row: As 4th row.

13th row: As 3rd row.

14th row: P2, k2, yf, k1, yf, k2tog, p2, *k6, p2, k2, yf, k1, yf, k2tog, p2; rep from * to end.

15th row: As 1st row.

16th row: P2, k6, p2, *yb, sl 1, k1, psso, [yf, sl 1, k1, psso] twice, p2, k6, p2; rep from * to end.

17th row: K2, p6, k2, *p5, k2, p6, k2; rep from * to end.

18th row: P2, C6F, p2, *yb, [sl 1, k1, psso, yf] twice, k1, p2, C6F, p2; rep from * to end.

19th row: As 17th row.

20th row: P2, k6, p2, *yb, [sl 1, k1, psso, yf] twice, k1, p2, k6, p2; rep from * to end.

Rep the last 2 rows twice more, then 19th row again.

26th row: As 18th row.

27th row: As 17th row.

28th row: P2, k6, p2, *k2, yf, sl 1, k1, psso, yf, k1, p2, k6, p2; rep from * to end.

Rep these 28 rows.

Frost Flower Pattern

Multiple of 34 sts + 2.

1st row (right side): K4, *k2tog, k4, yfrn, p2, [k2, yf, sl 1, k1, psso] 3 times, p2, yon, k4, sl 1, k1, psso, k6; rep from * but ending last rep with k4 instead of k6.

2nd row: P3, *p2tog tbl, p4, yrn, p1, k2, [p2, yrn, p2tog] 3 times, k2, p1, yrn, p4, p2tog, p4; rep from * but ending last rep with p3 instead of p4.

3rd row: K2, *k2tog, k4, yf, k2, p2, [k2, yf, sl 1, k1, psso] 3 times, p2, k2, yf, k4, sl 1, k1, psso, k2; rep from * to end.

4th row: P1, *p2tog tbl, p4, yrn, p3, k2, [p2, yrn, p2tog] 3 times, k2, p3, yrn, p4, p2tog; rep from * to last st, p1.

Rep the last 4 rows twice more.

13th row: K1, *yf, sl 1, k1, psso, k2, yf, sl 1, k1, psso, p2, yon, k4, sl 1, k1, psso, k6, k2tog, k4, yfrn, p2, k2, yf, sl 1, k1, psso, k2; rep from * but ending last rep with k3 instead of k2.

14th row: P1, *yrn, p2tog, p2, yrn, p2tog, k2, p1, yrn, p4, p2tog, p4, p2tog tbl, p4, yrn, p1, k2, p2, yrn, p2tog, p2; rep from * but ending last rep with p3 instead of p2.

15th row: K1, *yf, sl 1, k1, psso, k2, yf, sl 1, k1, psso, p2, k2, yf, k4, sl 1, k1, psso, k2, k2tog, k4, yf, k2, p2, k2, yf, sl 1, k1, psso, k2; rep from * but ending last rep with k3

---

instead of k2.

16th row: P1, *yrn, p2tog, p2, yrn, p2tog, k2, p3, yrn, p4, p2tog, p4, p2tog tbl, p4, yrn, p3, k2, p2, yrn, p2tog, p2; rep from * but ending last rep with p3 instead of p2.

Rep the last 4 rows twice more.

Rep these 24 rows.

Corona Pattern Stitch

Multiple of 10 sts + 1.

1st row (right side): K3, k2tog, yf, k1, yf, sl 1, k1, psso, *k5, k2tog, yf, k1, yf, sl 1, k1, psso; rep from * to last 3 sts, k3.

2nd, 4th, 6th and 8th rows: Purl.

3rd row: K2, k2tog, yf, k3, yf, sl 1, k1, psso, *k3, k2tog, yf, k3, yf, sl 1, k1, psso; rep from * to last 2 sts, k2.

5th row: K1, *k2tog, yf, k5, yf, sl 1, k1, psso, k1; rep from * to end.

7th row: Knit.

9th row: K6, *insert right-hand needle in first space of 5th row, yrn and draw through to make a long loop which is kept on needle; rep from * into each of remaining 5 spaces of leaf from right to left, k10; rep from * to last 5 sts, take up a long loop as before in next 6 spaces, knit to end.

10th row: P5, purl tog the 6 long loops with the next st, *p9, purl tog the 6 long loops with the next st; rep from * to last 5 sts, p5.

11th row: Knit.

12th, 14th, 16th, 18th and 20th rows: Purl.

13th row: K1, *yf, sl 1, k1, psso, k5, k2tog, yf, k1; rep from * to end.

15th row: K2, yf, sl 1, k1, psso, k3, k2tog, yf, *k3, yf, sl 1, k1, psso, k3, k2tog, yf; rep from * to last 2 sts, k2.

17th row: K3, yf, sl 1, k1, psso, k1, k2tog, yf, *k5, yf, sl 1, k1, psso, k1, k2tog, yf; rep from * to last 3 sts, k3.

19th row: Knit.

21st row: K1, take up a long loop as before in next 3 spaces, k10, *take up a long loop in each of next 6 spaces, k10; rep from * to last st, take up a long loop in each of next 3 spaces.

22nd row: Purl tog the first 3 long loops with the next st, p9, *purl tog the 6 long loops with the next st, p9; rep from * to last st, purl tog the last 3 long loops with the last st.

23rd row: Knit.

24th row: Purl.

Rep these 24 rows.

All-over Lace Patterns

Ornamental Parasols

Multiple of 18 sts + 1.

Note: Sts should only be counted after the 5th, 6th, 11th, 12th, 13th, 14th, 25th, 26th, 27th and 28th rows.

1st row (right side): K1, *[p2, k1] twice, yf, k2tog, yf, k1, yf, sl 1, k1, psso, yf, [k1, p2] twice, k1; rep from * to end.

2nd row: [P1, k2] twice, p9, *k2, [p1, k2] 3 times, p9; rep from * to last 6 sts, [k2, p1] twice.

3rd row: K1, *[p2, k1] twice, yf, k2tog, yf, k3, yf, sl 1, k1, psso, yf, [k1, p2] twice, k1; rep from * to end.

4th row: [P1, k2] twice, p11, *k2, [p1, k2] 3 times, p11; rep from * to last 6 sts, [k2, p1] twice.

5th row: K1, *[p2tog, k1] twice, yf, k2tog, yf, sl 1, k1, psso, k1, k2tog, yf, sl 1, k1, psso, yf, [k1, p2tog] twice, k1; rep from * to end.

6th row: [P1, k1] twice, p11, *k1, [p1, k1] 3 times, p11; rep from * to last 4 sts, [k1, p1] twice.

7th row: K1, *[p1, k1] twice, yf, k2tog, yf, KB1, yf, sl 1, k2tog, psso, yf, KB1, yf, sl 1, k1, psso, yf, [k1, p1] twice, k1; rep from * to end.

8th row: [P1, k1] twice, p13, *k1, [p1, k1] 3 times, p13; rep from * to last 4 sts, [k1, p1] twice.

9th row: K1, *[k2tog] twice, yf, k2tog, yf, k3, yf, k1, yf, k3, yf, sl 1, k1, psso, yf, [sl 1, k1, psso] twice, k1; rep from * to end.

10th row: Purl.

11th row: K1, *[k2tog, yf] twice, sl 1, k1, psso, k1, k2tog, yf, k1, yf, sl 1, k1, psso, k1, k2tog, [yf, sl 1, k1, psso] twice, k1; rep from * to end.

12th row: Purl.

13th row: [K2tog, yf] twice, KB1, yf, sl 1, k2tog, psso, yf, k3, yf, sl 1, k2tog, psso, yf, KB1, yf, sl 1, k1, psso, *yf, sl 1, k2tog, psso, yf, k2tog, yf, KB1, yf, sl 1, k2tog, psso, yf, k3, yf, sl 1, k2tog, psso, yf, KB1, yf, sl 1, k1, psso; rep from * to last 2 sts, yf, sl 1, k1, psso.

14th row: Purl.

15th row: K1, *yf, sl 1, k1, psso, yf, [k1, p2] 4 times, k1, yf, k2tog, yf, k1; rep from * to end.

16th row: P5, [k2, p1] 3 times, k2, *p9, [k2, p1] 3 times, k2; rep from * to last 5 sts, p5.

17th row: K2, yf, sl 1, k1, psso, yf, [k1, p2] 4 times, k1, yf, k2tog, *yf, k3, yf, sl 1, k1, psso, yf, [k1, p2] 4 times, k1, yf, k2tog; rep from * to last 2 sts, yf, k2.

18th row: P6, [k2, p1] 3 times, k2, *p11, [k2, p1] 3 times, k2; rep from * to last 6 sts, p6.

19th row: K1, *k2tog, yf, sl 1, k1, psso, yf, [k1, p2tog] 4 times, k1, yf, k2tog, yf, sl 1, k1, psso, k1; rep from * to end.

20th row: P6, [k1, p1] 3 times, k1, *p11, [k1, p1] 3 times, k1; rep from * to last 6 sts, p6.

21st row: K2tog, yf, KB1, yf, sl 1, k1, psso, yf, [k1, p1] 4 times, k1, yf, k2tog, yf, KB1, *yf, sl 1, k2tog, psso, yf, KB1, yf, sl 1, k1, psso, yf, [k1, p1] 4 times, k1, yf, k2tog, yf, KB1; rep from * to last 2 sts, yf, sl 1, k1, psso.

22nd row: P7, [k1, p1] 3 times, k1, *p13, [k1, p1] 3 times, k1; rep from * to last 7 sts, p7.

23rd row: K1, *yf, k3, yf, sl 1, k1, psso, yf, [sl 1, k1, psso] twice, k1, [k2tog] twice, yf, k2tog, yf, k3, yf, k1; rep from * to end.

24th row: Purl.

25th row: K1, *yf, sl 1, k1, psso, k1, k2tog, [yf, sl 1, k1, psso] twice, k1, [k2tog, yf] twice, sl 1, k1, psso, k2tog, yf, k1; rep from * to end.

26th row: Purl.

27th row: K2, yf, sl 1, k2tog, psso, yf, KB1, yf, sl 1, k1, psso, yf, sl 1, k2tog, psso, yf, k2tog, yf, KB1, yf, sl 1, k2tog, psso, *yf, k3, yf, sl 1, k2tog, psso, yf, KB1, yf, sl 1, k1, psso, yf, sl 1, k2tog, psso, yf, k2tog, yf, KB1, yf, sl 1, k2tog, psso; rep from * to last 2 sts, yf, k2.

28th row: Purl.

Rep these 28 rows.

Crowns of Glory (Cats Paw)

Multiple of 14 sts + 1.

Note: Sts should only be counted after the 7th, 8th, 9th, 10th, 11th and 12th rows.

1st row (right side): K1, *sl 1, k1, psso, k9, k2tog, k1; rep from * to end.

2nd row: P1, *p2tog, p7, p2tog tbl, p1; rep from * to end.

3rd row: K1, *sl 1, k1, psso, k2, [yf] 3 times, k3, k2tog, k1; rep from * to end.

4th row: P1, *p2tog, p2, [k1, p1, k1, p1, k1] into [yf] 3 times making 5 sts, p1, p2tog tbl, p1; rep from * to end.

5th row: K1, *sl 1, k1, psso, k6, k2tog, k1; rep from * to end.

6th row: P1, *p2tog, p7; rep from * to end.

7th row: K2, [yf, k1] 5 times, yf, *k3, [yf, k1] 5 times, yf; rep from * to last 2 sts, k2.

8th row: Purl.

9th and 10th rows: Knit.

11th row: Purl.

12th row: Knit.

Rep these 12 rows.

Ornamental Tulip Pattern

Multiple of 13 sts.

Note: Sts should only be counted after the 1st, 2nd, 9th and 10th rows of this pattern.

1st row (right side): Purl.

2nd row: Knit.

3rd row: P6, [p1, k1] 3 times into next st, *p12, [p1, k1] 3 times into next st; rep from * to last 6 sts, p6.

4th row: K6, p6, *k12, p6; rep from * to last 6 sts, k6.

5th row: P6, k6, *p12, k6; rep from * to last 6 sts, p6.

6th row: As 4th row.

7th row: [P2tog] twice, p2, [k2, yf] twice, k2, *p2, [p2tog] 4 times, p2, [k2, yf] twice, k2; rep from * to last 6 sts, p2, [p2tog] twice.

8th row: K4, p8, *k8, p8; rep from * to last 4 sts, k4.

9th row: [P2tog] twice, [k2tog, yf, k1, yf] twice, k2tog, *[p2tog] 4 times, [k2tog, yf, k1, yf] twice, k2tog; rep from * to last 4 sts, [p2tog] twice.

10th row: K2, p9, *k4, p9; rep from * to last 2 sts, k2.

Rep these 10 rows.

Canterbury Bells

Multiple of 5 sts.

Note: Sts should only be counted after the 1st, 2nd and 10th rows.

1st row (right side): P2, KB1, *p4, KB1; rep from * to last 2 sts, p2.

2nd row: K2, PB1, *k4, PB1; rep from * to last 2 sts, k2.

3rd row: P2, KB1, *p2, turn, cast on 8 sts cable method, turn, p2, KB1; rep from * to last 2 sts, p2.

4th row: K2, PB1, *k2, p8, k2, PB1; rep from * to last 2 sts, k2.

5th row: P2, KB1, *p2, k8, p2, KB1; rep from * to last 2 sts, p2.

6th row: As 4th row.

7th row: P2, KB1, *p2, yb, sl 1, k1, psso, k4, k2tog, p2, KB1; rep from * to last 2 sts, p2.

8th row: K2, PB1, *k2, p2tog, p2, p2tog tbl, k2, PB1; rep from * to last 2 sts, k2.

9th row: P2, KB1, *p2, yb, sl 1, k1, psso, k2tog, p2, KB1; rep from * to last 2 sts, p2.

10th row: K2, PB1, *k1, sl 1, k1, psso, k2tog, k1, PB1; rep from * to last 2 sts, k2.

Rep these 10 rows.

Embossed Leaf Pattern

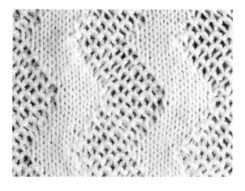

Multiple of 7 sts + 6.

Note: Sts should only be counted after the 15th and 16th rows of this pattern.

1st row (right side): P6, *yon, k1, yfrn, p6; rep from * to end.

2nd row: K6, *p3, k6; rep from * to end.

3rd row: P6, *[k1, yf] twice, k1, p6; rep from * to end.

4th row: K6, *p5, k6; rep from * to end.

5th row: P6, *k2, yf, k1, yf, k2, p6; rep from * to end.

6th row: K6, *p7, k6; rep from * to end.

7th row: P6, *k3, yf, k1, yf, k3, p6; rep from * to end.

8th row: K6, *p9, k6; rep from * to end.

9th row: P6, *sl 1, k1, psso, k5, k2tog, p6; rep from * to end.

10th row: K6, *p7, k6; rep from * to end.

11th row: P6, *sl 1, k1, psso, k3, k2tog, p6; rep from * to end.

12th row: K6, *p5, k6; rep from * to end.

13th row: P6, *sl 1, k1, psso, k1, k2tog, p6; rep from * to end.

14th row: K6, *p3, k6; rep from * to end.

15th row: P6, *sl 1, k2tog, psso, p6; rep from * to end.

16th row: Knit.

17th row: Purl.

Rep the last 2 rows once more then the 16th row again.

Rep these 20 rows.

Hyacinth Blossom Stitch

Multiple of 6 sts + 2.

1st row (wrong side): K1, *p5tog, [k1, p1, k1, p1, k1] into next st; rep from * to last st, k1.

2nd row: Purl.

3rd row: K1, *[k1, p1, k1, p1, k1] into next st, p5tog; rep from * to last st, k1.

4th row: As 2nd row.

5th row: Knit this row winding yarn round the needle 3 times for each st.

6th row: Purl to end dropping extra loops.

Rep these 6 rows.

Mesh Zigzag Stitch

Multiple of 11 sts.

Special Abbreviation

KW5 = knit 5 sts wrapping yarn twice round needle for each st.

1st row (right side): K1, KW5, *k6, KW5; rep from * to last 5 sts, k5.

2nd row: P5, k5 dropping extra loops, *p6, k5 dropping extra loops; rep from * to last st, p1.

3rd row: K2, KW5, *k6, KW5; rep from * to last 4 sts, k4.

4th row: P4, k5 dropping extra loops, *p6, k5 dropping extra loops; rep from * to last 2 sts, p2.

5th row: K3, KW5, *k6, KW5; rep from * to last 3 sts, k3.

6th row: P3, k5 dropping extra loops, *p6, k5 dropping extra loops; rep from * to last 3 sts, p3.

7th row: K4, KW5, *k6, KW5; rep from * to last 2 sts, k2.

8th row: P2, k5 dropping extra loops, *p6, k5 dropping extra loops; rep from * to last 4 sts, p4.

9th row: K5, KW5, *k6, KW5; rep from * to last st, k1.

10th row: P1, k5 dropping extra loops, *p6, k5 dropping extra loops; rep from * to last 5 sts, p5.

11th row: As 7th row.

12th row: As 8th row.

13th row: As 5th row.

14th row: As 6th row.

15th row: As 3rd row.

16th row: As 4th row.

17th row: As 1st row.

18th row: As 2nd row.

Rep these 18 rows.

Wave Stitch

Multiple of 6 sts + 1.

Special Abbreviations

KW2 = knit next st wrapping yarn twice around needle.

KW3 = knit next st wrapping yarn 3 times around needle.

1st row (right side): K1, *KW2, [KW3] twice, KW2, k2; rep from * to end.

2nd row: Knit dropping all extra loops of previous row.

3rd row: KW3, KW2, k2, KW2, *[KW3] twice, KW2, k2, KW2; rep from * to last 2 sts, KW3, k1.

4th row: As 2nd row.

Rep these 4 rows.

All-over Lace Patterns

Vertical Ripple Stripes

Multiple of 4 sts + 3.

Note: Do not count yf and sts resulting from yf as a stitch.

1st Foundation row (right side): K3, *yf, k4; rep from * to end.

2nd, 3rd and 4th Foundation rows: Work 3 rows in st st, starting purl.

Commence Pattern

1st row: *K5, yf; rep from * to last 3 sts, k3.

2nd and every alt row: Purl.

3rd row: K3, *slip next st off left-hand needle and allow it to drop down to the loop made 6 rows below, k5, rep from * to end.

5th row: K3, *yf, k5; rep from * to end.

7th row: *K5, slip next st off left-hand needle as before; rep from * to last 3 sts, k3.

8th row: Purl.

Rep the last 8 rows.

Snow Shoe Pattern

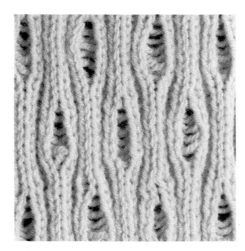

Multiple of 8 sts + 4.

Note: Sts should only be counted after the 8th, 9th, 10th, 18th, 19th or 20th rows.

1st row (right side): K2, M1, *k1, p2, k2, p2, k1, M1; rep from * to last 2 sts, k2.

2nd row: P4, k2, p2, k2, *p3, k2, p2, k2; rep from * to last 4 sts, p4.

3rd row: K4, p2, k2, p2, *k3, p2, k2, p2; rep from * to last 4 sts, k4.

Rep the last 2 rows twice more.

8th row: P2, drop next st down 7 rows, *p1, k2, p2, k2, p1, drop next st down 7 rows; rep from * to last 2 sts, p2.

9th row: K3, p2, *k2, p2; rep from * to last 3 sts, k3.

10th row: P3, k2, *p2, k2; rep from * to last 3 sts, p3.

11th row: K3, p2, k1, M1, k1, p2, *k2, p2, k1, M1, k1, p2; rep from * to last 3 sts, k3.

12th row: P3, k2, p3, k2, *p2, k2, p3, k2; rep from * to last 3 sts, p3.

13th row: K3, p2, k3, p2, *k2, p2, k3, p2; rep from * to last 3 sts, k3.

Rep the last 2 rows twice more.

18th row: P3, k2, p1, drop next st down 7 rows, p1, k2, *p2, k2, p1, drop next st down 7 rows, p1, k2; rep from * to last 3 sts, p3.

19th row: K3, p2, *k2, p2; rep from * to last 3 sts, k3.

20th row: P3, k2, *p2, k2; rep from * to last 3 sts, p3.

Rep these 20 rows.

Reversed Diamonds

Multiple of 12 sts + 1.

1st row (right side): K1, *yf, k3, sl 1, k1, psso, k1, k2tog, k3, yf, k1; rep from * to end.

2nd row: P2, k9, *p3, k9; rep from * to last 2 sts, p2.

3rd row: K2, yf, k2, sl 1, k1, psso, k1, k2tog, k2, yf, *k3, yf, k2, sl 1, k1, psso, k1, k2tog, k2, yf; rep from * to last 2 sts, k2.

4th row: P3, k7, *p5, k7; rep from * to last 3 sts, p3.

5th row: K3, yf, k1, sl 1, k1, psso, k1, k2tog, k1, yf, *k5, yf, k1, sl 1, k1, psso, k1, k2tog, k1, yf; rep from * to last 3 sts, k3.

6th row: P4, k5, *p7, k5; rep from * to last 4 sts, p4.

7th row: K4, yf, sl 1, k1, psso, k1, k2tog, yf, *k7, yf, sl 1, k1, psso, k1, k2tog, yf; rep from * to last 4 sts, k4.

8th row: P5, k3, *p9, k3; rep from * to last 5 sts, p5.

9th row: K5, yf, sl 1, k2tog, psso, yf, *k9, yf, sl 1, k2tog, psso, yf; rep from * to last 5 sts, k5.

10th row: P6, k1, *p11, k1; rep from * to last 6 sts, p6.

11th row: K1, *k2tog, k3, yf, k1, yf, k3, sl 1, k1, psso, k1; rep from * to end.

12th row: As 8th row.

13th row: K1, *k2tog, k2, yf, k3, yf, k2, sl 1, k1, psso, k1; rep from * to end.

14th row: As 6th row.

15th row: K1, *k2tog, k1, yf, k5, yf, k1, sl 1, k1, psso, k1; rep from * to end.

16th row: As 4th row.

17th row: K1, *k2tog, yf, k7, yf, sl 1, k1, psso, k1; rep from * to end.

18th row: As 2nd row.

19th row: K2tog, yf, k9, *yf, sl 1, k2tog, psso, yf, k9; rep from * to last 2 sts, yf, sl 1, k1, psso.

20th row: P1, *k11, p1; rep from * to end.

Rep these 20 rows.

Puff Stitch Check I

Multiple of 10 sts + 7.

Special Abbreviation

K5W = knit next 5 sts wrapping yarn twice around needle for each st.

1st row (right side): P6, k5W, *p5, k5W; rep from * to last 6 sts, p6.

2nd row: K6, p5 dropping extra loops, *k5, p5 dropping extra loops; rep from * to last 6 sts, k6.

Rep the last 2 rows 3 times more.

9th row: P1, k5W, *p5, k5W; rep from * to last st, p1.

10th row: K1, p5 dropping extra loops, *k5, p5 dropping extra loops; rep from * to last st, k1.

Rep the last 2 rows 3 times more.

Rep these 16 rows.

Puff Stitch Check II

Worked as Puff Stitch Check I, using reverse side as right side.

Bluebell Insertion

Worked over 8 sts on a background of reversed st st.

1st row (right side): P2, [k1, p2] twice.
2nd row: K2, [p1, k2] twice.
Rep the last 2 rows once more.
5th row: P1, yon, sl 1, k1, psso, p2, k2tog, yfrn, p1.
6th row: K1, p2, k2, p2, k1.
7th row: P2, yon, sl 1, k1, psso, k2tog, yfrn, p2.
8th row: K2, p4, k2.
Rep these 8 rows.

Little Shell Insertion

Worked over 7 sts on a background of st st.
1st row (right side): Knit.
2nd row: Purl.
3rd row: K1, yfrn, p1, p3tog, p1, yon, k1.
4th row: Purl.
Rep these 4 rows.

Zigzag Insertion

Worked over 5 sts on a background of reverse st st.
1st row: Knit.
2nd and every alt row: Purl.
3rd row: K1, k2tog, yf, k2.
5th row: K2tog, yf, k3.
7th row: Knit.
9th row: K2, yf, sl 1, k1, psso, k1.
11th row: K3, yf, sl 1, k1, psso.
12th row: Purl.
Rep these 12 rows.

Eyelet Lattice Insertion

Worked over 8 sts on a background of st st.
1st row (right side): K1, [k2tog, yf] 3 times, k1.
2nd row: Purl.
3rd row: K2, [k2tog, yf] twice, k2.
4th row: Purl.
Rep these 4 rows.

Eyelet Twist Panel

Worked over 13 sts on a background of st st.
1st and every alt row (wrong side): Purl.
2nd row: K1, [yf, sl 1, k1, psso] twice, k3, [k2tog, yf] twice, k1.
4th row: K2, [yf, sl 1, k1, psso] twice, k1, [k2tog, yf] twice, k2.
6th row: K3, yf, sl 1, k1, psso, yf, sl 1, k2tog, psso, yf, k2tog, yf, k3.
8th row: K4, yf, sl 1, k2tog, psso, yf, k2tog, yf, k4.
10th row: K4, [k2tog, yf] twice, k5.
12th row: K3, [k2tog, yf] twice, k1, yf, sl 1, k1, psso, k3.
14th row: K2, [k2tog, yf] twice, k1, [yf, sl 1, k1, psso] twice, k2.
16th row: K1, [k2tog, yf] twice, k3, [yf, sl 1, k1, psso] twice, k1.
18th row: [K2tog, yf] twice, k5, [yf, sl 1, k1, psso] twice.
Rep these 18 rows.

Braided Lace Panel

Worked over 20 sts on a background of st st.
1st and every alt row (wrong side): Purl.
2nd row: K4, [yf, sl 1, k1, psso] twice, k3, [k2tog, yf] twice, k5.
4th row: K2, [k2tog, yf] twice, k4, [k2tog, yf] twice, k1, yf, sl 1, k1, psso, k3.
6th row: K1, [k2tog, yf] twice, k4, [k2tog, yf] twice, k1, [yf, sl 1, k1, psso] twice, k2.
8th row: [K2tog, yf] twice, k4, [k2tog, yf] twice, k3, [yf, sl 1, k1, psso] twice, k1.
10th row: K2, [yf, sl 1, k1, psso] twice, k1, [k2tog, yf] twice, k5, [yf, sl 1, k1, psso] twice.
12th row: K3, yf, sl 1, k1, psso, yf, sl 1, k2tog, psso, yf, k2tog, yf, k4, [k2tog, yf] twice, k2.
14th row: K4, yf, sl 1, k1, psso, yf, sl 1, k2tog, psso, yf, k4, [k2tog, yf] twice, k3.
16th row: K5, [yf, sl 1, k1, psso] twice, k3, [k2tog, yf] twice, k4.
18th row: K3, k2tog, yf, k1, [yf, sl 1, k1, psso] twice, k4, [yf, sl 1, k1, psso] twice, k2.
20th row: K2, [k2tog, yf] twice, k1, [yf, sl 1, k1, psso] twice, k4, [yf, sl 1, k1, psso] twice, k1.
22nd row: K1, [k2tog, yf] twice, k3, [yf, sl 1, k1, psso] twice, k4, [yf, sl 1, k1, psso] twice.
24th row: [K2tog, yf] twice, k5, [yf, sl 1, k1, psso] twice, k1, [k2tog, yf] twice, k2.
26th row: K2, [yf, sl 1, k1, psso] twice, k4, yf, sl 1, k1, psso, yf, k3tog, yf, k2tog, yf, k3.
28th row: K3, [yf, sl 1, k1, psso] twice, k4, yf, k3tog, yf, k2tog, yf, k4.
Rep these 28 rows.

Lace Panels

Zigzag Panel

Worked over 9 sts on a background of st st.
1st row (right side): K3, sl 1, k1, psso, yf, k2tog, yf, k2.
2nd and every alt row: Purl.
3rd row: K2, sl 1, k1, psso, yf, k2tog, yf, k3.
5th row: K1, sl 1, k1, psso, yf, k2tog, yf, k4.
7th row: Sl 1, k1, psso, yf, k2tog, yf, k5.
9th row: K2, yf, sl 1, k1, psso, yf, k2tog, k3.
11th row: K3, yf, sl 1, k1, psso, yf, k2tog, k2.
13th row: K4, yf, sl 1, k1, psso, yf, k2tog, k1.
15th row: K5, yf, sl 1, k1, psso, yf, k2tog.
16th row: Purl.
Rep these 16 rows.

Zigzag Panel with Diamonds

Worked over 9 sts on a background of st st.
1st row (right side): K2, yf, sl 1, k1, psso, k5.
2nd and every alt row: Purl.
3rd row: K3, yf, sl 1, k1, psso, k4.
5th row: K4, yf, sl 1, k1, psso, k3.
7th row: K5, yf, sl 1, k1, psso, k2.
9th row: K2, yf, sl 1, k1, psso, k2, yf, sl 1, k1, psso, k1.
11th row: K1, [yf, sl 1, k1, psso] twice, k2, yf, sl 1, k1, psso.
13th row: K2, yf, sl 1, k1, psso, k2, k2tog, yf, k1.

15th row: K5, k2tog, yf, k2.
17th row: K4, k2tog, yf, k3.
19th row: K3, k2tog, yf, k4.
21st row: K2, k2tog, yf, k5.
23rd row: K1, k2tog, yf, k3, yf, sl 1, k1, psso, k1.
25th row: K2tog, yf, k3, [yf, sl 1, k1, psso] twice.
27th row: K1, yf, sl 1, k1, psso, k3, yf, sl 1, k1, psso, k1.
28th row: Purl.
Rep these 28 rows.

Eyelet Fan Panel

Worked over 13 sts on a background of st st.
Work 4 rows in garter st (1st row is right side).
5th row: Sl 1, k1, psso, k4, yf, k1, yf, k4, k2tog.
6th, 8th, 10th and 12th rows: Purl.
7th row: Sl 1, k1, psso, [k3, yf] twice, k3, k2tog.
9th row: Sl 1, k1, psso, k2, yf, k2tog, yf, k1, yf, sl 1, k1, psso, yf, k2, k2tog.
11th row: Sl 1, k1, psso, k1, yf, k2tog, yf, k3, yf, sl 1, k1, psso, yf, k1, k2tog.
13th row: Sl 1, k1, psso, [yf, k2tog] twice, yf, k1, [yf, sl 1, k1, psso] twice, yf, k2tog.
14th row: Purl.
Rep these 14 rows.

Lyre Panel

Worked over 21 sts on a background of st st.
1st and every alt row (wrong side): Purl.
2nd row: K1, yf, k2tog, k5, k2tog, yf, k1, yf, sl 1, k1, psso, k5, sl 1, k1, psso, yf, k1.
4th row: K1, yf, k2tog, k4, k2tog, yf, k3, yf, sl 1, k1, psso, k4, sl 1, k1, psso, yf, k1.
6th row: K1, yf, k2tog, k3, k2tog, yf, k5, yf, sl 1, k1, psso, k3, sl 1, k1, psso, yf, k1.
8th row: K1, yf, k2tog, k2, [k2tog, yf] twice, k3, [yf, sl 1, k1, psso] twice, k2, sl 1, k1, psso, yf, k1.
10th, 12th, 14th, 16th and 18th rows: K1, yf, k2tog, k3, yf, k2tog, yf, sl 1, k1, psso, k1, k2tog, yf, sl 1, k1, psso, yf, k3, sl 1, k1, psso, yf, k1.
20th row: K1, yf, k2tog, k1, k2tog, yf, k9, yf, sl 1, k1, psso, k1, sl 1, k1, psso, yf, k1.
Rep these 20 rows.

Pyramid Panel

Worked over 17 sts on a background of st st.
1st row (right side): [K1, yf, sl 1, k1, psso] twice, p5, [k2tog, yf, k1] twice.
2nd row: P6, k5, p6.
3rd row: K2, yf, sl 1, k1, psso, k1, yf, sl 1, k1, psso, p3, k2tog, yf, k1, k2tog, yf, k2.
4th row: P7, k3, p7.
5th row: K3, yf, sl 1, k1, psso, k1, yf, sl 1, k1, psso, p1, k2tog, yf, k1, k2tog, yf, k3.
6th row: P8, k1, p8.
7th row: K4, yf, sl 1, k1, psso, k1, yf, sl 1, k1, psso, k2tog, psso, yf, k1, k2tog, yf, k4.
8th and every alt row: Purl.
9th row: K5, yf, sl 1, k1, psso, k3, k2tog, yf, k5.
11th row: K6, yf, sl 1, k1, psso, k1, k2tog, yf, k6.
13th row: K7, yf, sl 1, k2tog, psso, yf, k7.
14th row: Purl.
Rep these 14 rows.

Lace Loops

Worked over 20 sts on a background of st st.
1st and every alt row (wrong side): Purl.
2nd row: K2, yf, sl 1, k1, psso, k1, k2tog, yf, k1, yf, sl 1, k1, psso, k10.
4th row: K3, yf, sl 1, k2tog, psso, yf, k3, yf, sl 1, k1, psso, k3, k2tog, yf, k4.
6th row: K4, yf, sl 1, k1, psso, k4, yf, sl 1, k1, psso, k1, k2tog, yf, k1, yf, sl 1, k1, psso, k2.
8th row: K11, yf, k3tog, yf, k3, yf, sl 1, k1, psso, k1.
10th row: K11, k2tog, yf, k5, yf, sl 1, k1, psso.
12th row: K10, k2tog, yf, k1, yf, sl 1, k1, psso, k1, k2tog, yf, k2.
14th row: K4, yf, sl 1, k1, psso, k3, k2tog, yf, k3, yf, k3tog, yf, k3.
16th row: K2, k2tog, yf, k1, yf, sl 1, k1, psso, k1, k2tog, yf, k4, k2tog, yf, k4.
18th row: K1, k2tog, yf, k3, yf, sl 1, k2tog, yf, k11.
20th row: K2tog, yf, k5, yf, sl 1, k1, psso, k11.
Rep these 20 rows.

Ribbed Diamond Panel

Worked over 17 sts on a background of st st.
1st row (right side): K6, k2tog, yf, k1, yf, sl 1, k1, psso, k6.
2nd row: P7, k1, p1, k1, p7.
3rd row: K5, k2tog, yfrn, p1, k1, p1, yon, sl 1, k1, psso, k5.
4th row: As 2nd row.
5th row: K4, k2tog, yf, [k1, p1] twice, k1, yf, sl 1, k1, psso, k4.
6th row: P5, k1, [p1, k1] 3 times, p5.
7th row: K3, k2tog, yfrn, [p1, k1] 3 times, p1, yon, sl 1, k1, psso, k3.
8th row: As 6th row.
9th row: K2, k2tog, yf, [k1, p1] 4 times, k1, yf, sl 1, k1, psso, k2.
10th row: P3, k1, [p1, k1] 5 times, p3.
11th row: K1, k2tog, yfrn, [p1, k1] 5 times, p1, yon, sl 1, k1, psso, k1.
12th row: As 10th row.
13th row: K1, yf, sl 1, k1, psso, [p1, k1] 5 times, p1, k2tog, yf, k1.
14th row: As 10th row.

15th row: K2, yf, sl 1, k1, psso, [k1, p1] 4 times, k1, k2tog, yf, k2.
16th row: As 6th row.
17th row: K3, yf, sl 1, k1, psso, [p1, k1] 3 times, p1, k2tog, yf, k3.
18th row: As 6th row.
19th row: K4, yf, sl 1, k1, psso, [k1, p1] twice, k1, k2tog, yf, k4.
20th row: As 2nd row.
21st row: K5, yf, sl 1, k1, psso, p1, k1, p1, k2tog, yf, k5.
22nd row: As 2nd row.
23rd row: K6, yf, sl 1, k1, psso, k1, k2tog, yf, k6.
24th row: Purl.
Rep these 24 rows.

Moss Stitch Diamond Panel

Worked over 19 sts on a background of st st.
1st row (right side): K8, yf, sl 1, k2tog, psso, yf, k8.
2nd, 4th, 6th and 8th rows: Purl.
3rd row: K7, k2tog, yf, k1, yf, sl 1, k1, psso, k7.
5th row: K6, k2tog, yf, k3, yf, sl 1, k1, psso, k6.
7th row: K5, k2tog, yf, k5, yf, sl 1, k1, psso, k5.
9th row: K4, k2tog, yf, k3, p1, k3, yf, sl 1, k1, psso, k4.
10th row: P9, k1, p9.
11th row: K3, k2tog, yf, k3, p1, k1, p1, k3, yf, sl 1, k1, psso, k3.
12th row: P8, k1, p1, k1, p8.
13th row: K2, k2tog, yf, k3, [p1, k1] twice, p1, k3, yf, sl 1, k1, psso, k2.
14th row: P7, [k1, p1] twice, k1, p7.
15th row: K1, k2tog, yf, k3, [p1, k1] 3 times, p1, k3, yf, sl 1, k1, psso, k1.
16th row: P6, [k1, p1] 3 times, k1, p6.
17th row: K2tog, yf, k3, [p1, k1] 4 times, p1, k3, yf, sl 1, k1, psso.
18th row: P5, [k1, p1] 4 times, k1, p5.
19th row: K2, yf, sl 1, k1, psso, k2, [p1, k1] 3 times, p1, k2, k2tog, yf, k2.
20th row: As 16th row.
21st row: K3, yf, sl 1, k1, psso, k2, [p1, k1] twice, p1, k2, k2tog, yf, k3.

22nd row: As 14th row.
23rd row: K4, yf, sl 1, k1, psso, k2, p1, k1, p1, k2, k2tog, yf, k4.
24th row: As 12th row.
25th row: K5, yf, sl 1, k1, psso, k2, p1, k2, k2tog, yf, k5.
26th row: As 10th row.
27th row: K6, yf, sl 1, k1, psso, k3, k2tog, yf, k6.
28th row: Purl.
29th row: K7, yf, sl 1, k1, psso, k1, k2tog, yf, k7.
30th row: Purl.
Rep these 30 rows.

Bishops Mitre Panel

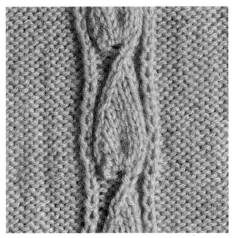

Worked over 9 sts on a background of reverse st st.

Foundation row (wrong side): K1, p1, k5, p1, k1.
Commence Pattern

1st row: P1, KB1, p2, [k1, KB1, k1, KB1, k1, KB1, k1, KB1] into next st, p2, KB1, p1. (16 sts).
2nd row: K1, p1, k2, p8, k2, p1, k1.
3rd row: P1, KB1, p2, k6, k2tog, p2, KB1, p1. (15 sts).
4th row: K1, p1, k2, p7, k2, p1, k1.
5th row: P1, KB1, p2, k5, k2tog, p2, KB1, p1. (14 sts).
6th row: K1, p1, k2, p6, k2, p1, k1.
7th row: P1, KB1, p2, k4, k2tog, p2, KB1, p1. (13 sts).
8th row: K1, p1, k2, p5, k2, p1, k1.
9th row: P1, KB1, p2, k3, k2tog, p2, KB1, p1. (12 sts).
10th row: K1, p1, k2, p4, k2, p1, k1.
11th row: P1, KB1, p2, k2, k2tog, p2, KB1, p1. (11 sts).
12th row: K1, p1, k2, p3, k2, p1, k1.
13th row: P1, KB1, p2, k1, k2tog, p2, KB1, p1. (10 sts).
14th row: K1, p1, k2, p2, k2, p1, k1.
15th row: P1, KB1, p2, k2tog, p2, KB1, p1. (9 sts).
16th row: K1, p1, [k2, p1] twice, k1.
Rep these 16 rows.

Lace Panels

Ascending Arrow Panel

Worked over 13 sts on a background of reverse st st.

1st row (right side): P2, yon, sl 1, k1, psso, k5, k2tog, yfrn, p2.
2nd and every alt row: K2, p9, k2.
3rd row: P2, k1, yf, sl 1, k1, psso, k3, k2tog, yf, k1, p2.
5th row: P2, k2, yf, sl 1, k1, psso, k1, k2tog, yf, k2, p2.
7th row: P2, k3, yf, sl 1, k2tog, psso, yf, k3, p2.
8th row: K2, p9, k2.
Rep these 8 rows.

Twig and Leaf Insertion

Worked over 13 sts on a background of st st.
1st and every alt row (wrong side): Purl.
2nd row: [K1, yf] twice, sl 1, k2tog, psso, k3, k3tog, [yf, k1] twice.
4th row: K1, yf, k3, yf, sl 1, k1, psso, k1, k2tog, yf, k3, yf, k1. (15 sts).
6th row: K1, yf, sl 1, k1, psso, k1, k2tog, yf, sl 1, k2tog, psso, yf, sl 1, k1, psso, k1, k2tog, yf, k1. (13 sts).
8th row: K1, [yf, sl 1, k1, psso, k1, k2tog, yf, k1] twice.
10th row: As 8th row.
Rep these 10 rows.

Raised Tyre Track Panel

12th row: Purl.
Rep these 12 rows.

Worked over 10 sts on a background of st st.
1st row (right side): K4, yf, k1, sl 1, k1, psso, k3.
2nd row: P2, p2tog tbl, p1, yrn, p5.
3rd row: K6, yf, k1, sl 1, k1, psso, k1.
4th row: P2tog tbl, p1, yrn, p7.
5th row: K3, k2tog, k1, yf, k4.
6th row: P5, yrn, p1, p2tog, p2.
7th row: K1, k2tog, k1, yf, k6.
8th row: P7, yrn, p1, p2tog.
Rep these 8 rows.

Vertical Arrow Panel

Worked over 13 sts on a background of st st.
1st row (right side): K1, yf, k4, sl 2tog, k1, p2sso, k4, yf, k1.
2nd and every alt row: Purl.
3rd row: K2, yf, k3, sl 2tog, k1, p2sso, k3, yf, k2.
5th row: K3, yf, k2, sl 2tog, k1, p2sso, k2, yf, k3.
7th row: K4, yf, k1, sl 2tog, k1, p2sso, k1, yf, k4.
9th row: K5, yf, sl 2tog, k1, p2sso, yf, k5.
10th row: Purl.
Rep these 10 rows.

Branch Panel

Worked over 12 sts on a background of reverse st st.

1st row (right side): K2tog, k5, yf, k1, yf, k2, sl 1, k1, psso.
2nd and every alt row: Purl.
3rd row: K2tog, k4, yf, k3, yf, k1, sl 1, k1, psso.
5th row: K2tog, k3, yf, k5, yf, sl 1, k1, psso.
7th row: K2tog, k2, yf, k1, yf, k5, sl 1, k1, psso.
9th row: K2tog, k1, yf, k3, yf, k4, sl 1, k1, psso.
11th row: K2tog, yf, k5, yf, k3, sl 1, k1, psso.

Comb Panel

Worked over 8 sts on a background of reverse st st.
1st row (wrong side): K1, p6, k1.
2nd row: P1, yb, sl 1, k1, psso, k4, yfrn, p1.
3rd row: K1, p1, yrn, p3, p2tog tbl, k1.
4th row: P1, yb, sl 1, k1, psso, k2, yf, k2, p1.
5th row: K1, p3, yrn, p1, p2tog tbl, k1.
6th row: P1, yb, sl 1, k1, psso, yf, k4, p1.
7th row: As 1st row.
8th row: P1, yon, k4, k2tog, p1.
9th row: K1, p2tog, p3, yrn, p1, k1.
10th row: P1, k2, yf, k2, k2tog, p1.
11th row: K1, p2tog, p1, yrn, p3, k1.
12th row: P1, k4, yf, k2tog, p1.
Rep these 12 rows.

Fishtails

Worked over 15 sts on a background of st st.

1st row (right side): K6, yf, sl 1, k2tog, psso, yf, k6.

2nd and every alt row: Purl.

Rep these 2 rows 3 times more.

9th row: [K1, yf] twice, sl 1, k1, psso, k2, sl 1, k2tog, psso, k2, k2tog, [yf, k1] twice.

11th row: K2, yf, k1, yf, sl 1, k1, psso, k1, sl 1, k2tog, psso, k1, k2tog, yf, k1, yf, k2.

13th row: K3, yf, k1, yf, sl 1, k1, psso, sl 1, k2tog, psso, k2tog, yf, k1, yf, k3.

15th row: K4, yf, sl 1, k1, psso, yf, sl 1, k2tog, psso, yf, k2tog, yf, k4.

16th row: Purl.

Rep these 16 rows.

Fountains Panel

Worked over 16 sts on a background of st st.

1st row (right side): K1, yf, k1, sl 1, k1, psso, p1, k2tog, k1, yfrn, p1, yb, sl 1, k1, psso, p1, k2tog, [yf, k1] twice.

2nd row: P5, k1, p1, k1, p3, k1, p4.

3rd row: K1, yf, k1, sl 1, k1, psso, p1, k2tog, k1, p1, yb, sl 1, k2tog, psso, yf, k3, yf, k1. (15 sts).

4th row: P7, k1, p2, k1, p4.

5th row: [K1, yf] twice, sl 1, k1, psso, p1, [k2tog] twice, yf, k5, yf, k1. (16 sts).

6th row: P8, k1, p1, k1, p5.

7th row: K1, yf, k3, yf, sl 1, k2tog, psso, p1, yon, k1, sl 1, k1, psso, p1, k2tog, k1, yf, k1.

8th row: P4, k1, p3, k1, p7.

9th row: K1, yf, k5, yf, sl 1, k1, psso, k1, sl 1, k1, psso, p1, k2tog, k1, yf, k1.

10th row: P4, k1, p2, k1, p8.

Rep these 10 rows.

Gardenia Lace Panel

Worked over 12 sts on a background of st st.

Note: Sts should not be counted after 1st row.

1st row (right side): K3, [k2tog, yf] twice, sl 1, k1, psso, k3.

2nd row: P2, p2tog tbl, yrn, p1, inc 1 in next st, p1, yrn, p2tog, p2.

3rd row: K1, k2tog, yf, k6, yf, sl 1, k1, psso, k1.

4th row: P2tog tbl, yrn, p8, yrn, p2tog.

5th row: K1, yf, k3, k2tog, sl 1, k1, psso, k3, yf, k1.

6th row: P2, yrn, p2, p2tog tbl, p2tog, p2, yrn, p2.

7th row: K3, yf, k1, k2tog, sl 1, k1, psso, k1, yf, k3.

8th row: P4, yrn, p2tog tbl, p2tog, yrn, p4.

Rep these 8 rows.

Cascading Leaves

Worked over 16 sts on a background of reverse st st.

1st row (right side): P1, k3, k2tog, k1, yfrn, p2, yon, k1, sl 1, k1, psso, k3, p1.

2nd and every alt row: K1, p6, k2, p6, k1.

3rd row: P1, k2, k2tog, k1, yf, k1, p2, k1, yf, k1, sl 1, k1, psso, k2, p1.

5th row: P1, k1, k2tog, k1, yf, k2, p2, k2, yf, k1, sl 1, k1, psso, k1, p1.

7th row: P1, k2tog, k1, yf, k3, p2, k3, yf, k1, sl 1, k1, psso, p1.

8th row: K1, p6, k2, p6, k1.

Rep these 8 rows.

Butterfly Panel

Worked over 15 sts on a background of reverse st st.

1st row (right side): Yb, sl 1, k1, psso, k4, yf, k3, yf, k4, k2tog.

2nd row: P2tog, p3, yrn, p5, yrn, p3, p2tog tbl.

3rd row: Yb, sl 1, k1, psso, k2, yf, k7, yf, k2, k2tog.

4th row: P2tog, p1, yrn, p9, yrn, p1, p2tog tbl.

5th row: Yb, sl 1, k1, psso, yf, k11, yf, k2tog.

6th row: P1, yrn, p4, p2tog, k1, p2tog tbl, p4, yrn, p1.

7th row: K2, yf, k3, sl 1, k1, psso, p1, k2tog, k3, yf, k2.

8th row: P3, yrn, p2, p2tog, k1, p2tog tbl, p2, yrn, p3.

9th row: K4, yf, k1, sl 1, k1, psso, p1, k2tog, k1, yf, k4.

10th row: P5, yrn, p2tog, k1, p2tog tbl, yrn, p5.

Rep these 10 rows.

Ostrich Plume Panel

Worked over 13 sts on a background of reverse st st.

1st row (right side): Knit.

2nd row: Purl.

3rd row: K4tog, [yf, k1] 5 times, yf, k4tog.

4th row: Purl.

Rep these 4 rows.

Lace Panels

Cockleshells

Worked over 19 sts on a background of garter stitch.

1st row (right side): Knit.

2nd row: Knit.

3rd row: K1, yfrn, yrn, p2tog tbl, k13, p2tog, yrn, yon, k1. (21 sts).

4th row: K2, p1, k15, p1, k2.

5th and 6th rows: Knit.

7th row: K1, yfrn, yrn, p2tog tbl, [yrn] twice, p2tog tbl, k11, p2tog, [yrn] twice, p2tog, yrn, yon, k1. (25 sts).

8th row: [K2, p1] twice, k13, [p1, k2] twice.

9th row: Knit.

10th row: K5, k15 wrapping yarn 3 times around needle for each st, k5.

11th row: K1, yfrn, yrn, p2tog tbl, [yrn] twice, p2tog tbl, [yrn] twice, pass next 15 sts to right-hand needle dropping extra loops, pass same 15 sts back to left-hand needle and purl all 15 sts tog, [yrn] twice, p2tog, [yrn] twice, p2tog, yrn, yon, k1. (19 sts).

12th row: K1, p1, [k2, p1] twice, k3, [p1, k2] twice, p1, k1.

Rep these 12 rows.

Arched Windows

Worked over 13 sts on a background of reverse st st.

Note: Stitches should not be counted after the 3rd, 4th, 7th or 8th rows.

T5R (Twist 5 Right) = slip next 3 sts onto cable needle and hold at back of work, knit next 2 sts from left-hand needle, then p1, k2 from cable needle.

1st row (right side): K2, p2, k2tog, yf, k1, yf, sl 1, k1, psso, p2, k2.

2nd row: P2, k2, p5, k2, p2.

3rd row: K2, p2, k1, yf, k3, yf, k1, p2, k2.

4th row: P2, k2, p7, k2, p2.

5th row: K2, p2, yb, sl 1, k1, psso, yf, sl 1, k2tog, psso, yf, k2tog, p2, k2.

6th row: As 2nd row.

7th row: T3F, p1, k1, yf, k3, yf, k1, p1, T3B.

8th row: K1, p2, k1, p7, k1, p2, k1.

9th row: P1, T3F, sl 1, k1, psso, yf, sl 1, k2tog, psso, yf, k2tog, T3B, p1.

10th row: K2, p9, k2.

11th row: P2, T3F, p3, T3B, p2.

12th row: [K3, p2] twice, k3.

13th row: P3, T3F, p1, T3B, p3.

14th row: K4, p2, k1, p2, k4.

15th row: P4, T5R, p4.

16th row: Knit.

Rep these 16 rows.

Catherine Wheels

Worked across 13 sts on a background of st st.

Special Abbreviations

Inc 1 (Increase 1) = knit into front and back of next st.

Inc 2 (Increase 2) = knit into front, back and front of next st.

Work 5tog = sl 1, k1, psso, k3tog, pass the st resulting from sl 1, k1, psso over the st resulting from k3tog.

1st and every alt row (wrong side): Purl.

2nd row: K5, sl 3, yf, pass same slipped sts back to left-hand needle, yb, knit 3 slipped sts, k5.

4th row: K3, k3tog, yf, Inc 2, yf, k3tog tbl, k3.

6th row: K1, k3tog, yf, k2tog, yf, Inc 2, yf, sl 1, k1, psso, yf, k3tog tbl, k1.

8th row: [K2tog, yf] 3 times, KB1, [yf, sl 1, k1, psso] 3 times.

10th row: K1, [yf, k2tog] twice, yf, sl 1, k2tog, psso, [yf, sl 1, k1, psso] twice, yf, k1.

12th row: [Sl 1, k1, psso, yf] 3 times, KB1, [yf, k2tog] 3 times.

14th row: K1, Inc 1, yf, sl 1, k1, psso, yf, Work 5tog, yf, k2tog, yf, Inc 1, k1.

16th row: K3, Inc 1, yf, Work 5tog, yf, Inc 1, k3.

Rep these 16 rows.

Frost Flower Panel

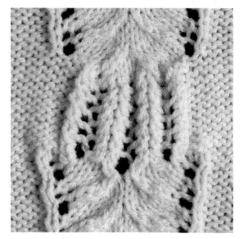

Worked over 18 sts on a background of reverse st st.

1st row (right side): K1, yf, k3, sl 1, k1, psso, k6, k2tog, k3, yf, k1.

2nd row: P1, yrn, p4, p2tog, p4, p2tog tbl, p4, yrn, p1.

3rd row: K2, yf, k4, sl 1, k1, psso, k2, k2tog, k4, yf, k2.

4th row: P3, yrn, p4, p2tog, p2tog tbl, p4, yrn, p3.

Rep these 4 rows twice more.

13th row: P3, [k2, yf, sl 1, k1, psso] 3 times, p3.

14th row: K3, [p2, yrn, p2tog] 3 times, k3.

Rep the last 2 rows 5 times more.

Rep these 24 rows.

Spiral and Eyelet Panel

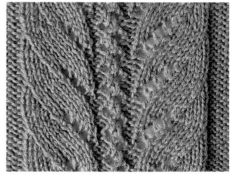

Worked over 24 sts on a background of reverse st st.

1st row (right side): K3, k2tog, k4, yfrn, p2, yon, k2tog, p2, yon, k4, sl 1, k1, psso, k3.

2nd and every alt row: P9, k2, p2, k2, p9.

3rd row: K2, k2tog, k4, yf, k1, p2, k2tog, yfrn, p2, k1, yf, k4, sl 1, k1, psso, k2.

5th row: K1, k2tog, k4, yf, k2, p2, yon, k2tog, p2, k2, yf, k4, sl 1, k1, psso, k1.

7th row: K2tog, k4, yf, k3, p2, k2tog, yfrn, p2, k3, yf, k4, sl 1, k1, psso.

8th row: P9, k2, p2, k2, p9.

Rep these 8 rows.

Embossed Rosebud Panel

Worked over 9 sts on a background of reverse st st.

1st row (wrong side): K3, p3, k3.

2nd row: P3, slip next st onto cable needle and hold at front of work, k1, [k1, yf, k1, yf, k1] into next st on left-hand needle, then knit st from cable needle, p3. (13 sts).

3rd row: K3, p1, [KB1] 5 times, p1, k3.

4th row: P3, [k1, yf] 6 times, k1, p3. (19 sts).

5th row: K3, p13, k3.

6th row: P3, k13, p3.

7th row: K3, p2tog, p9, p2tog tbl, k3. (17 sts).

8th row: P3, yb, sl 1, k1, psso, k7, k2tog, p3. (15 sts).

9th row: K3, p2tog, p5, p2tog tbl, k3. (13 sts).

10th row: P3, yb, sl 1, k1, psso, k3, k2tog, p3. (11 sts).

11th row: K3, p2tog, p1, p2tog tbl, k3. (9 sts).

12th row: P3, k3, p3.
Rep these 12 rows.

Snake Panel

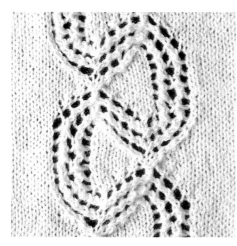

Worked over 22 sts on a background of st st.
Special Abbreviations
Work 5tog = sl 1, k1, psso, k3tog, pass the

st resulting from sl 1, k1, psso over the st resulting from k3tog.

Inc 1 (Increase 1) = knit into front and back of next st.

Inc 2 (Increase 2) = knit into front, back and front of next st.

Cluster 3 = sl 3, yf, slip same 3 sts back to left-hand needle, yb, k3.

1st row (right side): [K2tog, yf] 3 times, k3, [yf, sl 1, k1, psso] twice, yf, sl 1, k2tog, psso, yf, [k2tog, yf] twice, k2.

2nd and every alt row: Purl.

3rd row: K1, yf, k2tog, yf, sl 2, k1, p2sso, yf, k3, Inc 1, yf, sl 1, k1, psso, yf, Work 5tog, yf, k2tog, yf, Inc 1, yf.

5th row: K1, yf, sl 2, k1, p2sso, yf, sl 1, k1, psso, yf, k5, Inc 1, yf, Work 5tog, yf, Inc 1, k4.

7th row: K1, yf, k2tog, yf, sl 2, k1, p2sso, yf, k7, Cluster 3, k6.

9th row: K1, yf, sl 2, k1, p2sso, yf, sl·1, k1, psso, yf, k5, k3tog, yf, Inc 2, yf, k3tog tbl, k4.

11th row: K1, yf, k2tog, yf, sl 2, k1, p2sso, yf, k3, k3tog, yf, k2tog, yf, Inc 2, yf, sl 1, k1, psso, yf, k3tog tbl, k2.

13th row: K1, yf, sl 2, k1, p2sso, yf, sl 1, k1, psso, yf, k2 [k2tog, yf] 3 times, k1, [yf, sl 1, k1, psso] 3 times, k1.

15th row: K2, [yf, sl 1, k1, psso] twice, yf, sl 1, k2tog, psso, yf, [k2tog, yf] twice, k3, [yf, sl 1, k1, psso] 3 times.

17th row: K2, Inc 1, yf, sl 1, k1, psso, yf, Work 5tog, yf, k2tog, yf, Inc 1, k3, yf, sl 2, k1, p2sso, yf, sl 1, k1, psso, yf, k1.

19th row: K4, Inc 1, yf, Work 5tog, yf, Inc 1, k5, yf, k2tog, yf, sl 2, k1, p2sso, yf, k1.

21st row: K6, Cluster 3, k7, yf, sl 2, k1, p2sso, yf, sl 1, k1, psso, yf, k1.

23rd row: K4, k3tog, yf, Inc 2, yf, k3tog tbl, k5, yf, k2tog, yf, sl 2, k1, p2sso, yf, k1.

25th row: K2, k3tog, yf, k2tog, yf, Inc 2, yf, sl 1, k1, psso, yf, k3tog tbl, k3, yf, sl 2, k1, p2sso, yf, sl 1, k1, psso, yf, k1.

27th row: K1, [k2tog, yf] 3 times, k1, [yf, sl 1, k1, psso] 3 times, k2, yf, k2tog, yf, sl 2, k1, p2sso, yf, k1.

28th row: Purl.
Rep these 28 rows.

Bobble Tree Panel

Worked over 17 sts on a background of reverse st st.

1st row (right side): P6, k2tog, yfrn, p1, yon, sl 1, k1, psso, p6.

2nd row: K6, p1, k3, p1, k6.

3rd row: P5, k2tog, yfrn, p3, yon, sl 1, k1, psso, p5.

4th row: [K5, p1] twice, k5.

5th row: P4, k2tog, yfrn, [p1, k1] twice, p1, yon, sl 1, k1, psso, p4.

6th row: K4, p1, k2, p1, k1, p1, k2, p1, k4.

7th row: P3, k2tog, yfrn, p2, k1, p1, k1, p2, yon, sl 1, k1, psso, p3.

8th row: [K3, p1] twice, k1, [p1, k3] twice.

9th row: P2, k2tog, yfrn, p2, k2tog, yfrn, p1, yon, sl 1, k1, psso, p2, yon, sl 1, k1, psso, p2.

10th row: K2, [p1, k3] 3 times, p1, k2.

11th row: P2, [k1, p1] twice into next st, turn and p4, turn and k4, turn and p4, turn and sl 1, k1, psso, k2tog, turn and p2tog, turn and slip bobble st onto right-hand needle (bobble completed), p2, k2tog, yfrn, p3, yon, sl 1, k1, psso, p2, make bobble, p2.

12th row: [K5, p1] twice, k5.
Rep these 12 rows.

Bobble Spray Panel

Worked over 23 sts on a background of st st.
1st row (right side): Sl 1, k1, psso, k6, [yf, k1] twice, sl 1, k2tog, psso, [k1, yf] twice, k6, k2tog.

2nd and every alt row: Purl.

3rd row: Sl 1, k1, psso, k5, yf, k1, yf, k2, sl 1, k2tog, psso, k2, yf, k1, yf, k5, k2tog.

5th row: Sl 1, k1, psso, k4, yf, k1, yf, MB, k2, sl 1, k2tog, psso, k2, MB, yf, k1, yf, k4, k2tog.

7th row: Sl 1, k1, psso, k3, yf, k1, yf, MB, k3, sl 1, k2tog, psso, k3, MB, yf, k1, yf, k3, k2tog.

9th row: Sl 1, k1, psso, k2, yf, k1, yf, MB, k4, sl 1, k2tog, psso, k4, MB, yf, k1, yf, k2, k2tog.

11th row: Sl 1, k1, psso, [k1, yf] twice, MB, k5, sl 1, k2tog, psso, k5, MB, [yf, k1] twice, k2tog.

13th row: Sl 1, k1, psso, yf, k1, yf, MB, k6, sl 1, k2tog, psso, k6, MB, yf, k1, yf, k2tog.

14th row: Purl.
Rep these 14 rows.

Patterns for Texture and Colour

Loop Pattern I

Multiple of 2 sts.
Note: Slip all sts purlwise.
1st row (right side): Knit.
2nd row: *K1, sl 1; rep from * to last 2 sts, k2.
3rd row: Knit.
4th row: K2, *sl 1, k1; rep from * to end.
Rep these 4 rows.

Loop Pattern II

Multiple of 3 sts + 1.
1st row (right side): Knit.
2nd row: *K1, sl 2 purlwise; rep from * to last st, k1.
Rep these 2 rows.

2-Colour Loop Pattern

Multiple of 2 sts + 1.
Note: All slip sts should be slipped purlwise.
1st row (right side): Using A knit.
2nd row: Using A purl.

3rd row: Using B k1, *sl 1, k1; rep from * to end.
4th row: As 3rd row.
5th row: Using B knit.
6th row: Using B purl.
7th row: Using A k2, sl 1, *k1, sl 1; rep from * to last 2 sts, k2.
8th row: Using A p1, k1, *sl 1, k1; rep from * to last st, p1.
Rep these 8 rows.

2-Colour Loop Pattern Variation

Multiple of 4 sts + 1.
Note: All slip sts should be slipped purlwise.
1st row (right side): Using A knit.
2nd row: Using A purl.
3rd row: Using B k1, *sl 3, k1; rep from * to end.
4th row: As 3rd row.
5th row: Using B knit.
6th row: Using B purl.
7th row: Using A k3, sl 3, *k1, sl 3,; rep from * to last 3 sts, k3.
8th row: Using A p2, k1, *sl 3, k1; rep from * to last 2 sts, p2.
Rep these 8 rows.

3-Colour Loop Pattern

Multiple of 2 sts + 1.
1st row (right side): Using A knit.
2nd row: Using A purl.
3rd row: Using B k1, *sl 1, k1; rep from * to end.

4th row: As 3rd row.
5th row: Using B knit.
6th row: Using B purl.
7th and 8th rows: As 3rd row **but** using A instead of B.
9th row: Using A knit.
10th row: Using A purl.
11th and 12th rows: As 3rd row **but** using C instead of B.
13th row: Using C knit.
14th row: Using C purl.
15th and 16th rows: As 3rd row **but** using A instead of B.
Rep these 16 rows.

Bee Stitch

Multiple of 2 sts + 1.
1st row (wrong side): Knit.
2nd row: K1, *K1B, k1; rep from * to end.
3rd row: Knit.
4th row: K2, K1B, *k1, K1B; rep from * to last 2 sts, k2.
Rep these 4 rows.

2-Colour Bee Stitch

Multiple of 2 sts + 1.
1st Foundation row (right side): Using A knit.
2nd Foundation row: Using A knit.
Commence Pattern
1st row: Using B k1, *K1B, k1; rep from * to end.
2nd row: Using B knit.
3rd row: Using A k2, K1B, *k1, K1B; rep from * to last 2 sts, k2.
4th row: Using A knit.
Rep the last 4 rows.

Texture Stitch

Multiple of 2 sts + 1.
1st row (right side): Purl.
2nd row: K1, *yf, sl 1 purlwise, yb, k1; rep from * to end.
Rep these 2 rows.

Knot Ridges I

Multiple of 2 sts + 1.
Using A work 4 rows in st st, starting knit (right side).
5th row Using B k1, [k1, yf, k1] into next st, *sl 1, [k1, yf, k1] into next st; rep from * to last st, k1.
6th row: Using B k1, k3tog tbl, *sl 1, k3tog tbl; rep from * to last st, k1.
Rep these 6 rows.

Knot Ridges II

Multiple of 2 sts + 1.
1st row (right side): Using A knit.
2nd row: Using A purl.
3rd row: Using B k1, [k1, yf, k1] into next st, *sl 1, [k1, yf, k1] into next st; rep from
* to last st, k1.
4th row: Using B k1, k3tog tbl, *sl 1, k3tog tbl; rep from * to last st, k1.
5th row: Using A knit.
6th row: Using A purl.
7th row: Using B k2, [k1, yf, k1] into next st, *sl 1, [k1, yf, k1] into next st; rep from * to last 2 sts, k2.
8th row: Using B p2, k3tog tbl, *sl 1, k3tog tbl; rep from * to last 2 sts, p2.
Rep these 8 rows.

Knot Ridges with Twists

Multiple of 8 sts + 5.
Note: Slip all stitches purlwise.
1st row (right side): Using A k5, *C3R, k5; rep from * to end.
2nd row: Using A purl.
3rd row: Using B [k1, sl 1] twice, k1, *sl 3, [k1, sl 1] twice, k1; rep from * to end.
4th row: Using B [k1, sl 1] twice, k1, *yf, sl 3, yb, [k1, sl 1] twice, k1; rep from * to end.
Rep these 4 rows.

Thick Woven Blanket Fabric I

Multiple of 4 sts + 1.
Note: Slip all sts purlwise.
Foundation row (wrong side): Using B purl.
Commence Pattern
1st row: Using A k2, sl 1, *k1, sl 1; rep from * to last 2 sts, k2.
2nd row: Using A p1, k1, *yf, sl 1, yb, k1; rep from * to last st, p1.
3rd row: Using B k1, *sl 1, k1; rep from * to end.
4th row: Using B p1, *sl 1, p1; rep from * to end.
5th row: Using C k1, yf, sl 1, yb, sl 1, yf, *sl 3, yb, sl 1, yf; rep from * to last 2 sts, sl 1, yb, k1.
6th row: Using C p1, yb, sl 1, yf, sl 1, yb, *sl 3, yf, sl 1, yb; rep from * to last 2 sts, sl 1, yf, p1.
Rep the first 4 rows once more.
11th row: Using C k1, yf, sl 3, yb, *sl 1, yf, sl 3, yb; rep from * to last st, k1.
12th row: Using C p1, yb, sl 3, yf, *sl 1, yb, sl 3, yf; rep from * to last st, p1.
Rep the last 12 rows.

Thick Woven Blanket Fabric II

Worked as Thick Woven Blanket Fabric I but using one colour throughout.

Plain Triple Slip

Multiple of 6 sts + 5.
Note: Slip all sts purlwise.
1st row (right side): Using A knit.
2nd row: Using A purl.
3rd row: Using B k1, sl 3, *yf, sl 3, yb, sl 3; rep from * to last st, k1.
4th row: Using B p1, sl 3, *yb, sl 3, yf, sl 3; rep from * to last st, p1.
5th row: As 1st row.
6th row: As 2nd row.
7th row: Using B k1, yf, sl 3, yb, *sl 3, yf, sl 3, yb; rep from * to last st, k1.
8th row: Using B p1, yb, sl 3, yf, *sl 3, yb, sl 3, yf; rep from * to last st, p1.
Rep these 8 rows.

Patterns for Texture and Colour

Dotted Triple Slip I

Multiple of 6 sts + 5.
Note: Slip all sts purlwise.
1st row (right side): Using A knit.
2nd row: Using A purl.
3rd row: Using B k1, yf, sl 3, yb, *sl 1, k1, sl 1, yf, sl 3, yb; rep from * to last st, k1.
4th row: Using B p1, yb, sl 3, *yf, sl 1, yb, k1, yf, sl 1, yb, sl 3; rep from * to last st, yf, p1.
5th row: As 1st row.
6th row: As 2nd row.
7th row: Using B [k1, sl 1] twice, *yf, sl 3, yb, sl 1, k1, sl 1; rep from * to last st, k1.
8th row: Using B p1, sl 1, yb, k1, yf, sl 1, *yb, sl 3, yf, sl 1, yb, k1, yf, sl 1; rep from * to last st, p1.
Rep these 8 rows.

Dotted Triple Slip II

Work as Dotted Triple Slip I but using one colour throughout.

Berry Stitch

Multiple of 4 sts + 3.
Note: Sts should only be counted after the 2nd and 4th rows.
1st row (right side): K1, [k1, KB1, k1] into next st, *p3, [k1, KB1, k1] into next st; rep from * to last st, k1.
2nd row: K4, p3tog, *k3, p3tog; rep from * to last 4 sts, k4.
3rd row: K1, p3, *[k1, KB1, k1] into next st, p3; rep from * to last st, k1.
4th row: K1, p3tog, *k3, p3tog; rep from * to last st, k1.
Rep these 4 rows.

Star Stitch Pattern I

Multiple of 4 sts + 1.
Special Abbreviation
Make Star = p3tog leaving sts on needle, yrn, then purl the same 3 sts together again.
1st row (right side): Knit.
2nd row: P1, *Make Star, p1; rep from * to end.
3rd row: Knit.
4th row: P3, Make Star, *p1, Make Star; rep from * to last 3 sts, p3.
Rep these 4 rows.

2-Colour Star Stitch Pattern

Worked as Star Stitch Pattern I.
1st and 2nd rows in colour A, 3rd and 4th rows in colour B throughout.

Star Stitch Pattern II

Multiple of 4 sts + 1.
Special Abbreviation
Make Star = p3tog leaving sts on needle, yrn, then purl the same 3 sts together again.
1st row (right side): P1, *k1, p1; rep from * to end.
2nd row: K1, *Make Star, k1; rep from * to end.
3rd row: As 1st row.
4th row: K1, p1, k1, *Make Star, k1; rep from * to last 2 sts, p1, k1.
Rep these 4 rows.

Textured Acorn Stitch

Multiple of 6 sts + 3.
Note: Sts should only be counted after 1st, 2nd, 7th and 8th rows.
Special Abbreviation
M3 (Make 3) = knit into front, back and front of next st.
1st row (right side): P3, *k3, p3; rep from * to end.
2nd row: K3, *p3, k3; rep from * to end.
3rd row: P1, M3, p1, *sl 1, k2tog, psso, p1, M3, p1; rep from * to end.
4th row: K1, p3, *k3, p3; rep from * to last st, k1.
5th row: P1, k3, *p3, k3; rep from * to last st, p1.
6th row: As 4th row.
7th row: P1, sl 1, k2tog, psso, p1, *M3, p1, sl 1, k2tog, psso, p1; rep from * to end.

8th row: As 2nd row.
Rep these 8 rows.

Diagonal Knot Stitch III

See Diagonal Knot Stitches I and II on page 39 of The Harmony Guide to Knitting Stitches.

Multiple of 4 sts + 1.
1st row (right side): K4, p1, *k3, p1; rep from * to last 4 sts, k4.
2nd row: P4, k1, *p3, k1; rep from * to last 4 sts, p4.
3rd row: P1, *MK, p1; rep from * to end.
4th row: As 2nd row.
5th row: K2, p1, *k3, p1; rep from * to last 2 sts, k2.
6th row: P2, k1, *p3, k1; rep from * to last 2 sts, p2.
7th row: K2, p1, *MK, p1; rep from * to last 2 sts, k2.
8th row: As 6th row.
Rep these 8 rows.

Treble Slip Knot Pattern

Multiple of 8 sts + 3.
Note: Stitches should not be counted after 4th, 5th, 12th and 13th rows.
Special Abbreviation
D2 (Draw 2) = yb, insert needle into st 2 rows below next st, yrn and draw through loop, yf, knit into same st dropping st above off needle (2 sts increased).

Work 3 rows in reversed st st, starting knit (1st row is wrong side).
4th row: P1, D2, *p7, D2; rep from * to last st, p1.
5th row: K1, p3, *k7, p3; rep from * to last st, k1.
6th row: P1, yb, sl 2tog knitwise, k1, p2sso, *p7, yb, sl 2tog knitwise, k1, p2sso; rep from * to last st, p1.
Work 5 rows in reversed st st, starting knit.
12th row: P5, D2, *p7, D2; rep from * to last 5 sts, p5.
13th row: K5, p3, *k7, p3; rep from * to last 5 sts, k5.
14th row: P5, yb, sl 2tog knitwise, k1, p2sso, *p7, yb, sl 2tog knitwise, k1, p2sso; rep from * to last 5 sts, p5.
Work 2 rows in reversed st st, starting knit.
Rep these 16 rows.

Ringlet Pillars

Multiple of 5 sts + 1.
1st row (wrong side): Purl.
2nd row: K2, Make Ringlet as follows: p2, [keeping yf slip last 2 sts worked back onto left-hand needle, yb, slip same 2 sts back onto right-hand needle] 3 times (Ringlet completed), *k3, Make Ringlet as before; rep from * to last 2 sts, k2.
Rep these 2 rows.

Flagon Stitch

Multiple of 6 sts + 4.
Note: Slip all sts purlwise.
1st row (wrong side): K1, *p2, k1; rep from * to end.
2nd row: P1, k2, p1, *sl 1, p1, yon, psso the p1 and the yon, p1, k2, p1; rep from * to end.

Rep the last 2 rows 3 times more, then the 1st row again.
10th row: P1, sl 1, p1, yon, psso the p1 and the yon, p1, *k2, p1, sl 1, p1, yon, psso the p1 and the yon, p1; rep from * to end.
11th row: As 1st row.
Rep the last 2 rows twice more, then the 10th row again.
Rep these 16 rows.

Hindu Pillar Stitch

Multiple of 4 sts + 1.
1st row (right side): K1, *p3tog without slipping sts from left-hand needle, knit them tog then purl them tog, k1; rep from * to end.
2nd row: Purl.
Rep these 2 rows.

Drawn Loop Pattern

Multiple of 6 sts + 5.
Special Abbreviation
DR (Draw Loop) = insert needle between 3rd and 4th st on left-hand needle, yrn, draw through loop and place on left-hand needle, k2tog tbl (the loop and next st on left-hand needle), k2.
1st row (right side): Knit.
2nd row: Purl.
3rd row: K1, DR, *k3, DR; rep from * to last st, k1.
Work 3 rows in st st, starting purl.
7th row: K4, DR, *k3, DR; rep from * to last 4 sts, k4.
8th row: Purl.
Rep these 8 rows.

Patterns for Texture and Colour

Oyster Pattern

Multiple of 6 sts + 1.

1st row (right side): Knit.

2nd row: P1, *p5 wrapping yarn twice around needle for each st, p1; rep from * to end.

3rd row: K1, *Cluster 5 as follows: pass next 5 sts onto right-hand needle dropping extra loops, pass these 5 sts back onto left-hand needle, [k1, p1, k1, p1, k1] into all 5 sts together wrapping yarn twice around needle for each st, k1; rep from * to end.

4th row: P1, *k5 dropping extra loops, p1; rep from * to end.

5th row: Knit.

6th row: P4, p5 wrapping yarn twice around needle for each st, *p1, p5 wrapping yarn twice around needle for each st; rep from * to last 4 sts, p4.

7th row: K4, Cluster 5 as before, *k1, Cluster 5 as before; rep from * to last 4 sts, k4.

8th row: P4, k5 dropping extra loops, *p1, k5 dropping extra loops; rep from * to last 4 sts, p4.

Rep these 8 rows.

Pique Squares

Multiple of 12 sts + 8.

1st row (right side): K7, [p2, slip these sts onto left-hand needle, yb, slip the 2 sts back onto right-hand needle] 3 times, *k6, [p2, slip these sts onto left-hand needle, yb, slip the 2 sts back onto right-hand needle] 3 times; rep from * to last 7 sts, k7.

2nd row: Purl.

Rep these 2 rows twice more.

7th row: K1, [p2, slip these sts onto left-hand needle, yb, slip the 2 sts back onto right-hand needle] 3 times, *k6, [p2, slip these sts onto left-hand needle, yb, slip the

2 sts back onto right-hand needle] 3 times; rep from * to last st, k1.

8th row: Purl.
Rep these 2 rows twice more.
Rep these 12 rows.

Crowns I

Multiple of 5 sts.
Work 4 rows in garter stitch.

5th row: K1, *k1 winding yarn round needle 3 times; rep from * to end.

6th row: *Sl 5 sts purlwise dropping extra loops, return these 5 sts to left-hand needle then work into these 5 sts together as follows: k1, [p1, k1] twice; rep from * to end.

Work 2 rows in garter stitch.
Rep these 8 rows.

Crowns II

Multiple of 10 sts + 7.

Specal Abbreviations

KW5 = knit 5 sts wrapping yarn 3 times round needle for each st.

Twist 5 = slip 5 sts purlwise dropping extra loops, return these 5 sts to left-hand needle, then k1, [p1, k1] twice into same 5 sts tog.

1st row: K6, KW5, *k5, KW5; rep from * to last 6 sts, k6.

2nd row: P6, Twist 5, *p5, Twist 5; rep from * to last 6 sts, p6.

3rd row: Knit.

4th row: K6, p5, *k5, p5; rep from * to last 6 sts, k6.

5th row: K1, KW5, *k5, KW5; rep from * to last st, k1.

6th row: P1, Twist 5, *p5, Twist 5; rep from * to last st, p1.

7th row: Knit.

8th row: K1, p5, *k5, p5; rep from * to last st, k1.

Rep these 8 rows.

Little Crowns

Multiple of 3 sts + 2.

1st row (right side): Knit.

2nd row: Knit.

3rd row: K1, knit to last st wrapping yarn twice around needle for each st, k1.

4th row: K1, *pass next 3 sts to right-hand needle dropping extra loops, pass these 3 sts back to left-hand needle, k1, p1, k1 through 3 sts tog; rep from * to last st, k1.

Rep these 4 rows.

Knotted Boxes I

Multiple of 8 sts + 5.

1st row (right side): Knit.

2nd row: Purl.

3rd row: K1, p3, *k5, p3; rep from * to last st, k1.

4th row: P1, k3, *p5, k3; rep from * to last st, p1.

5th row: K1, yf, k3tog, yf, *k5, yf, k3tog, yf; rep from * to last st, k1.

Work 3 rows in st st, starting purl.

9th row: K5, *p3, k5; rep from * to end.

10th row: P5, *k3, p5; rep from * to end.

11th row: K5, *yf, k3tog, yf, k5; rep from * to end.

12th row: Purl.

Rep these 12 rows.

Knotted Boxes II

Multiple of 6 sts + 5.

1st row (right side): K1, p3, *k3, p3; rep from * to last st, k1.

2nd row: P1, k3, *p3, k3; rep from * to last st, p1.

3rd row: K1, yf, k3tog, yf, *k3, yf, k3tog, yf; rep from * to last st, k1.

4th row: Purl.

5th row: K4, p3, *k3, p3; rep from * to last 4 sts, k4.

6th row: P4, k3, *p3, k3; rep from * to last 4 sts, p4.

7th row: K4, yf, k3tog, yf, *k3, yf, k3tog, yf; rep from * to last 4 sts, k4.

8th row: Purl.

Rep these 8 rows.

Bobble and Ridge Stitch

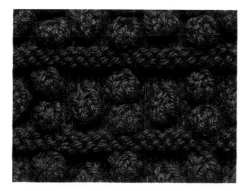

Multiple of 6 sts + 5.

Special Abbreviation

MB (Make Bobble) = knit into front, back and front of next st, turn and p3, turn and k3, turn and p3, turn and sl 1, k2tog, psso (bobble completed).

1st row (right side): Knit.

2nd row: Purl.

3rd row: K5, *MB, k5; rep from * to end.

4th row: Purl.

5th row: K2, MB, *k5, MB; rep from * to last 2 sts, k2.

6th, 7th and 8th rows: As 2nd, 3rd and 4th rows.

9th row: Purl.

10th row: Knit.

Rep these 10 rows.

2-Colour Bobble and Ridge Stitch

Worked as Bobble and Ridge Stitch but using a second colour for bobbles.

Ridge Stitch

Any number of sts.

Work 3 rows in st st, starting purl (1st row is wrong side).

4th row: Knit into front and back of each st (thus doubling the number of sts).

5th row: *K2tog; rep from * to end (original number of sts restored).

6th row: Knit.

Rep these 6 rows.

Twisted Texture

Multiple of 3 sts + 1.

1st row (wrong side): Purl.

2nd row: P1, *C2B, p1; rep from * to end.

3rd row: K1, *purl into 2nd st on needle then purl first st, slipping both sts off needle at the same time, k1; rep from * to end.

4th row: Knit.

Rep these 4 rows.

Triangle Pleats

Multiple of 10 sts + 4.

1st row (right side): K1, *C2F, k7, p1; rep from * to last 3 sts, C2F, k1.

2nd row: P3, *k2, p8; rep from * to last st, p1.

3rd row: K1, *C2F, k5, p3; rep from * to last 3 sts, C2F, k1.

4th row: P3, k4, *p6, k4; rep from * to last 7 sts, p7.

5th row: K1, *C2F, k3, p5; rep from * to last 3 sts, C2F, k1.

6th row: P3, k6, *p4, k6; rep from * to last 5 sts, p5.

7th row: K1, *C2F, k1, p7; rep from * to last 3 sts, C2F, k1.

8th row: P3, k8, *p2, k8; rep from * to last 3 sts, p3.

Rep these 8 rows.

Granite Stitch

Multiple of 2 sts.

1st row (right side): Knit.

2nd row: *K2tog; rep from * to end.

3rd row: *[K1, p1] into each st; rep from * to end.

4th row: Purl.

Rep these 4 rows.

Patterns for Texture and Colour

Mock Rib Checks I

Multiple of 2 sts.
Foundation row: Purl.
Commence Pattern
1st row (wrong side): *K1, K1B; rep from * to last 2 sts, k2.
Rep this row 5 times more.
7th row: K2, *K1B, k1; rep from * to end.
Rep this row 5 times more.
Rep the last 12 rows.

Mock Rib Checks II

Worked as Mock Rib Checks I, using reverse side as right side.

Blanket Moss Stitch

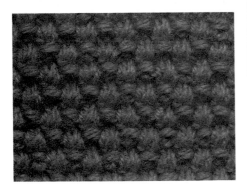

Multiple of 2 sts + 1.
Note: Sts should only be counted after the 2nd and 4th rows.

1st row (right side): Knit into front and back of each st (thus doubling the number of sts).
2nd row: K2tog, *p2tog, k2tog; rep from * to end (original number of sts restored).
3rd row: As 1st row.
4th row: P2tog, *k2tog, p2tog; rep from * to end.
Rep these 4 rows.

Puff Stitch

Multiple of 4 sts + 3.
1st row (right side): P1, k1, p1, *M5 (make 5) as follows: [k1, yf, k1, yf, k1] into next st, p1, k1, p1; rep from * to end.
2nd row: K1, p1, k1, *D4 (dec 4) as follows: p2tog, p3tog, pass the first of the 2 last sts on right-hand needle over the 2nd and off needle, k1, p1, k1; rep from * to end.
3rd row: P1, M5, p1, *k1, p1, M5, p1; rep from * to end.
4th row: K1, D4, k1, *p1, k1, D4, k1; rep from * to end.
Rep these 4 rows.

Crocus Buds

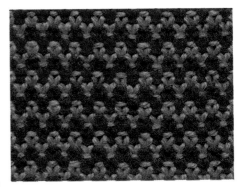

Multiple of 2 sts + 1.
1st row (right side): K1, *yf, k2; rep from * to end.
2nd row: P1, *p3, pass the 3rd st on right-hand needle over the first 2 sts; rep from * to end.
3rd row: *K2, yf; rep from * to last st, k1.
4th row: *P3, pass the 3rd st on right-hand needle over the first 2 sts on right-hand needle; rep from * to last st, p1.
Rep these 4 rows.

Slip Stitch Stripes

Multiple of 5 sts.
1st row (right side): K2, *p1, k4; rep from * to last 3 sts, p1, k2.
2nd row: K2, *sl 1 purlwise, k4; rep from * to last 3 sts, sl 1 purlwise, k2.
Rep these 2 rows.

Coloured Tweed Stitch

Multiple of 2 sts + 1.
1st row (right side): Using A k1, *yf, sl 1p, yb, k1; rep from * to end.
2nd row: Using A p2, *yb, sl 1p, yf, p1; rep from * to last st, p1.
Rep these 2 rows using B.
Rep these 4 rows.

Slip Stitch Tweed

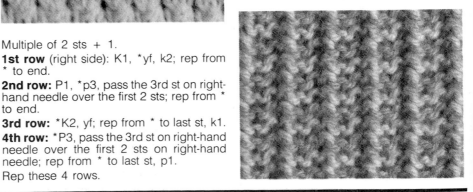

Multiple of 3 sts + 2.
1st row (right side): Using A k2, *sl 1 purlwise, k2; rep from * to end.
2nd row: Using A knit.
3rd row: Using B k2, *sl 1 purlwise, k2; rep from * to end.
4th row: Using B knit.
Rep these 4 rows.

Pinstripes

Multiple of 2 sts + 1.
Note: Slip all sts purlwise.
1st Foundation row (right side): Using A knit.
2nd Foundation row: Using A purl.
Commence Pattern
1st row: Using B k1, *sl 1, k1; rep from * to end.
2nd row: Using B p1, *sl 1, p1; rep from * to end.
3rd row: Using A k2, sl 1, *k1, sl 1; rep from * to last 2 sts, k2.
4th row: Using A p2, sl 1, *p1, sl 1; rep from * to last 2 sts, p2.
Rep the last 4 rows.

Wide Slip Stitch Stripes

Multiple of 4 sts.
Note: Slip all sts purlwise.
1st Foundation row (right side): Using A knit.
2nd Foundation row: Using A purl.
Commence Pattern
1st row: Using B k3, sl 2, *k2, sl 2; rep from

* to last 3 sts, k3.
2nd row: Using B p3, sl 2, *p2, sl 2; rep from * to last 3 sts, p3.
3rd row: Using A k1, sl 2, *k2, sl 2; rep from * to last st, k1.
4th row: Using A p1, sl 2, *p2, sl 2; rep from * to last st, p1.
Rep the last 4 rows.

Slip Stitch Check Pattern

Multiple of 4 sts.
Note: Slip all sts purlwise.
1st row (wrong side): Using A purl.
2nd row: Using B k3, sl 2, *k2, sl 2; rep from * to last 3 sts, k3.
3rd row: Using B p3, sl 2, *p2, sl 2; rep from * to last 3 sts, p3.
4th row: Using A knit.
5th row: Using C p1, sl 2, *p2, sl 2; rep from * to last st, p1.
6th row: Using C k1, sl 2, *k2, sl 2; rep from * to last st, k1.
Rep these 6 rows.

Tongue and Groove Stitch

Multiple of 6 sts + 2.
Note: Slip all sts purlwise.
Foundation row (wrong side): Using A purl.
Commence Pattern
1st row: Using B k4, sl 1, k1, sl 1, *k3, sl 1, k1, sl 1; rep from * to last st, k1.
2nd row: Using B [p1, sl 1] twice, *p3, sl 1,

p1, sl 1; rep from * to last 4 sts, p4.
3rd row: Using A [k1, sl 1] twice, *k3, sl 1, k1, sl 1; rep from * to last 4 sts, k4.
4th row: Using A p4, sl 1, p1, sl 1, *p3, sl 1, p1, sl 1; rep from * to last st, p1.
5th row: Using B k2, *sl 1, k3, sl 1, k1; rep from * to end.
6th row: Using B *p1, sl 1, p3, sl 1; rep from * to last 2 sts, p2.
7th row: Using A *k3, sl 1, k1, sl 1; rep from * to last 2 sts, k2.
8th row: Using A p2, *sl 1, p1, sl 1, p3; rep from * to end.
9th row: Using B k2, *sl 1, k1, sl 1, k3; rep from * to end.
10th row: Using B *p3, sl 1, p1, sl 1; rep from * to last 2 sts, p2.
11th row: Using A *k1, sl 1, k3, sl 1; rep from * to last 2 sts, k2.
12th row: Using A p2, *sl 1, p3, sl 1, p1; rep from * to end.
Rep the last 12 rows.

Raised Tongue and Groove Stitch

Multiple of 6 sts + 2.
Note: Slip all sts purlwise.
Foundation row (wrong side): Using A purl.
Commence Pattern
1st row: Using B k3, sl 1, *k5, sl 1; rep from * to last 4 sts, k4.
2nd row: Using B k4, yf, sl 1, yb, *k5, yf, sl 1, yb; rep from * to last 3 sts, k3.
3rd row: Using A k6, sl 1, *k5, sl 1; rep from * to last st, k1.
4th row: Using A k1, yf, sl 1, yb, *k5, yf, sl 1, yb; rep from * to last 6 sts, k6.
5th row: Using B k1, sl 1, *k5, sl 1; rep from * to last 6 sts, k6.
6th row: Using B k6, yf, sl 1, yb, *k5, yf, sl 1, yb; rep from * to last st, k1.
7th row: Using A k4, sl 1, *k5, sl 1; rep from * to last 3 sts, k3.
8th row: Using A k3, yf, sl 1, yb, *k5, yf, sl 1, yb; rep from * to last 4 sts, k4.
9th row: Using B *k5, sl 1; rep from * to last 2 sts, k2.
10th row: Using B k2, *yf, sl 1, yb, k5; rep from * to end.
11th row: Using A k2, *sl 1, k5; rep from * to end.
12th row: Using A *k5, yf, sl 1, yb; rep from * to last 2 sts, k2.
Rep the last 12 rows.

Patterns for Texture and Colour

Flecked Tweed

Multiple of 4 sts + 3.
Note: Slip all sts purlwise.
1st row (wrong side): Using A p1, yb, sl 1, yf, *p3, yb, sl 1, yf; rep from * to last st, p1.
2nd row: Using A k1, sl 1, *k3, sl 1; rep from * to last st, k1.
3rd row: Using B p3, *yb, sl 1, yf, p3; rep from * to end.
4th row: Using B k3, *sl 1, k3; rep from * to end.
Rep these 4 rows.

3-Colour Flecked Tweed

Worked as Flecked Tweed.
Beginning with the 1st row work 2 rows in A, 2 rows in B and 2 rows in C throughout.

3-Colour Scottie Tweed

Multiple of 3 sts + 2.
Note: Slip all sts purlwise.
1st row (wrong side): Using A purl.
2nd row: Using B k2, *sl 1, k2; rep from * to end.
3rd row: Using B purl.
4th row: Using C k1, sl 1, *k2, sl 1; rep from * to last 3 sts, k3.
5th row: Using C purl.
6th row: Using A k3, sl 1, *k2, sl 1; rep from * to last st, k1.
Rep these 6 rows.

2-Colour Flecked Garter Stitch

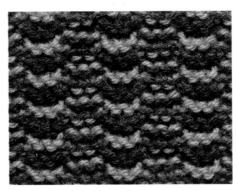

Multiple of 6 sts + 3.
1st row (right side): Using A k3, *p3, k3; rep from * to end.
2nd row: As 1st row.
3rd row: Using B k3, *p3, k3; rep from * to end.
4th row: As 3rd row.
Rep these 4 rows.

T-Square

Multiple of 10 sts + 2.
Note: Slip all sts purlwise.
Foundation row (wrong side): Using A purl.
Commence Pattern
1st row: Using B k4, sl 1, k2, sl 1, *k6, sl 1, k2, sl 1; rep from * to last 4 sts, k4.
2nd row: Using B p4, sl 1, p2, sl 1, *p6, sl 1, p2, sl 1; rep from * to last 4 sts, p4.
3rd row: Using A k5, sl 2, *k8, sl 2; rep from * to last 5 sts, k5.
4th row: Using A p5, sl 2, *p8, sl 2; rep from * to last 5 sts, p5.
5th row: Using B k2, *sl 1, k6, sl 1, k2; rep from * to end.
6th row: Using B p2, *sl 1, p6, sl 1, p2; rep from * to end.
7th row: Using A k1, sl 1, k8, *sl 2, k8; rep from * to last 2 sts, sl 1, k1.
8th row: Using A p1, sl 1, p8, *sl 2, p8; rep from * to last 2 sts, sl 1, p1.
Rep the last 8 rows.

Blister Check Pattern

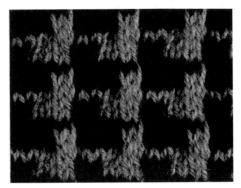

Multiple of 6 sts + 2.
Note: Slip all sts purlwise.
1st row (wrong side): Using A purl.
2nd row: Using B k3, sl 2, *k4, sl 2; rep from * to last 3 sts, k3.
3rd row: Using B p3, sl 2, *p4, sl 2; rep from * to last 3 sts, p3.
4th row: As 2nd row.
5th row: Using B purl.
6th row: Using A k5, sl 2, *k4, sl 2; rep from * to last st, k1.
7th row: Using A p1, sl 2, *p4, sl 2; rep from * to last 5 sts, p5.
8th row: As 6th row.
Rep these 8 rows.

Moroccan Pattern

Multiple of 6 sts + 5.
Note: Slip all sts purlwise.

Foundation row (wrong side): Using A purl.
Commence Pattern
1st row: Using B k6, sl 1, *k5, sl 1; rep from * to last 4 sts, k4.
2nd row: Using B k4, yf, sl 1, yb, *k5, yf, sl 1, yb; rep from * to last 6 sts, k6.
3rd row: Using A k3, sl 1, k1, *sl 1, k3, sl 1, k1; rep from * to end.
4th row: Using A k1, yf, sl 1, yb, k3, *yf, sl 1, yb, k1, yf, sl 1, yb, k3; rep from * to end.
5th row: Using B k2, sl 1, *k5, sl 1; rep from * to last 2 sts, k2.
6th row: Using B k2, yf, sl 1, yb, *k5, yf, sl 1, yb; rep from * to last 2 sts, k2.
7th row: Using A [k1, sl 1] twice, *k3, sl 1, k1, sl 1; rep from * to last st, k1.
8th row: Using A [k1, yf, sl 1, yb] twice, *k3, yf, sl 1, yb, k1, yf, sl 1, yb; rep from * to last st, k1.
9th row: Using B k4, sl 1, *k5, sl 1; rep from * to last 6 sts, k6.
10th row: Using B k6, yf, sl 1, yb, *k5, yf, sl 1, yb; rep from * to last 4 sts, k4.
11th row: Using A k1, sl 1, k3, *sl 1, k1, sl 1, k3; rep from * to end.
12th row: Using A k3, yf, sl 1, yb, k1, *yf, sl 1, yb, k3, yf, sl 1, yb, k1; rep from * to end.
Rep the last 12 rows.

Simulated Basketweave

Multiple of 10 sts + 5.
Note: Slip all sts purlwise.
Foundation row (wrong side): Using A purl.
Commence Pattern
1st row: Using B k4, sl 2, *k8, sl 2; rep from * to last 9 sts, k9.
2nd row: Using B p9, sl 2, *p8, sl 2; rep from * to last 4 sts, p4.
3rd row: Using A [k1, sl 1] twice, *k2, sl 1, k1, sl 1; rep from * to last st, k1.
4th row: Using A [p1, sl 1] twice, *p2, sl 1, p1, sl 1; rep from * to last st, p1.
5th row: Using B k9, sl 2, *k8, sl 2; rep from * to last 4 sts, k4.
6th row: Using B p4, sl 2, *p8, sl 2; rep from * to last 9 sts, p9.
7th row: Using A k1, sl 1, *k6, sl 1, k2, sl 1; rep from * to last 3 sts, k3.
8th row: Using A p3, sl 1, *p2, sl 1, p6, sl 1; rep from * to last st, p1.
9th row: As 5th row.
10th row: As 6th row.
11th row: As 3rd row.

12th row: As 4th row.
13th row: As 1st row.
14th row: As 2nd row.
15th row: Using A k3, sl 1, *k2, sl 1, k6, sl 1; rep from * to last st, k1.
16th row: Using A p1, sl 1, *p6, sl 1, p2, sl 1; rep from * to last 3 sts, p3.
Rep the last 16 rows.

Raised Brick Stitch

Multiple of 4 sts + 3.
Note: Slip all sts purlwise.
1st row (right side): K3, *sl 1, k3; rep from * to end.
2nd row: K3, *yf, sl 1, yb, k3; rep from * to end.
3rd row: K1, sl 1, *k3, sl 1; rep from * to last st, k1.
4th row: K1, yf, sl 1, yb, *k3, yf, sl 1, yb; rep from * to last st, k1.
Rep these 4 rows.

3-Colour Ladders

Multiple of 4 sts + 3.
Note: Slip all sts purlwise.
Foundation row (wrong side): Using A purl.
Commence Pattern
1st row: Using B k3, *sl 1, k3; rep from * to end.
2nd row: Using B k3, *yf, sl 1, yb, k3; rep from * to end.
3rd row: Using A k1, sl 1, *k3, sl 1; rep from * to last st, k1.
4th row: Using A p1, sl 1, *p3, sl 1; rep from * to last st, p1.

5th row: Using C as 1st row.
6th row: Using C as 2nd row.
7th row: As 3rd row.
8th row: As 4th row.
Rep the last 8 rows.

2-Colour Ladders

Multiple of 6 sts + 5.
Note: Slip all sts purlwise.
1st row (right side): Using A k2, sl 1, *k5, sl 1; rep from * to last 2 sts, k2.
2nd row: Using A p2, sl 1, *p5, sl 1; rep from * to last 2 sts, p2.
3rd row: Using B k5, *sl 1, k5; rep from * to end.
4th row: Using B k5, *yf, sl 1, yb, k5; rep from * to end.
Rep these 4 rows.

2-Colour Ladders with Twists

Multiple of 6 sts.
Note: Slip all sts purlwise.
1st Foundation row (right side): Using A knit.
2nd Foundation row: Using A purl.
Commence Pattern
1st row: Using B k2, sl 2, *k4, sl 2; rep from * to last 2 sts, k2.
2nd row: Using B k1, p1, sl 2, p1, *k2, p1, sl 2, p1; rep from * to last st, k1.
3rd row: Using A k1, C2F, C2B, *k2, C2F, C2B; rep from * to last st, k1.
4th row: Using A purl.
Rep the last 4 rows.

Patterns for Texture and Colour

Nubbly Tweed I

Multiple of 2 sts + 1.
Note: Slip all sts purlwise.
1st row (wrong side): Using A p1, *k1, p1; rep from * to end.
2nd row: Using B k1, *sl 1, k1; rep from * to end.
3rd row: Using B k1, *p1, k1; rep from * to end.
4th row: Using A k2, sl 1, *k1, sl 1; rep from * to last 2 sts, k2.
Rep these 4 rows.

Nubbly Tweed II

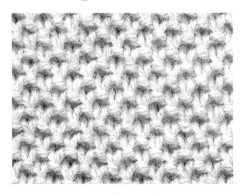

Work as Nubbly Tweed I but using one colour throughout.

Nubbly Tweed III

Multiple of 4 sts + 1.
Note: Slip all sts purlwise.
1st row (right side): Using B k4, sl 1, *k3, sl 1; rep from * to last 4 sts, k4.

2nd row: Using B k4, yf, sl 1, yb, *k3, yf, sl 1, yb; rep from * to last 4 sts, k4.
3rd row: Using A k1, *sl 1, k1; rep from * to end.
4th row: Using A k1, *yf, sl 1, yb; k1; rep from * to end.
Rep these 4 rows.

Tweed Checks

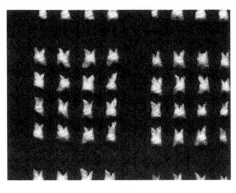

Multiple of 10 sts + 9.
Note: Slip all sts purlwise.
Using A work 4 rows in st st, starting knit (1st row is right side).
5th row: Using B k1, sl 1, k1, sl 3, *[k1, sl 1] 3 times, k1, sl 3; rep from * to last 3 sts, k1, sl 1, k1.
6th row: Using B k1, yf, sl 1, yb, k1, yf, sl 3, yb, *[k1, yf, sl 1, yb] 3 times, k1, yf, sl 3, yb; rep from * to last 3 sts, k1, yf, sl 1, yb, k1.
Using A work 2 rows in st st, starting knit.
Rep the last 4 rows twice more then 5th and 6th rows again.
Rep these 18 rows.

Basket Twists

Multiple of 8 sts + 5.
Special Abbreviation
Twist 3 = knit into front of 3rd st on left-hand needle, then knit 2nd st, then knit 1st st, slipping all 3 sts off needle together.
1st row (right side): P5, *Twist 3, p5; rep from * to end.
2nd row: K5, *p3, k5; rep from * to end.
Rep the last 2 rows once more.
5th row: P1, Twist 3, *p5, Twist 3; rep from * to last st, p1.
6th row: K1, p3, *k5, p3; rep from * to last st, k1.
Rep the last 2 rows once more.
Rep these 8 rows.

Slip Stitch Crosses

Multiple of 6 sts.
Note: Slip all sts purlwise.
1st Foundation row (right side): Using A knit.
2nd Foundation row: Using A purl.
Commence Pattern
1st row: Using B k2, *sl 2, k4; rep from * to last 4 sts, sl 2, k2.
2nd row: Using B p2, *sl 2, p4; rep from * to last 4 sts, sl 2, p2.
3rd row: Using A k1, C2F, C2B, *k2, C2F, C2B; rep from * to last st, k1.
4th row: Using A purl.
5th row: Using B k5, sl 2, *k4, sl 2; rep from * to last 5 sts, k5.
6th row: Using B p5, *sl 2, p4; rep from * to last 7 sts, sl 2, p5.
7th row: Using A k4, C2F, C2B, *k2, C2F, C2B; rep from * to last 4 sts, k4.
8th row: Using A purl.
Rep the last 8 rows.

Slip Stitch Zigzags

See Little Cable Fabric on page 43 of the Harmony Guide to Knitting Stitches.
Multiple of 4 sts + 1.
1st row (right side): Using A k1, *sl 1 purlwise, k3; rep from * to end.
2nd row: Using A *p3, sl 1 purlwise; rep from * to last st, p1.
3rd row: Using B k1, *C3L, k1; rep from * to end.
4th row: Using B purl.
5th row: Using A k5, *sl 1, k3; rep from * to end.
6th row: Using A *p3, sl 1; rep from * to last 5 sts, p5.

7th row: Using B k3, *C3R, k1; rep from * to last 2 sts, k2.
8th row: Using B purl.
Rep these 8 rows.

Snowballs

Multiple of 5 sts + 1.
Note: Sts should not be counted after 4th, 5th and 6th rows.
1st row (wrong side): Using A purl.
2nd row: Using A knit.
3rd row: Using A p1, *p1 wrapping yarn twice around needle, p2, p1 wrapping yarn twice around needle, p1; rep from * to end.
4th row: Using B k1, sl 1 (dropping extra loop), k2, sl 1 (dropping extra loop), *[k1, yf, k1, yf, k1] into next st, sl 1 (dropping extra loop), k2, sl 1 (dropping extra loop); rep from * to last st, k1.
5th row: Using B p1, sl 1, p2, sl 1, *yb, k5, yf, sl 1, p2, sl 1; rep from * to last st, p1.
6th row: Using B k1, sl 1, k2, sl 1, *yf, p5, yb, sl 1, k2, sl 1; rep from * to last st, k1.
7th row: Using B p1, sl 1, p2, sl 1, *yb, k2tog, k3tog, pass k2tog st over k3tog st, yf, sl 1, p2, sl 1; rep from * to last st, p1.
8th row: Using A k1, *drop first elongated st off needle, with yb sl 2, drop next elongated st off needle, with left-hand needle pick up first elongated st, pass the slipped sts from right-hand needle back to left-hand needle, then pick up second elongated st on left-hand needle, k5; rep from * to end.
Rep these 8 rows.

Trellis Stitch III

See Trellis Stitches I and II on page 34 of the Harmony Guide to Knitting Stitches.

Multiple of 6 sts + 5.
Special Abbreviation
Pull up loop = insert point of right-hand needle under the 2 strands of B, then knit the next st at the same time slipping the B strands over to the back of the work.
Using A cast on and work 1 row knit, 1 row purl.
Commence Pattern
1st row (right side): Using B p4, *keeping yarn at front sl 3 purlwise, p3; rep from * to last st, p1.
2nd row: Using B k4, *keeping yarn at back sl 3 purlwise, k3; rep from * to last st, k1.
3rd row: Using A knit.
4th row: Using A purl.
5th row: Using A k5, *pull up loop, k5; rep from * to end.
6th row: Using A purl.
7th row: Using B p1, *keeping yarn at front sl 3 purlwise, p3; rep from * to last 4 sts, sl 3 purlwise, p1.
8th row: Using B k1, *keeping yarn at back sl 3 purlwise, k3; rep from * to last 4 sts, sl 3, k1.
9th row: Using A knit.
10th row: Using A purl.
11th row: Using A, k2, *pull up loop, k5; rep from * to last 3 sts, pull up loop, k2.
12th row: Using A purl.
Rep the last 12 rows.

Trellis Stitch IV

Multiple of 6 sts + 5.
Special Abbreviation
Pull up loop = insert point of right-hand needle under the 2 strands of B, then knit the next st at the same time slipping the B strands over to the back of the work.
Cast on using A and work 1 row knit, 1 row purl.
Commence Pattern
1st row (right side): Using B, k4, *yf, sl 3 purlwise, yb, k3; rep from * to last st, k1.
2nd row: Using B p4, *yb, sl 3 purlwise, yf, p3; rep from * to last st, p1.
3rd row: Using A knit.
4th row: Using A purl.
5th row: Using A k5, *pull up loop, k5; rep from * to end.
6th row: Using A purl.
7th row: Using B k1, *yf, sl 3 purlwise, yb, k3; rep from * to last 4 sts, yf, sl 3 purlwise, yb, k1.
8th row: Using B p1, *yb, sl 3 purlwise, yf, p3; rep from * to last 4 sts, yb, sl 3 purlwise, yf, p1.
9th row: Using A knit.
10th row: Using A purl.
11th row: Using A, k2, *pull up loop, k5; rep from * to last 3 sts, pull up loop, k2.
12th row: Using A purl.
Rep the last 12 rows.

Slip Stitch Bubbles I

Multiple of 8 sts + 4.
Note: Slip all sts purlwise.
1st row (right side): Knit.
2nd row: Purl.
3rd row: P1, yb, sl 2, yf, *p6, yb, sl 2, yf; rep from * to last st, p1.
4th row: K1, yf, sl 2, yb, *k6, yf, sl 2, yb; rep from * to last st, k1.
Rep the last 2 rows twice more.
9th row: Knit.
10th row: Purl.
11th row: P5, yb, sl 2, yf, *p6, yb, sl 2, yf; rep from * to last 5 sts, p5.
12th row: K5, yf, sl 2, yb, *k6, yf, sl 2, yb; rep from * to last 5 sts, k5.
Rep the last 2 rows twice more.
Rep these 16 rows.

Slip Stitch Bubbles II

Worked as Slip Stitch Bubbles I, using reverse side as right side.

Patterns for Texture and Colour

Slip Stitch Bubbles with Garter Stitch

Multiple of 6 sts + 4.
Note: Slip all sts purlwise.
1st row (right side): Knit.
2nd row: K1, yf, sl 2, yb, *k4, yf, sl 2, yb; rep from * to last st, k1.
3rd row: K1, sl 2, *k4, sl 2; rep from * to last st, k1.
Rep the last 2 rows once more.
6th row: As 2nd row.
7th row: Knit.
8th row: K4, *yf, sl 2, yb, k4; rep from * to end.
9th row: K4, *sl 2, k4; rep from * to end.
Rep the last 2 rows once more.
12th row: As 8th row.
Rep these 12 rows.

Bubble Pattern I

Multiple of 4 sts + 3.
Special Abbreviation
K5B (Knit 5th St Below) = slip next st off left-hand needle and drop 4 rows down. Insert point of right-hand needle under strands and into the st on the 5th row down, insert left-hand needle under the strands and into the stitch. Knit the st normally catching the strands at the same time.
Cast on and purl 1 row.
Commence Pattern
Work 4 rows in st st, starting knit (1st row is right side).
5th row: K3, *K5B, k3; rep from * to end.
6th row: Purl.
Work 4 rows in st st, starting knit.
11th row: K1, *K5B, k3; rep from * to last 2 sts, K5B, k1.

12th row: Purl.
Rep the last 12 rows.

Bubble Pattern II

Worked as Bubble Pattern I, but using 3 colours.
Cast on and purl 1 row in A.
Commence Pattern
Work 4 rows in B, 2 rows in A, 4 rows in C, 2 rows in A.
Rep the last 12 rows.

Bubble Pattern III

Multiple of 4 sts + 3.
Special Abbreviation
K5B (Knit 5th St Below) = slip next st off left-hand needle and drop 4 rows down. Insert point of right-hand needle under strands and into the st on the 5th row down, insert left-hand needle under the strands and into the stitch. Knit the st normally catching the strands at the same time.
Cast on and knit 1 row in A.
Commence Pattern
Using B work 4 rows in st st, starting knit.
5th row: Using A k3, *K5B, k3; rep from * to end.
6th row: Using A knit.
Using C work 4 rows in st st, starting knit.
11th row: Using A k1, *K5B, k3; rep from * to last 2 sts, K5B, k1.
12th row: Using A knit.
Rep the last 12 rows.

Basket Stitch

Multiple of 10 sts + 7.
Note: Slip all sts purlwise.
Work 3 rows in reversed st st, starting knit (1st row is wrong side).
4th row: K6, sl 5, *k5, sl 5; rep from * to last 6 sts, k6.
5th row: P6, sl 5, *p5, sl 5; rep from * to last 6 sts, p5.
Rep the last 2 rows once more then 4th row again.
Work 3 rows in reversed st st, starting knit.
12th row: K1, sl 5, *k5, sl 5; rep from * to last st, k1.
13th row: P1, sl 5, *p5, sl 5; rep from * to last st, p1.
Rep the last 2 rows once more then the 12th row again.
Rep these 16 rows.

3-Colour Honeycomb I

Multiple of 8 sts + 4.
Note: Slip all sts purlwise.
1st and 2nd rows: Using A knit (1st row is right side).
3rd row: Using B k1, sl 2, *k6, sl 2; rep from * to last st, k1.
4th row: Using B p1, sl 2, *p6, sl 2; rep from * to last st, p1.
Rep the last 2 rows twice more.
9th and 10th rows: Using A knit.
11th row: Using C k5, sl 2, *k6, sl 2; rep from * to last 5 sts, k5.
12th row: Using C p5, sl 2, *p6, sl 2; rep from * to last 5 sts, p5.
Rep the last 2 rows twice more.
Rep these 16 rows.

3-Colour Honeycomb II

Multiple of 8 sts + 4.
Note: Slip all sts purlwise.
1st row (right side): Using A knit.
2nd row: Using A purl.
3rd row: Using B k1, sl 2, *k6, sl 2; rep from * to last st, k1.
4th row: Using B p1, sl 2, *p6, sl 2; rep from * to last st, p1.
Rep the last 2 rows twice more.
9th row: Using A knit.
10th row: Using A purl.
11th row: Using C k5, sl 2, *k6, sl 2; rep from * to last 5 sts, k5.
12th row: Using C p5, sl 2, *p6, sl 2; rep from * to last 5 sts, p5.
Rep the last 2 rows twice more.
Rep these 16 rows.

Brick Pattern I

Multiple of 6 sts + 3.
Note: Slip all sts purlwise.
1st row (right side): Using A knit.
2nd row: Using A purl.
3rd row: Using B k4, sl 1, *k5, sl 1; rep from * to last 4 sts, k4.
4th row: Using B k4, yf, sl 1, yb, *k5, yf, sl 1, yb; rep from * to last 4 sts, k4.
5th row: Using B p4, yb, sl 1, yf, *p5, yb, sl 1, yf; rep from * to last 4 sts, p4.
6th row: As 4th row.
7th row: Using A knit.
8th row: Using A purl.
9th row: Using B k1, sl 1, *k5, sl 1; rep from * to last st, k1.
10th row: Using B k1, yf, sl 1, yb, *k5, yf, sl 1, yb; rep from * to last st, k1.

11th row: Using B p1, yb, sl 1, yf, *p5, yb, sl 1, yf; rep from * to last st, p1.
12th row: As 10th row.
Rep these 12 rows.

Brick Pattern II

Multiple of 16 sts + 7.
Note: Slip all sts purlwise.
1st row (right side): Using A knit.
2nd row: Using A purl.
3rd row: Using B k2, sl 3, *k13, sl 3; rep from * to last 2 sts, k2.
4th row: Using B k2, yf, sl 3, yb, *k13, yf, sl 3, yb; rep from * to last 2 sts, k2.
5th row: Using B p2, yb, sl 3, yf, *p13, yb, sl 3, yf; rep from * to last 2 sts, p2.
Rep the last 2 rows twice more then 4th row again.
Using A work 4 rows in st st, starting knit.
15th row: Using B k10, sl 3, *k13, sl 3; rep from * to last 10 sts, k10.
16th row: Using B k10, yf, sl 3, yb, *k13, yf, sl 3, yb; rep from * to last 10 sts, k10.
17th row: Using B p10, yb, sl 3, yf, *p13, yb, sl 3, yf; rep from * to last 10 sts, p10.
Rep the last 2 rows twice more then 16th row again.
23rd row: Using A knit.
24th row: Using A purl.
Rep these 24 rows.

Surface Quilting Stitch I

Multiple of 10 sts + 7.
Note: Slip all sts purlwise.
Cast on in A and purl 1 row.

Foundation row (right side): Using B k6, sl 2, yf, sl 1, yb, sl 2, *k5, sl 2, yf, sl 1, yb, sl 2; rep from * to last 6 sts, k6.
Commence Pattern
1st row: Using B k6, sl 5, *k5, sl 5; rep from * to last 6 sts, k6.
Using A work 4 rows in st st, starting knit.
6th row: Using B k1, sl 2, yf, sl 1, yb, sl 2, *k2, insert point of right-hand needle upwards under loose strand in B in front of the slipped sts 4 rows down, place onto left-hand needle and knit this loop together with next st on left-hand needle tbl (called pull up loop), k2, sl 2, yf, sl 1, yb, sl 2; rep from * to last st, k1.
7th row: Using B k1, sl 5, *k5, sl 5; rep from * to last st, k1.
Using A work 4 rows in st st, starting knit.
12th row: Using B k3, pull up loop, *k2, sl 2, yf, sl 1, yb, sl 2, k2, pull up loop; rep from * to last 3 sts, k3.
Rep the last 12 rows.

Surface Quilting Stitch II

Multiple of 10 sts + 7.
Note: Slip all sts purlwise.
Cast on with A and purl 1 row.
Foundation row (right side): Using B k6, yf, sl 5, yb, *k5, yf, sl 5, yb; rep from * to last 6 sts, k6.
Commence pattern
1st row: Using B k6, sl 5, *k5, sl 5; rep from * to last 6 sts, k6.
Using A work 4 rows in st st, starting knit.
6th row: Using B k1, yf, sl 5, yb, *k2, insert point of right-hand needle upwards under loose strands in B in front of the slip sts 4 and 5 rows down, place onto left-hand needle and knit these loops together with next st on left-hand needle tbl (called pull up loops), k2, yf, sl 5, yb; rep from * to last st, k1.
7th row: Using B k1, sl 5, *k5, sl 5; rep from * to last st, k1.
Using A work 4 rows in st st, starting knit.
12th row: Using B k3, pull up loops, *k2, yf, sl 5, yb, k2, pull up loops; rep from * to last 3 sts, k3.
Rep the last 12 rows.

Patterns for Texture and Colour

Slip Stitch Plaid

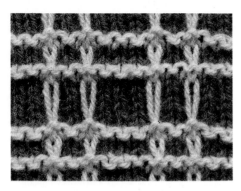

Multiple of 8 sts + 6.

Note: Slip all sts purlwise.

Special Abbreviation

KW = k1 wrapping yarn twice round needle.

Using A work 2 rows in garter st (1st row is right side).

3rd row: Using B k1, sl 1, k2, sl 1, *k4, sl 1, k2, sl 1; rep from * to last st, k1.

4th row: Using B p1, sl 1, p2, sl 1, *p4, sl 1, p2, sl 1; rep from * to last st, p1.

5th row: Using A knit.

6th row: Using A k1, KW, k2, KW, *k4, KW, k2, KW; rep from * to last st, k1.

7th row: Using B k1, sl 1, k2, sl 1, *k4, sl 1, k2, sl 1; rep from * to last st, k1 (dropping extra loops off needle when slipping sts).

8th row: As 4th row.

9th row: As 3rd row.

Rep the last 2 rows once more then 4th row again.

Rep these 12 rows.

2-Colour Herringbone Twists

Multiple of 8 sts + 2.

Note: Slip all sts purlwise.

1st Foundation row (wrong side): Using A k4, p2 wrapping yarn twice around needle for each st, *k6, p2 wrapping yarn twice around needle for each st; rep from * to last 4 sts, k4.

2nd Foundation row: Using A k4, sl 2 dropping extra loops, *k6, sl 2 as before; rep from * to last 4 sts, k4.

Commence Pattern

1st row: Using A k4, yf, sl 2, yb, *k6, yf, sl 2, yb; rep from * to last 4 sts, k4.

2nd row: Using A k4, sl 2, *k6, sl 2; rep from * to last 4 sts, k4.

3rd row: Using A k3, p1 wrapping yarn twice around needle (PW1), sl 2, PW1, *k4, PW1, sl 2, PW1; rep from * to last 3 sts, k3.

4th row: Using B k1, *slip next 3 sts onto cable needle dropping extra loop and hold at back of work, knit next st from left-hand needle, then k2 and sl 1 from cable needle, slip next st onto cable needle and hold at front of work, sl 1 dropping extra loop, k2 from left-hand needle, then knit st from cable needle; rep from * to last st, k1.

5th row: As 1st row but using B.

6th row: As 2nd row but using B.

7th Row: As 3rd row but using B.

8th row: As 4th row but using A.

Rep the last 8 rows.

Herringbone Twists

Worked as given for 2-Colour Herringbone Twists but using one colour only throughout.

Zigzag Chevron Stripes I

Multiple of 14 sts + 2.

1st row (wrong side): Using A purl.

2nd row: Using A k1, inc in next st (by knitting into front and back of st), k4, sl 1, k1, psso, k2tog, k4, *inc in each of next 2 sts, k4, sl 1, k1, psso, k2tog, k4; rep from * to last 2 sts, inc in next st, k1.

3rd row: Using A purl.

4th row: Using B as 2nd row.

5th row: Using B knit.

6th row: Using A knit.

7th row: Using A purl.

8th row: As 2nd row.

Rep these 8 rows.

Zigzag Chevron Stripes II

Multiple of 14 sts + 2.

Note: This example is worked using a multiple of 14 sts but any multiple of 2 can be added or subtracted to make the zig-zags wider or narrower.

1st row (wrong side): Using A purl.

2nd row: Using A k1, inc in next st (by knitting into front and back of st), k4, sl 1, k1, psso, k2tog, k4, *inc in each of next 2 sts, k4, sl 1, k1, psso, k2tog, k4; rep from * to last 2 sts, inc in next st, k1.

3rd row: Using A purl.

4th row: As 2nd row.

Rep the last 4 rows using B.

Rep these 8 rows.

Wigwams

Multiple of 16 sts.

1st row (right side): Knit.

2nd row: K4, p8, *k8, p8; rep from * to last 4 sts, k4.

3rd row: P3, k2tog, k3, pick up horizontal strand of yarn lying between stitch just worked and next st and knit into back and front of it (Inc 2), k3, sl 1, k1, psso, *p6, k2tog, k3, inc 2 as before, k3, sl 1, k1, psso; rep from * to last 3 sts, p3.

4th row: K3, p10, *k6, p10; rep from * to last 3 sts, k3.

5th row: P2, k2tog, k3, M1, k2, M1, k3, sl 1, k1, psso, *p4, k2tog, k3, M1, k2, M1, k3, sl 1, k1, psso; rep from * to last 2 sts, p2.

6th row: K2, p12, *k4, p12; rep from * to last 2 sts, k2.

7th row: P1, k2tog, k3, M1, k4, M1, k3, sl 1, k1, psso, *p2, k2tog, k3, M1, k4, M1, k3, sl 1, k1, psso; rep from * to last st, p1.

8th row: K1, p14, *k2, p14; rep from * to last st, k1.

9th row: *K2tog, k3, M1, k6, M1, k3, sl 1, k1, psso; rep from * to end.

10th row: Purl.

Rep these 10 rows.

Foxgloves

Multiple of 10 sts + 6.

Note: Sts should only be counted after the 10th row of pattern.

1st row (right side): P6, *yon, k1, p2, k1, yfrn, p6; rep from * to end.

2nd row: P6, *yrn, p2, k2, p2, yrn, p6; rep from * to end.

3rd row: P6, *yon, k3, p2, k3, yfrn, p6; rep from * to end.

4th row: P6, *yrn, p4, k2, p4, yrn, p6; rep from * to end.

5th row: P6, *k5, p2, k5, p6; rep from * to end.

6th row: P11, *k2, p11; rep from * to end.

7th row: P6, *sl 1, k1, psso, k3, p2, k3, k2tog, p6; rep from * to end.

8th row: P6, *p2tog, p2, k2, p2, p2tog tbl, p6; rep from * to end.

9th row: P6, *sl 1, k1, psso, k1, p2, k1, k2tog, p6; rep from * to end.

10th row: P6, *p2tog, k2, p2tog tbl, p6; rep from * to end.

Rep these 10 rows.

Butterfly Wings

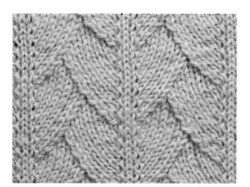

Multiple of 26 sts.

1st and every alt row (wrong side): Purl.

2nd row: K1, *M1, sl 1, k1, psso, k4, k2tog, k3, M1, k2, M1, k3, sl 1, k1, psso, k4, k2tog,

---

M1, k2; rep from * but ending last rep with k1 instead of k2.

4th row: K1, *M1, k1, sl 1, k1, psso, k2, k2tog, k4, M1, k2, M1, k4, sl 1, k1, psso, k2, k2tog, k1, M1, k2; rep from * but ending last rep with k1 instead of k2.

6th row: K1, *M1, k2, sl 1, k1, psso, k2tog, k5, M1, k2, M1, k5, sl 1, k1, psso, k2tog, k2, M1, k2; rep from * but ending last rep with k1 instead of k2.

8th row: K1, *M1, k3, sl 1, k1, psso, k4, k2tog, M1, k2, M1, sl 1, k1, psso, k4, k2tog, k3, M1, k2; rep from * but ending last rep with k1 instead of k2.

10th row: K1, *M1, k4, sl 1, k1, psso, k2, k2tog, k1, M1, k2, M1, k1, sl 1, k1, psso, k2, k2tog, k4, M1, k2; rep from * but ending last rep with k1 instead of k2.

12th row: K1, *M1, k5, sl 1, k1, psso, k2tog, [k2, M1] twice, k2, sl 1, k1, psso, k2tog, k5, M1, k2; rep from * but ending last rep with k1 instead of k2.

Rep these 12 rows.

Shell Pattern

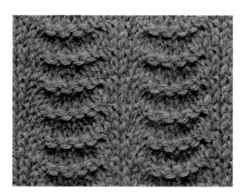

Multiple of 11 sts.

1st row (right side): Knit.

2nd row: Purl.

3rd row: [P2tog] twice, [inc 1 (by lifting horizontal thread lying between last st worked and next st and knitting into back of it), k1] 3 times, inc 1, *[p2tog] 4 times, [inc 1, k1] 3 times, inc 1; rep from * to last 4 sts, [p2tog] twice.

4th row: Purl.

Rep these 4 rows.

Coloured Turn Pattern

Multiple of 22 sts + 15.

Using A work 4 rows in st st, starting knit (1st row is right side).

5th row: Using B k2, turn pattern as follows: k7, turn, with yf sl 1, p2, turn, with yb sl 1, k4, turn, with yf sl 1, p6, turn, with yb sl 1, k8, turn, with yf sl 1, p10, turn, with yb sl 1, k10 (pattern completed), *k11, turn pattern as before; rep from * to last 2 sts, k2.

6th row: Using B k2, p11, *k11, p11; rep from * to last 2 sts, k2.

Using A work 4 rows in st st, starting knit.

11th row: Using B k13, turn pattern, *k11, turn pattern; rep from * to last 13 sts, k13.

12th row: Using B k13, p11, *k11, p11; rep from * to last 13 sts, k13.

Rep these 12 rows.

Pleat Pattern I

Multiple of 8 sts + 6.

Work 9 rows in st st, starting knit (1st row is right side).

Commence Pattern

1st row (wrong side): P5, *[with right-hand needle pick up loop of next st 7 rows below, place on left-hand needle, then purl together picked up loop and next st on left-hand needle] 4 times, p4; rep from * to last st, p1.

Work 7 rows in st st, starting knit.

9th row: P1, [pick up loop and purl as before] 4 times, *p4, [pick up loop and purl] 4 times; rep from * to last st, p1.

Work 7 rows in st st, starting knit.

Rep the last 16 rows.

Pleat Pattern II

Worked as Pleat Pattern I, using reverse side as right side.

Patterns for Texture and Colour

Fur Stitch

Multiple of 2 sts.

1st row (wrong side): Knit.

2nd row: *K1, k1 keeping st on left-hand needle bring yf, pass yarn over left thumb to make a loop (approx 4 cms) yb and knit this st again, slipping st off the needle, yfon pass the 2 sts just worked over this loop (1 loop made = ML); rep from * to last 2 sts, k2.

3rd row: Knit.

4th row: K2, *ML, k1; rep from * to end. Rep these 4 rows.

Large Trellis Pattern

Multiple of 12 sts.

Note: Sts should be cast on **loosely**.

Base Triangles: Using A *p2 (wrong side of work), turn and k2, turn and p3, turn and k3, turn and p4, turn and k4, continue in this way working 1 more st on every wrong side row until the row 'turn and p12' has been worked; rep from * to end. Break off A.

1st row of Rectangles: Using B k2, turn and p2, turn, inc in first st (by knitting into front and back of st), sl 1, k1, psso; turn and p3, turn, inc in first st, k1, sl 1, k1, psso, turn and p4, turn, inc in first st, k2, sl 1, k1, psso, turn and p5, turn, inc in first st, k3, sl 1, k1, psso, turn and p6, continue in this way working 1 more st on every right side row until the row 'inc in first st, k9, sl 1, k1, psso' has

been worked (1 edge triangle complete), then continue as follows: *pick up and k12 sts evenly along edge of next triangle, [turn and p12, turn and k11, sl 1, k1, psso] 12 times (1 rectangle complete); rep from * to edge of last triangle, pick up and k12 sts evenly along edge of last triangle, turn and p2tog, p10, turn and k11, turn and p2tog, p9, turn and k10, turn and p2tog, p8, turn and k9, continue in this way until the row 'turn and k2' has been worked, turn and p2tog (1 st remains on right-hand needle and edge triangle is complete). Break off B.

2nd row of Rectangles: Using A and continuing on from st on right-hand needle, pick up and p11 sts evenly along edge of triangle just worked, [turn and k12, turn and p11, p2tog] 12 times, then continue as follows: *pick up and p12 sts evenly along side of next rectangle, [turn and k12, turn and p11, p2tog] 12 times; rep from * to end. Break off A.

3rd row of Rectangles: As 1st row but picking sts up side edge of rectangles instead of triangles.

Rep 2nd and 3rd rows for pattern.

Final row of Triangles: Using A *continuing on from st on right-hand needle, pick up and p11 sts evenly along edge of triangle just worked, turn and k12, turn and p2tog, p9, p2tog, turn and k11, turn and p2tog, p8, p2tog, turn and k10, turn and p2tog, p7, p2tog, continue in this way working 1 st less on every wrong side row until the row 'turn and k3' has been worked, turn and [p2tog] twice, turn and k2, turn and p1, p2tog, p1, turn and k3, turn and p3tog; rep from * but picking up sts along side of rectangle instead of triangle. Fasten off remaining st.

Small Trellis Pattern

Multiple of 6 sts.

Note: Sts should be cast on **loosely**.

Base Triangles: Using A *p2 (wrong side of work), turn and k2, turn and p3, turn and k3, turn and p4, turn and k4, continue in this way working 1 more st on next and following alt row, thus ending with the row 'turn and p6'; rep from * to end. Break off A.

1st row of Rectangles: Using B k2, turn and p2, turn, inc in first st (by knitting into front and back of st), sl 1, k1, psso, turn and p3, turn, inc in first st, k1, sl 1, k1, psso, turn

and p4, turn, inc in first st, k2, sl 1, k1, psso, turn and p5, turn, inc in first st, k3, sl 1, k1, psso, (1 edge triangle complete), then continue as follows: *pick up and k6 sts evenly along edge of next triangle, [turn and p6, turn and k5, sl 1, k1, psso] 6 times (1 rectangle complete); rep from * to edge of last triangle, pick up and k6 sts evenly along edge of last triangle, turn and p2tog, p4, turn and k5, turn and p2tog, p3, turn and k4, turn and p2tog, p2, turn and k3, turn, p2tog, p1, turn and k2, turn and p2tog (1 st remains on right-hand needle and edge triangle is complete). Break off B.

2nd row of Rectangles: Using A and continuing on from st on right-hand needle, pick up and p5 sts evenly along edge of triangle just worked, [turn and k6, turn and p5, p2tog] 6 times, then continue as follows: *pick up and p6 sts evenly along side of next rectangle, [turn and k6, turn and p5, p2tog] 6 times; rep from * to end. Break off A.

3rd row of Rectangles: As 1st row but picking sts up side edge of rectangles instead of triangles.

Rep 2nd and 3rd rows for pattern.

Final row of Triangles: Using A *continuing on from st on right-hand needle, pick up and p5 sts evenly along edge of triangle just worked, turn and k6, turn and p2tog, p3, p2tog, turn and k5, turn and p2tog, p2, p2tog, turn and k4, turn and p2tog, p1, p2tog, turn and k3, turn and [p2tog] twice, turn and k2, turn and p1, p2tog, p1, turn and k3, turn and p3tog; rep from * but picking up sts along side of rectangle instead of triangle. Fasten off remaining st.

Reversible Stocking Stitch

Multiple of 2 sts.

Notes: This stitch must be worked on a circular needle or two double-pointed needles as the work is not turned at the end of rows 1 and 3.

When turning work make sure yarns are crossed around each other.

Slip all sts purlwise.

1st row: Using A *k1, yf, sl 1, yb; rep from * to end. Return to beg of row without turning work.

2nd row: Using B *yb, sl 1, yf, p1; rep from * to end, turn work.

3rd row: Using B as 1st row.

4th row: Using A as 2nd row.

Rep these 4 rows.

Reversible Checks

Multiple of 16 sts + 8.

Notes: This stitch must be worked on a circular needle or two double-pointed needles as the work is not turned on 1st and following alt rows.

When turning work make sure yarns are crossed around each other.

Slip all sts purlwise.

1st row: Using A [yb, k1, yf, sl 1] 4 times, *[yb, sl 1, yf, p1] 4 times, [yb, k1, yf, sl 1] 4 times; rep from * to end. Return to beg of row without turning work.

2nd row: Using B [yb, sl 1, yf, p1] 4 times, *[yb, k1, yf, sl 1] 4 times, [yb, sl 1, yf, p1] 4 times; rep from * to end. Turn work.

3rd row: Using B as 1st row.

4th row: Using A as 2nd row.

Rep last 4 rows once more.

9th row: Using B as 1st row.

10th row: Using A as 2nd row.

11th row: As 1st row.

12th row: As 2nd row.

Rep the last 4 rows once more.

Rep these 16 rows.

Reversible Motif

Multiple of 22 sts.

Notes: This stitch must be worked on a circular needle or two double-pointed needles as the work is not turned on 1st and following alt rows.

When turning work make sure yarns are crossed around each other.

Slip all sts purlwise.

1st row: Using A *yb, k1, yf, sl 1; rep from * to end. Return to beg of row without turning work.

2nd row: Using B *yb, sl 1, yf, p1; rep from * to end. Turn work.

3rd row: Using B as 1st row.

4th row: Using A as 2nd row.

Rep the last 4 rows twice more.

13th row: Using A [yb, k1, yf, sl 1] 4 times, [yb, sl 1, yf, p1] 3 times, *[yb, k1, yf, sl 1] 8 times, [yb, sl 1, yf, p1] 3 times; rep from * to last 8 sts, [yb, k1, yf, sl 1] 4 times. Do not turn.

14th row: Using B [yb, sl 1, yf, p1] 4 times, [yb, k1, yf, sl 1] 3 times, *[yb, sl 1, yf, p1] 8 times, [yb, k1, yf, sl 1] 3 times; rep from * to last 8 sts, [yb, sl 1, yf, p1] 4 times. Turn.

15th row: Using B as 13th row.

16th row: Using A as 14th row.

17th row: Using A [yb, k1, yf, sl 1] 3 times, [yb, sl 1, yf, p1] 5 times, *[yb, k1, yf, sl 1] 6 times, [yb, sl 1, yf, p1] 5 times; rep from * to last 6 sts, [yb, k1, yf, sl 1] 3 times. Do not turn.

18th row: Using B [yb, sl 1, yf, p1] 3 times, [yb, k1, yf, sl 1] 5 times, *[yb, sl 1, yf, p1] 6 times, [yb, k1, yf, sl 1] 5 times; rep from * to last 6 sts, [yb, sl 1, yf, p1] 3 times. Turn.

19th row: Using B as 17th row.

20th row: Using A as 18th row.

Rep the last 4 rows once more.

25th row: As 13th row.

26th row: As 14th row.

27th row: As 15th row.

28th row: As 16th row.

29th row: As 1st row.

30th row: As 2nd row.

31st row: As 3rd row.

32nd row: As 4th row.

Rep the last 4 rows twice more.

Rep these 40 rows.

Reversible Triangles I

Multiple of 12 sts + 10.

Notes: This stitch must be worked on a circular needle or two double-pointed needles as the work is not turned on 1st and following alt rows.

When turning work make sure yarns are crossed around each other.

Slip all sts purlwise.

1st row: Using A [yb, k1, yf, sl 1] 5 times, *yb, sl 1, yf, p1, [yb, k1, yf, sl 1] 5 times; rep from * to end. Return to beg of row without turning work.

2nd row: Using B [yb, sl 1, yf, p1] 5 times, *yb, k1, yf, sl 1, [yb, sl 1, yf, p1] 5 times; rep from * to end. Turn work.

3rd row: Using B as 1st row.

4th row: Using A as 2nd row.

5th row: Using A yb, sl 1, yf, p1, [yb, k1, yf, sl 1] 3 times, *[yb, sl 1, yf, p1] 3 times, [yb, k1, yf, sl 1] 3 times; rep from * to last 2 sts, yb, sl 1, yf, p1. Do not turn.

6th row: Using B yb, k1, yf, sl 1, [yb, sl 1, yf, p1] 3 times, *[yb, k1, yf, sl 1] 3 times, [yb, sl 1, yf, p1] 3 times; rep from * to last 2 sts, yb, k1, yf, sl 1, turn.

7th row: Using B as 5th row.

8th row: Using A as 6th row.

9th row: Using A [yb, sl 1, yf, p1] twice, yb, k1, yf, sl 1, *[yb, sl 1, yf, p1] 5 times, yb, k1, yf, sl 1; rep from * to last 4 sts, [yb, sl 1, yf, p1] twice. Do not turn work.

10th row: Using B [yb, k1, yf, sl 1] twice, *yb, sl 1, yf, p1, [yb, k1, yf, sl 1] 5 times, yb, sl 1, yf, p1; rep from * to last 4 sts, [yb, k1, yf, sl 1] twice, turn.

11th row: Using B as 9th row.

12th row: Using A as 10th row.

13th row: Using A as 10th row **but** do not turn work at end of row.

14th row: Using B as 9th row **but** turning work at end of row.

15th row: Using B as 10th row **but** do not turn work at end of row.

16th row: Using A as 9th row **but** turn work at end of row.

17th row: Using A as 6th row **but** do not turn work at end of row.

18th row: Using B as 5th row **but** turn work at end of row.

19th row: As 6th row **but** do not turn work at end of row.

20th row: As 5th row **but** turn work at end of row.

21st row: Using A as 2nd row **but** do not turn work at end of row.

22nd row: Using B as 1st row **but** turn work at end of row.

23rd row: Using B as 2nd row **but** do not turn work at end or row.

24th row: Using A as 1st row **but** turning work at end of row.

Rep these 24 rows.

Reversible Triangles II

Rep rows 1 to 12 only of Reversible Triangles I.

Edging Patterns

Picot Edging

Multiple of 2 sts + 1.

Note: This method can be used on either the cast on or cast off edge of fabric.

Work 4 rows in st st, starting knit.

5th row: K1, *yf, k2tog; rep from * to end.

Work 4 rows in st st, starting purl.

These 9 rows form the edging.

To Finish

Fold back edging along picot row and slip stitch in place.

Picot Point Cast Off

Used to cast off multiple of 3 sts + 2.

Cast off 2 sts, *slip remaining st on right-hand needle onto left-hand needle, cast on 2 sts, cast off 4 sts; rep from * to end and fasten off remaining st.

Picot Point Chain

Worked lengthways. Cast on 5 sts.

Note: Cast on using cable method.

*Cast off 4 sts, slip remaining st on right-hand needle onto left-hand needle, cast on 4 sts; rep from * until chain is of required length.

Chains of 5 or more picot points can be joined into circles. Several of these circles can be joined together and used in the same way as crochet wheels.

Crown Edging

Multiple of 5 sts.

Note: Cast on using cable method.

1st row: Knit.

2nd row: Cast off first 2 sts, *slip st remaining on right-hand needle onto left-hand needle, [cast on 2 sts, cast off next 2 sts, slip remaining st onto left-hand needle as before] 3 times, cast on 2 sts, cast off 6 sts; rep from * to end and fasten off remaining st.

These 2 rows form the edging.

Scalloped Edging in Garter Stitch

Worked lengthways. Cast on 7 sts.

Note: Increase by knitting into front and back of next st.

Foundation row: Knit.

Commence Pattern

1st row: K4, inc in next st, k2. (8 sts).

2nd row: K1, inc in next st, k6. (9 sts).

3rd row: K6, inc in next st, k2. (10 sts).

4th row: K1, inc in next st, k8. (11 sts).

5th row: K8, inc in next st, k2. (12 sts).

6th row: K1, inc in next st, k10. (13 sts).

7th row: K10, inc in next st, k2. (14 sts).

8th row: K1, inc in next st, k12. (15 sts).

9th row: K12, k2tog, k1. (14 sts).

10th row: K1, k2tog tbl, k11. (13 sts).

11th row: K10, k2tog, k1. (12 sts).

12th row: K1, k2tog tbl, k9. (11 sts).

13th row: K8, k2tog, k1. (10 sts).

14th row: K1, k2tog tbl, k7. (9 sts).

15th row: K6, k2tog, k1. (8 sts).

16th row: K1, k2tog tbl, k5. (7 sts).

Rep the last 16 rows.

Point Edging

Note: Each point is worked separately.

Cast on 2 sts.

1st row: K2.

2nd row: Yf (to make a stitch), k2.

3rd row: Yf, k3.

4th row: Yf, k4.

5th row: Yf, k5.

6th row: Yf, k6.

7th row: Yf, k7.

8th row: Yf, k8.

9th row: Yf, k9.

10th row: Yf, k10.

11th row: Yf, k11.

12th row: Yf, k12.

Rows 1 to 12 form one point. Break yarn and leave finished point on needle. On the same needle cast on 2 sts and work 2nd point. Continue in this way until there are as many points as desired. Do not break yarn after completing the last one but turn and knit across all points on needle. Work 9 rows in garter st.

To Finish

Sew back ends.

Castle Edging

Worked lengthways. Cast on 7 sts.

Note: Cast on using cable method.

Work 3 rows in garter st (every row knit — 1st row is right side).

4th row: Cast on 3 sts, knit across all sts. (10 sts).

Work 3 rows in garter st.

8th row: Cast on 3 sts, knit across all sts. (13 sts).

9th row: K1, *p1, k1; rep from * to end.

10th row: P1, *k1, p1; rep from * to end.

Rep the last 2 rows twice more then the 9th row again.

16th row: Cast off 3 sts knitwise, knit to end. (10 sts).

Work 3 rows in garter st.

20th row: Cast off 3 sts knitwise, knit to end. (7 sts).

Rep these 20 rows.

Two Colour Fringe

Worked lengthways. Cast on 12 sts using yarn double (1 strand each of A and B).

Note: The example shown is worked using 2 colours but this stitch can be worked using one single colour or 3 or more different colours.

1st row: K2, yf, k2tog, k1, yf, k2tog, k5.

2nd row: P4, k2, [yf, k2tog, k1] twice.

Rep these 2 rows ending with a 2nd row.

Final row: Cast off 8 sts, draw yarn through remaining st on right-hand needle. Slip remaining 3 sts off needle and unravel them all the way down to make fringe loops.

If desired, loops can be cut to single strands.

Cobweb Ruffle

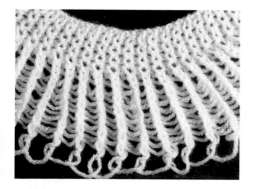

Multiple of 3 sts + 1.

1st row: KB1, *p2, KB1; rep from * to end.
2nd row: P1, *KB1, k1, p1; rep from * to end.

Rep the last 2 rows 5 times more.

13th row: KB1, *slip next st off needle and allow it to drop to cast on edge, p1, KB1; rep from * to end.

14th row: P1, *KB1, p1; rep from * to end.
15th row: KB1, *p1, KB1; rep from * to end.

Rep the last 2 rows twice more.
These 19 rows form the edging.

Bell Edging I

Cast on multiple of 12 sts + 3.

Note: 2 sts are decreased for every repeat on 3rd and following alt rows.

1st row (right side): P3, *k9, p3; rep from * to end.

2nd row: K3, *p9, k3; rep from * to end.
3rd row: P3, *yb, sl 1, k1, psso, k5, k2tog, p3; rep from * to end.
4th row: K3, *p7, k3; rep from * to end.
5th row: P3, *yb, sl 1, k1, psso, k3, k2tog, p3; rep from * to end.
6th row: K3, *p5, k3; rep from * to end.
7th row: P3, *yb, sl 1, k1, psso, k1, k2tog, p3; rep from * to end.
8th row: K3, *p3, k3; rep from * to end.
9th row: P3, *yb, sl 1, k2tog, psso, p3; rep from * to end.
10th row: K3, *p1, k3; rep from * to end.
11th row: P3, *k1, p3; rep from * to end.
12th row: As 10th row.
These 12 rows form the edging.

Bell Edging II

Multiple of 8 sts + 7.

Note: 2 sts are increased for each repeat on 3rd and following alt rows.

1st row (right side): P7, *k1, p7; rep from * to end.

2nd row: K7, *p1, k7; rep from * to end.
3rd row: P7, *yon, k1, yfrn, p7; rep from * to end.
4th row: K7, *p3, k7; rep from * to end.
5th row: P7, *yon, k3, yfrn, p7; rep from * to end.
6th row: K7, *p5, k7; rep from * to end.
7th row: P7, *yon, k5, yfrn, p7; rep from * to end.
8th row: K7, *p7, k7; rep from * to end.
9th row: P7, *yon, k7, yfrn, p7; rep from * to end.
10th row: K7, *p9, k7; rep from * to end.
11th row: P7, *yon, k9, yfrn, p7; rep from * to end.
12th row: K7, *p11, k7; rep from * to end.
13th row: P7, *yon, k11, yfrn, p7; rep from * to end.
14th row: K7, *p13, k7; rep from * to end.
These 14 rows form the edging.

Lace Bells

Cast on multiple of 14 sts + 3 thumb method.

Note: 2 sts are decreased for every repeat on 5th and following alt rows.

Work 2 rows in garter st (1st row is right side).

3rd row: P3, *k11, p3; rep from * to end.
4th row: K3, *p11, k3; rep from * to end.
5th row: P3, *yb, sl 1, k1, psso, k2, yf, sl 1, k2tog, psso, yf, k2, k2tog, p3; rep from * to end.
6th row: K3, *p9, k3; rep from * to end.
7th row: P3, *yb, sl 1, k1, psso, k1, yf, sl 1, k2tog, psso, yf, k1, k2tog, p3; rep from * to end.
8th row: K3, *p7, k3; rep from * to end.
9th row: P3, *yb, sl 1, k1, psso, yf, sl 1, k2tog, psso, yf, k2tog, p3; rep from * to end.
10th row: K3, *p5, k3; rep from * to end.
11th row: P3, *yb, sl 1, k1, psso, k1, k2tog, p3; rep from * to end.
12th row: K3, *p3, k3; rep from * to end.
13th row: P3, *yb, sl 1, k2tog, psso, p3; rep from * to end.
14th row: K3, *p1, k3; rep from * to end.
15th row: P3, *k1, p3; rep from * to end.
16th row: As 14th row.
These 16 rows form the edging.

Edging Patterns

Laburnum Edging

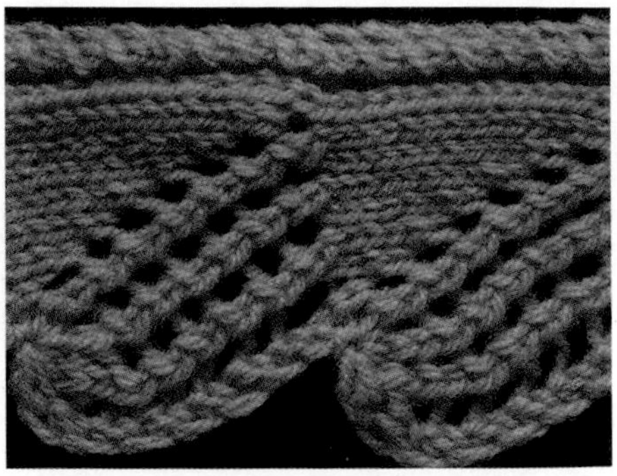

Worked lengthways. Cast on 13 sts.

1st row (right side): K2, yfrn, p2tog, k1, [yf, sl 1, k1, psso] 3 times, [yf] twice (to make 2 sts), k2tog. (14 sts).

2nd row: Yf (to make 1 st), k2tog, p9, yrn, p2tog, k1.

3rd row: K2, yfrn, p2tog, k2, [yf, sl 1, k1, psso] 3 times, [yf] twice, k2tog. (15 sts).

4th row: Yf, k2tog, p10, yrn, p2tog, k1.

5th row: K2, yfrn, p2tog, k3, [yf, sl 1, k1, psso] 3 times, [yf] twice, k2tog. (16 sts).

6th row: Yf, k2tog, p11, yrn, p2tog, k1.

7th row: K2, yfrn, p2tog, k4, [yf, sl 1, k1, psso] 3 times, [yf] twice, k2tog. (17 sts).

8th row: Yf, k2tog, p12, yrn, p2tog, k1.

9th row: K2, yfrn, p2tog, k5, [yf, sl 1, k1, psso] 3 times, [yf] twice, k2tog. (18 sts).

10th row: Yf, k2tog, p13, yrn, p2tog, k1.

11th row: K2, yfrn, p2tog, k6, [yf, sl 1, k1, psso] 3 times, [yf] twice, k2tog. (19 sts).

12th row: Yf, k2tog, p14, yrn, p2tog, k1.

13th row: K2, yfrn, p2tog, k7, [yf, sl 1, k1, psso] 3 times, [yf] twice, k2tog. (20 sts).

14th row: Yf, k2tog, p15, yrn, p2tog, k1.

15th row: K2, yfrn, p2tog, k8, yf, k1, slip last st worked back onto left-hand needle and with point of right-hand needle lift next 7 sts over this st and off needle, then slip st back onto right-hand needle. (14 sts).

16th row: P2tog, p9, yrn, p2tog, k1. (13 sts).

Rep these 16 rows.

Scalloped Shell Edging I

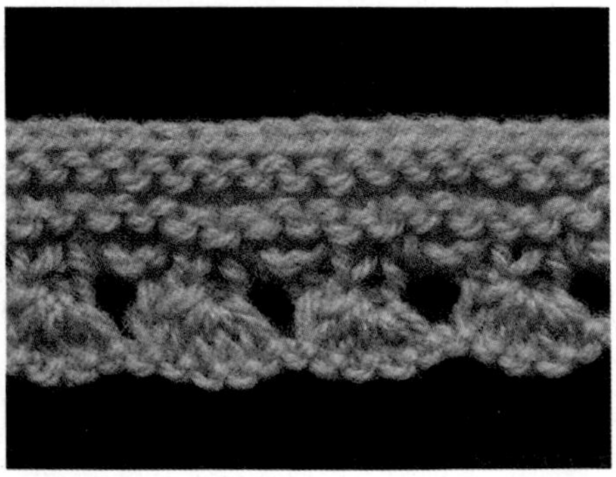

Multiple of 5 sts + 2.

Note: Cast on using thumb method.

1st row (right side): K1, yf, *k5, slip successively the 2nd, 3rd, 4th and 5th sts just worked over the 1st and off needle, yf; rep from * to last st, k1.

2nd row: P1, *[p1, yon, KB1] into next st, p1; rep from * to end.

3rd row: K2, KB1, *k3, KB1; rep from * to last 2 sts, k2.

Work 3 rows in garter st.

These 6 rows form the edging.

Scalloped Shell Edging II

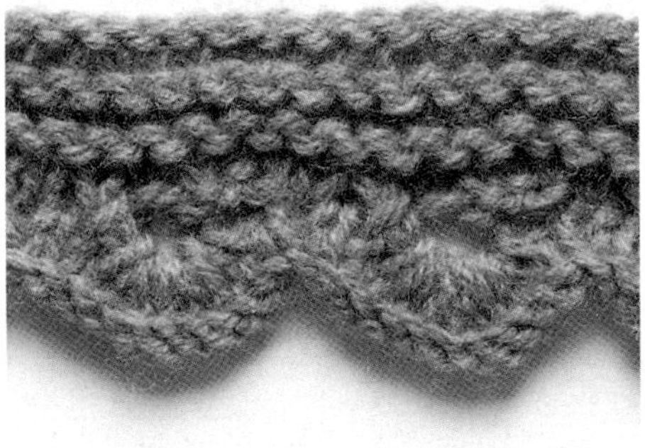

Multiple of 11 sts + 2.

Note: Cast on using thumb method.

1st row (right side): Purl.

2nd row: K2, *k1, slip this st back onto left-hand needle, lift the next 8 sts on left-hand needle over this st and off needle, [yf] twice, knit the first st again, k2; rep from * to end.

3rd row: K1, *p2tog, drop loop of 2 sts made in previous row and [k1, KB1] twice into it, p1; rep from * to last st, k1.

Work 5 rows in garter st (every row knit).

These 8 rows form the edging.

Double Beaded Edge

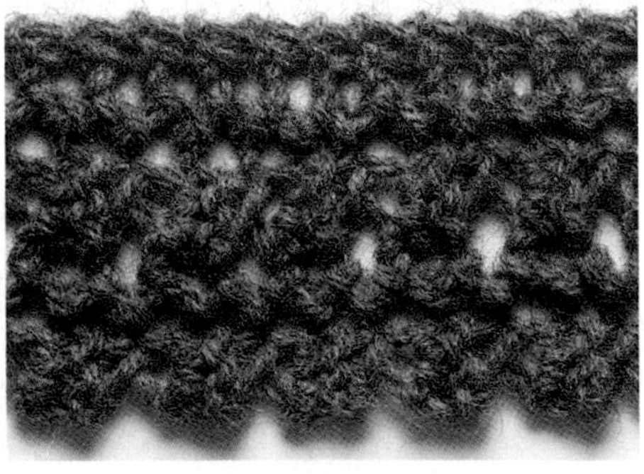

Worked lengthways. Cast on 8 sts.

1st row (right side): Sl 1, k1, *yfrn, p2tog, [k1, p1, k1] into next st; rep from * once more. (12 sts).

2nd row: [K3, yfrn, p2tog] twice, k2.

3rd row: Sl 1, k1, [yfrn, p2tog, k3] twice.

4th row: Cast off 2 sts knitwise (1 st remains on right-hand needle), yfrn, p2tog, cast off next 2 sts knitwise (4 sts on right-hand needle), yfrn, p2tog, k2.

Rep these 4 rows.

Zigzag Filigree Edging

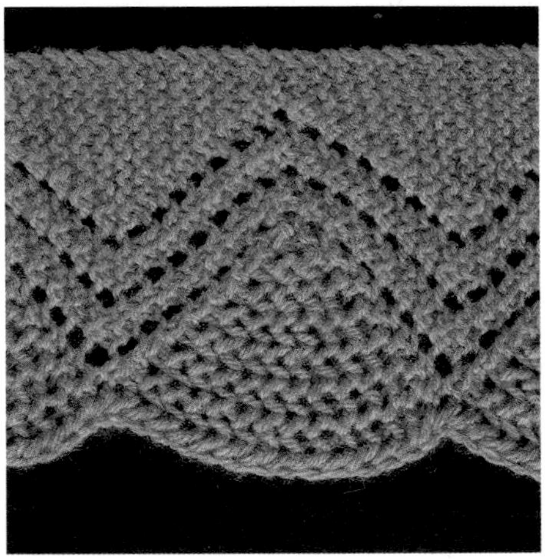

Worked lengthways. Cast on 20 sts.

1st row (right side): K9, [k2tog, yf, k1] 3 times, yf, sl 1, k1, psso.

2nd row: Yfon (to make 1 st), sl 1, k1, psso, k18.

3rd row: K8, [k2tog, yf, k1] 3 times, yf, k1, yf, sl 1, k1, psso. (21 sts).

4th row: Yfon, sl 1, k1, psso, yf, sl 1, k1, psso, k17.

5th row: K7, [k2tog, yf, k1] 3 times, yf, k1, [yf, sl 1, k1, psso] twice. (22 sts).

6th row: Yfon, sl 1, k1, psso, [yf, sl 1, k1, psso] twice, k16.

7th row: K6, [k2tog, yf, k1] 3 times, yf, k1, [yf, sl 1, k1, psso] 3 times. (23 sts).

8th row: Yfon, sl 1, k1, psso, [yf, sl 1, k1, psso] 3 times, k15.

9th row: K5, [k2tog, yf, k1] 3 times, yf, k1, [yf, sl 1, k1, psso] 4 times. (24 sts).

10th row: Yfon, sl 1, k1, psso, [yf, sl 1, k1, psso] 4 times, k14.

11th row: K4, [k2tog, yf, k1] 3 times, yf, k1, [yf, sl 1, k1, psso] 5 times. (25 sts).

12th row: Yfon, sl 1, k1, psso, [yf, sl 1, k1, psso] 5 times, k13.

13th row: K3, [k2tog, yf, k1] 3 times, yf, k1, [yf, sl 1, k1, psso] 6 times. (26 sts).

14th row: Yfon, sl 1, k1, psso, [yf, sl 1, k1, psso] 6 times, k12.

15th row: K2, [k2tog, yf, k1] 3 times, yf, k1, [yf, sl 1, k1, psso] 7 times. (27 sts).

16th row: Yfon, sl 1, k1, psso, [yf, sl 1, k1, psso] 7 times, k11.

17th row: K4, yf, [k2tog, k1, yf] twice, sl 1, k2tog, psso, [yf, sl 1, k1, psso] 7 times. (26 sts).

18th row: Yfon, sl 1, k1, psso, [yf, sl 1, k1, psso] 6 times, k12.

19th row: K5, yf, [k2tog, k1, yf] twice, sl 1, k2tog, psso, [yf, sl 1, k1, psso] 6 times. (25 sts).

20th row: Yfon, sl 1, k1, psso, [yf, sl 1, k1, psso] 5 times, k13.

21st row: K6, yf, [k2tog, k1, yf] twice, sl 1, k2tog, psso, [yf, sl 1, k1, psso] 5 times. (24 sts).

22nd row: Yfon, sl 1, k1, psso, [yf, sl 1, k1, psso] 4 times, k14.

23rd row: K7, yf, [k2tog, k1, yf] twice, sl 1, k2tog, psso, [yf, sl 1, k1, psso] 4 times. (23 sts).

24th row: Yfon, sl 1, k1, psso, [yf, sl 1, k1, psso] 3 times, k15.

25th row: K8, yf, [k2tog, k1, yf] twice, sl 1, k2tog, psso, [yf, sl 1, k1, psso] 3 times. (22 sts).

26th row: Yfon, sl 1, k1, psso, [yf, sl 1, k1, psso] twice, k16.

27th row: K9, yf, [k2tog, k1, yf] twice, sl 1, k2tog, psso, [yf, sl 1, k1, psso] twice. (21 sts).

28th row: Yfon, sl 1, k1, psso, yf, sl 1, k1, psso, k17.

29th row: K10, yf, [k2tog, k1, yf] twice, sl 1, k2tog, psso, yf, sl 1, k1, psso. (20 sts).

30th row: Yfon, sl 1, k1, psso, k18.

Rep these 30 rows.

5th row: K1, yf, k2tog, yf, k3, yf, sl 1, k1, psso, k2, yf, sl 1, k1, psso, k3, yf, k2tog, k2. (20 sts).

6th row: P3, yrn, p2tog, p15.

7th row: K1, yf, k2tog, yf, k3, [yf, sl 1, k1, psso] twice, k2, yf, sl 1, k1, psso, k2, yf, k2tog, k2. (21 sts).

8th row: P3, yrn, p2tog, p16.

9th row: K1, yf, k2tog, yf, k3, [yf, sl 1, k1, psso] 3 times, k2, yf, sl 1, k1, psso, k1, yf, k2tog, k2. (22 sts).

10th row: P3, yrn, p2tog, p17.

11th row: Sl 1, k1, psso, [yf, sl 1, k1, psso] twice, k2, [yf, sl 1, k1, psso] twice, k1, k2tog, yf, k3, yf, k2tog, k2. (21 sts).

12th row: P3, yrn, p2tog, p16.

13th row: Sl 1, k1, psso, [yf, sl 1, k1, psso] twice, k2, yf, sl 1, k1, psso, k1, k2tog, yf, k4, yf, k2tog, k2. (20 sts).

14th row: P3, yrn, p2tog, p15.

15th row: Sl 1, k1, psso, [yf, sl 1, k1, psso] twice, k3, k2tog, yf, k5, yf, k2tog, k2. (19 sts).

16th row: P3, yrn, p2tog, p14.

17th row: Sl 1, k1, psso, [yf, sl 1, k1, psso] twice, k1, k2tog, yf, k6, yf, k2tog, k2. (18 sts).

18th row: P3, yrn, p2tog, p13.

19th row: Sl 1, k1, psso, yf, sl 1, k1, psso, k1, k2tog, yf, k7, yf, k2tog, k2. (17 sts).

20th row: P3, yrn, p2tog, p12.

Rep the last 20 rows.

Butterfly Edging

Worked lengthways. Cast on 8 sts.

1st row (right side): Sl 1, k2, yf, k2tog, [yf] twice (to make 2 sts), k2tog, k1. (9 sts).

2nd row: K3, p1, k2, yf, k2tog, k1.

3rd row: Sl 1, k2, yf, k2tog, k1, [yf] twice, k2tog, k1. (10 sts).

4th row: K3, p1, k3, yf, k2tog, k1.

5th row: Sl 1, k2, yf, k2tog, k2, [yf] twice, k2tog, k1. (11 sts).

6th row: K3, p1, k4, yf, k2tog, k1.

7th row: Sl 1, k2, yf, k2tog, k6.

8th row: Cast off 3 sts (1 st on right-hand needle), k4, yf, k2tog, k1. (8 sts).

Rep these 8 rows.

Ornamental Diamond Edging

Worked lengthways. Cast on 17 sts.

1st foundation row (right side): K1, yf, sl 1, k1, psso, k1, k2tog, yf, k7, yf, k2tog, k2.

2nd foundation row: P3, yrn, p2tog, p12.

Commence Pattern

1st row: K1, yf, k2tog, yf, k3, yf, sl 1, k1, psso, k5, yf, k2tog, k2. (18 sts).

2nd row: P3, yrn, p2tog, p13.

3rd row: K1, yf, k2tog, yf, k5, yf, sl 1, k1, psso, k4, yf, k2tog, k2. (19 sts).

4th row: P3, yrn, p2tog, p14.

Lacy Arrow Edging

Worked lengthways. Cast on 21 sts.

1st row (right side): K3, yf, k2tog, p2, yon, sl 1, k1, psso, k3, k2tog, yfrn, p2, k1, yf, k2tog, k2.

2nd and every alt row: K3, yf, k2tog tbl, k2, p7, k3, yf, k2tog tbl, k2.

3rd row: K3, yf, k2tog, p2, k1, yf, sl 1, k1, psso, k1, k2tog, yf, k1, p2, k1, yf, k2tog, k2.

5th row: K3, yf, k2tog, p2, k2, yf, sl 1, k2tog, psso, yf, k2, p2, k1, yf, k2tog, k2.

6th row: As 2nd row.

Rep these 6 rows.

Scalloped Eyelet Edging

Worked lengthways. Cast on 11 sts.

1st row (right side): Sl 1, k2, yfrn, p2tog, yon, sl 1, k1, psso, [yf, sl 1, k1, psso] twice.

2nd row: Yfrn (to make 1 st), *p1, [k1, p1] into next st (made st of previous row); rep from * twice more, p2, yrn, p2tog, KB1. (15 sts).

3rd row: Sl 1, k2, yfrn, p2tog, k10.

4th row: Sl 1, p11, yrn, p2tog, KB1.

5th row: Sl 1, k2, yfrn, p2tog, k10.

6th row: Cast off 4 sts purlwise (1 st remains on right-hand needle), p7, yrn, p2tog, KB1. (11 sts).

Rep these 6 rows.

Edging Patterns

Lacy Leaf Edging

Worked lengthways. Cast on 13 sts.
1st row (right side): K1, sl 1, k2tog, psso, yf, k5, yf, KB1, yf, sl 1, k1, psso, k1.
2nd and every alt row: Purl.
3rd row: K1, KB1, yf, k1, k2tog tbl, p1, yb, sl 1, k1, psso, k1, yf, KB1, yf, sl 1, k1, psso, k1.
5th row: As 3rd row.
7th row: K1, sl 1, k1, psso, yf, k2tog tbl, p1, yb, sl 1, k1, psso, [yf, KB1] twice, yf, sl 1, k1, psso, k1.
9th row: K1, sl 1, k1, psso, yf, k3tog tbl, yf, k3, yf, KB1, yf, sl 1, k1, psso, k1.
10th row: Purl.
Rep these 10 rows.

Fancy Leaf Edging

Worked lengthways. Cast on 17 sts.
1st row (right side): K3, yfrn, p2tog, yrn, p2tog, yon, KB1, k2tog, p1, yb, sl 1, k1, psso, KB1, yf, k3.
2nd row: K3, p3, k1, p3, k2, yfrn, p2tog, yrn, p2tog, k1.
Rep the last 2 rows once more.
5th row: K3, yfrn, p2tog, yrn, p2tog, yon, KB1, yf, k2tog, p1, yb, sl 1, k1, psso, yf, k4. (18 sts).
6th row: K4, p2, k1, p4, k2, yfrn, p2tog, yrn, p2tog, k1.
7th row: K3, yfrn, p2tog, yrn, p2tog, yon, KB1, k1, KB1, yf, sl 1, k2tog, psso, yf, k5. (19 sts).
8th row: K5, p7, k2, yfrn, p2tog, yrn, p2tog, k1.
9th row: K3, yfrn, p2tog, yrn, p2tog, yon, KB1, k3, KB1, yf, k7. (21 sts).
10th row: Cast off 4 sts (1 st remains on right-hand needle), k2, p7, k2, yfrn, p2tog,

yrn, p2tog, k1. (17 sts).
Rep these 10 rows.

Puff Ball Cluster Edging

Worked lengthways. Cast on 13 sts.
Special Abbreviation
Yf2 = yarn forward twice to make 2 sts.
1st row (right side): K2, k2tog, yf2, k2tog, k7.
2nd row: K9, p1, k3.
3rd and 4th rows: Knit.
5th row: K2, k2tog, yf2, k2tog, k2, [yf2, k1] 3 times, yf2, k2. (21 sts).
6th row: K3, [p1, k2] 3 times, p1, k4, p1, k3.
7th and 8th rows: Knit.
9th row: K2, k2tog, yf2, k2tog, k15.
10th row: Knit 12 sts wrapping yarn twice round needle for each st, yf2, k5, p1, k3. (23 sts).
11th row: K10, [p1, k1] into next st, slip next 12 sts to right-hand needle dropping extra loops. Return sts to left-hand needle then k12tog. (13 sts).
12th row: Knit.
Rep these 12 rows.

Antique Edging

Worked lengthways. Cast on 13 sts.
1st row (wrong side): K2, yf, sl 1, k1, psso, yf, k1, yf, sl 1, k2tog, psso, yf, k3, yf, k2. (15 sts).
2nd row: K4, [k1, p1] 3 times into next st, p2, k1, p3, k4. (20 sts).
3rd row: K2, yf, sl 1, k1, psso, [k1, p1] 3 times into next st, yb, sl 1, k1, psso, p1,

k2tog, cast off next 5 sts, knit to last 2 sts, yf, k2. (19 sts).
4th row: K5, yf, [k1, p1] twice, cast off next 5 sts, knit to end. (15 sts).
5th row: K2, yf, sl 1, k1, psso, yf, k1, yf, sl 1, k2tog, psso, yf, k3, yf, k2tog, yf, k2. (17 sts).
6th row: K6, [k1, p1] 3 times into next st, p2, k1, p3, k4. (22 sts).
7th row: K2, yf, sl 1, k1, psso, [k1, p1] 3 times into next st, yb, sl 1, k1, psso, p1, k2tog, cast off next 5 sts, knit to last 4 sts, yf, k2tog, yf, k2. (21 sts).
8th row: Cast off 4 sts (1 st on right-hand needle after casting off), k2, yfrn, p2, k1, p1, cast off next 5 sts, knit to end. (13 sts).
Rep these 8 rows.

Fern and Bobble Edging

Worked lengthways. Cast on 21 sts.
1st row (right side): K2, k2tog, [yf] twice (to make 2 sts), [k2tog] twice, [yf] twice, k2tog, k2, [yf] twice, k2tog, k7. (22 sts).
2nd row: K9, p1, k4, [p1, k3] twice.
3rd row: K2, k2tog, [yf] twice, [k2tog] twice, [yf] twice, k2tog, k1, MB, k2, [yf] twice, k2tog, k6. (23 sts).
4th row: K8, p1, k6, [p1, k3] twice.
5th row: K2, k2tog, [yf] twice, [k2tog] twice, [yf] twice, k2tog, k3, MB, k2, [yf] twice, k2tog, k5. (24 sts).
6th row: K7, p1, k8, [p1, k3] twice.
7th row: K2, k2tog, [yf] twice, [k2tog] twice, [yf] twice, k2tog, k5, MB, k2, [yf] twice, k2tog, k4. (25 sts).
8th row: K6, p1, k10, [p1, k3] twice.
9th row: K2, k2tog, [yf] twice, [k2tog] twice, [yf] twice, k2tog, k7, MB, k2, [yf] twice, k2tog, k3. (26 sts).
10th row: K5, p1, k12, [p1, k3] twice.
11th row: K2, k2tog, [yf] twice, [k2tog] twice, [yf] twice, k2tog, k9, MB, k2, [yf] twice, k2tog, k2. (27 sts).
12th row: K4, p1, k14, [p1, k3] twice.
13th row: K2, k2tog, [yf] twice, [k2tog] twice, [yf] twice, k2tog, k11, MB, k2, [yf] twice, k2tog, k1. (28 sts).
14th row: K3, p1, k16, [p1, k3] twice.
15th row: K2, k2tog, [yf] twice, [k2tog] twice, [yf] twice, k2tog, k18. (28 sts).
16th row: Cast off 7 sts, knit until there are 13 sts on right-hand needle, [p1, k3] twice. (21 sts).
Rep these 16 rows.